The Drama of Democracy
Contention and Dispute in Community Planning

The drama of democracy seldom plays out as literally as it does in urban planning disputes. Yet these are complex dramas in which villains aren't clearly identified, protagonists are caught with ulterior motives, and fifth business runs rampant. In this book, Jill Grant uses a dramaturgical metaphor to show how community planning offers illuminating episodes of the workings of democracy.

Grant argues that planning provides a significant venue for debate about how we govern ourselves. She illustrates her theory with two case studies of planning disputes in Halifax. By examining the language and actions of the citizens, planners, and politicians involved in these disputes, Grant explores underlying motives and concerns. Overall, this work has much to say about the nature of cultural obstacles that prevent greater democracy. The author concludes that while democracy is a valued cultural concept, its practice proves weak.

Much of the work to date on urban planning takes a socio-economic perspective; the cultural implications of planning are still largely unexplored. By applying a cultural analysis to contemporary case studies, this book takes up the slack and provides a timely addition to the existing literature.

JILL GRANT is Associate Professor of Environmental Planning at the Nova Scotia College of Art and Design.

The Drama of Democracy

Contention and Dispute in Community Planning

JILL GRANT

UNIVERSITY OF TORONTO PRESS
Toronto Buffalo London

© University of Toronto Press Incorporated 1994
Toronto Buffalo London
Printed in Canada

ISBN 0-8020-0363-x (cloth)
ISBN 0-8020-7472-3 (paper)

Printed on acid-free paper

Canadian Cataloguing in Publication Data

Grant, Jill
    The drama of democracy : contention and
    dispute in community planning

    Includes bibliographical references and index.
    ISBN 0-8020-0363-X (bound)   ISBN 0-8020-7472-3 (pbk.)

    1. City planning – Citizen participation. 2. City
    planning – Nova Scotia – Halifax – Citizen
    participation

    HT166.G73 1994   307.1   C93-095569-2

Figure 7.1 is reprinted by courtesy of The Chronicle-Herald and The Mail-Star. Figures 8.1 and 8.2 are reprinted with permission from *And on the Eighth Day*, copyright 1967 by the American Planning Association, 1313 E. 60th St, Chicago, IL 60637.

University of Toronto Press acknowledges the financial assistance to its publishing program of the Canada Council and the Ontario Art Council.

This book has been published with the help of a grant from the Social Science Federation of Canada, using funds provided by the Social Sciences and Humanities Research Council of Canada.

For Marty, Sari, and Caleb,
my father, Alex,
and in loving memory of my mother

Contents

Tables, Maps, Photographs, and Figures

Acknowledgments

Many people helped in countless ways to make this work possible. For intellectual encouragement, I thank Bill Shalinsky, Sally Lerner, Pierre Filion, Beth Moore Milroy, Dorothy Counts, Linda Christiansen Ruffman, Marty Zelenietz, Mary McGeown, and Dave Balser. Through years of trying to learn about community planning, I've enjoyed exciting discussions with many colleagues and students about the nature of our profession. I am sure some will find their arguments reflected here.

Without the cooperation of many planners, citizen activists, and politicians in Halifax, I could never have collected the data presented in this book. I couldn't help but admire the sincerity and commitment of those I interviewed: I hope the participants in the study will find the results informative, and will begin to see that those on the other sides of disputes also have legitimate dreams and fears.

For help with illustrations and permission to reproduce original material, I thank Kerri Allen, Moritz Gaetz, Darrell Joudrey, Andy Lynch, Darren Parker, Lesley Staples, the journal *Environments*, the *Halifax Herald*, and the American Planning Association.

My greatest thanks I save for my family. They tolerated long hours of work and provided encouragement and diversion as required. Marty Zelenietz challenged in all the right places, and supported me endlessly. Sari and Caleb, my children, seldom complained about my obsession (although they had just cause). My parents launched me on the right road long ago, and for that I remain eternally grateful.

Part 1

All the World's a Stage

Introduction

'Everyone Loves a Mystery'

What is the nature of democracy in modern industrial societies? The dictionary says that supreme power in a democracy vests in the people. Democratic theory offers two principal models of modern representative democracy: the 'participatory' model suggests that the sovereign people can and should participate actively in making decisions that affect their lives; the 'elitist' model holds that the people lack the skills to rule and should not participate in daily governance. These two models compete for the loyalty of those who talk and write about democracy in modern society. The theorists have varying pronouncements about the meaning of democracy; we will not add to the extensive theoretical debate here. Instead, we intend to look at democracy in practice to discover disputed interpretations of its meaning in everyday life.

How do communities make decisions about appropriate uses of urban spaces? What arguments do people make to influence planning decisions? Community planning activities offer illuminating episodes of the drama of local democracy. In the context of planning episodes, people dispute who should make decisions about community spaces and resources; they argue about the circumstances and the ends of decision making. Actors in the drama have their own perspectives on the meaning of 'democracy,' influenced by their personal values and significant cultural themes. We seek to understand and interpret local democratic practice. What role do 'the people' have in local decision making? How do people use concepts like democracy as they participate in community activities? Our drama reveals the nature of community planning practice in one setting: we explore the concerns of participants in disputes about development in Halifax, Nova Scotia.

Valued as it is, democracy does not make the job of managing our communities easy. Rather than generating consensus, democratic participation nurtures contention and dispute. People fight about the character and future of communities. They argue about the balance between the rights of the people, the responsibilities of elected representatives, and the authority of appointed bureaucrats. The laws of the land in democratic societies give citizens opportunities to participate in developing public policies and implementing civic plans. That said, we find great diversity in community planning practice. In many communities, civic leaders reconsider proposed developments in the face of public pressure from citizens. Most local governments advertise public meetings. Politicians invite citizens to volunteer for advisory committees dealing with everything from community hospital management to constitutional affairs. City staff urge people to get involved in civic issues and make their concerns known to City Council. All the clues lead one to suspect that citizens should play an important and influential role in community decision making. Nevertheless, in some communities citizens find it virtually impossible to affect the outcomes of planning disputes. In certain circumstances city councils ignore lengthy petitions, noisy protest rallies, and well-reasoned arguments. Rather than finding participation in local government rewarding, citizens may get frustrated by the process of democratic decision making.

This is the mystery of community planning: why do citizens in some communities feel they have so little control over changes in the use of land? As we seek to solve this mystery, we find the drama of community planning compelling. Sometimes the mystery takes unusual twists. No white knights and villains here. Good guys have skeletons hidden in their closets. Bad guys have alibis. Following our leads, we discover a complex cultural drama emerging. In exploring planning disputes in Halifax, we use dramaturgical metaphors to illustrate our thesis that community planning provides venues in which actors stage debates over important cultural values, beliefs, and meanings. Case-studies of specific dramas can shed light on some of the mysteries of local democracy. All of the actors (citizens, politicians, and planners) come to the drama with their own interests and visions of the community good. As they work their way through planning disputes, people engage in public debate about major cultural themes, like 'democracy' itself.

Our quest to solve this mystery compels us to ask what the function of planning is in a democratic society. Our society has institutionalized community planning as part of a cultural apparatus for dealing with conflict and social control. Sometimes we reassure each other that planning gives people democratic control over urban form, but we also acknowledge that through planning we monitor deviance and engineer conformity (J. Bailey 1975). By grounding planning in its cultural context, by investigating the way that community members communicate varied and complex messages through planning activities, we come to understand that the problems of community planning derive in large part from its function within democratic societies.

Examining the planning drama, we find actors playing roles whose characters and behaviours seem partially predetermined, as if by script. By times, for instance, the planner acts the 'pompous technocrat'; at other times the 'genial civil servant.' Actors play their parts with divergent styles, using varied rhetorical devices and language. Sometimes displays of passion steal the show; at other times, cool reason rules. Planning activities in our communities serve as stages on which we play out significant cultural themes. In the course of planning disputes, people produce and reproduce values, beliefs, and meanings. Actors argue about the kind of community they want, about who should benefit (or lose) from change, and even about how to make decisions. By studying the language of disputes, we come to understand the ways in which people use 'planning,' 'the plan,' 'planners,' 'the public,' and even 'democracy' as cultural categories to justify or challenge continuity and change.

As we learn more about the drama of everyday life, some of the mystery of community planning disappears. We realize that communities sometimes experience frustrations because people have unrealistic expectations of local democracy and community planning. Providing venues for public input in local governance has not removed structural or systemic barriers to influence. Our political economy continues to encourage growth, regardless of local opposition. Community planning cannot solve the problems of contention and dispute in a democratic society: it simply accommodates the debate.

Chapter One

The Planning Drama

Modern societies face relentless demands for change in urban land-scapes. Planning provides mechanisms communities use to manage pressures for new development and to make decisions about preferred options. 'As part of our public *culture*' (Hodge 1986: 15), community planning generally perpetuates cultural 'myths' of progress, rationality, efficiency, expertise, independence, and democracy. We rely on such socially constructed 'realities' and 'myths' in order to make sense of the jumble of our lives (Horne 1986). Community members negotiate the meaning of cultural activities such as planning through their interactions with others. While cultural institutions such as children's literature and the mass media help generate mind-scapes of our cultural values, through planning we shape landscapes and townscapes reflecting those values. Communities are, in effect, cultural artefacts fashioned with planning tools.

In the course of everyday life, each of us plays various roles depending upon our situation, and especially upon the other actors with whom we interact. Life is a series of performances in which we give off impressions to sustain our preferred definitions of situations (Goffman 1959). We alter our language and presentation of self to suit the stage upon which we find ourselves. As people engage in planning activities, they style their performances into typical roles for their community.

Most residents in our communities don't participate actively in planning matters. A small minority engages regularly in discussions of land-use issues. A larger minority emerges to play roles in significant local disputes. People who learn that their local government has decided to make some change in their community may adopt the role of 'citizen.' Citizens who decide to become 'activists' put their days as tennis nuts or couch potatoes temporarily behind them as they devote their energies to some form of civic action. Citizen activists depart the anonymous comfort of 'the public' or the 'silent majority' for the stage of real politics. They put their ideas of local democracy to the test.

Proposals to change the use of land in built-up areas of a community commonly trigger civic action from citizens concerned about their interests. The battles that ensue may turn vicious and ugly. They offer fascinating insight into the way our society uses planning activities to manage conflicts over resources. Planning disputes expose episodes of the drama of democracy.

We need not stretch reality to consider planning disputes as dramas (Bolan 1980), for they are indeed tense and contentious stories. Within modern industrial societies, planning activities have become important venues through which communities work out conflicts over resources. To participants, each planning dispute represents an opportunity to stage a performance designed to influence the outcome of the process. Within the drama, actors improvise scripts through which they communicate key themes and messages.

Actors in different roles in the planning drama have divergent perceptions of the planning process. They use different tactics and argue for various ends. Citizens, for example, may see the plan as a shield that they wield to defend their neighbourhood from enemy incursions. This metaphor of 'plan as shield' captures a host of values, beliefs, and meanings: protection of family, heritage, and tradition through formalized community policies and regulations. Those who view the plan as armour reiterate plan policies self-righteously in public meetings. They feel betrayed and wounded when they lose a battle.

Where do actors' various perceptions of planning aims and roles originate? By and large we take actors' ideas as a given of the planning drama. Actors come to a planning dispute with particular views of the world, partly shared and partly idiosyncratic. Certainly self-interest plays a role in influencing their values and perceptions. Under largely unpredictable conditions they may change their opinions. While we might learn a great deal about the process of planning transactions from investigating the individual or the mass psychology of those participating, that is not our objective here.[1]

Instead, we try to articulate some of the values, beliefs, and meanings publicly and privately transacted through planning disputes. We argue that we cannot explain the meaning nor the outcomes of particular planning activities without elucidating the cultural context in which they occur. The difficulties of democratic participation in community planning are not simply 'planning problems': they arise out of the context in which our society uses planning as a way of making decisions. If we hope to overcome those problems, we first must understand their nature in our culture.

The reader who seeks a rigorous, quantitative analysis of planning disputes in Halifax will find this book disappointing. Instead of attempting an 'objective' analysis, we offer an interpretation of cultural events based upon 'insider knowledge.' Through systematic investigation and presentation, we try to convey to the reader a sense of how the actors involved see themselves and others engaged in planning activities. We offer interpretive explanation, as Geertz (1983: 22) calls it, 'systematic unpackings of the conceptual world.' We show the reader the subjective experience of participants to convey a qualitative understanding of the values, beliefs, and meanings that drive interactions.

Meaning and Explanation

In Akira Kurosawa's 1950 film, *Rashomon*, four people describe the murder of a man. The accounts differ in minor and major details. Each of the actors interprets reality differently. Those listening to the accounts learn something from each interpretation. The film does not distinguish between 'fact' and 'opinion.' No interpretation is definitive, but each informs. *Rashomon* offers a lesson for those seeking to account for behaviour: examine all perspectives before rendering judgment; accept uncertainty.

People continually construct and reconstruct meaning through their interactions. As Blumer (1969) explains, people adjust meanings and expectations as they participate in a situation. Situations have a dual character: partly defined by the actors in them, they also exist apart from the actors as cultural constructs (Morrione 1988). Explaining the nature of a situation involves both describing the institutions involved, as people think of them, and also exploring the meanings people give those institutions as they operate within them.

When we try to understand the details of human behaviour and thought, we encounter problems of interpretation peculiar to the study of culture. A scientist can measure the percentage of a chemical in a millilitre of solution[2], but a social scientist attempts to capture ephemeral phenomena that defy easy definition, measurement, and quantification. 'Facts' elude the investigator. One person's fact is another's opinion. No one has a monopoly on 'truth' – not the participant nor the observer. We therefore accept that some interpretations are more useful than others. Some are simpler than others. Some provide more telling insights. If we cannot achieve objectivity, then we attempt an intersubjectivity that offers satisfactory explanations of actors' interpretations.

What do we look for in a satisfactory explanation? We need adequate data[3] clearly expressed to provide a slice of reality that we can test against a proffered explanation. We require systematic and logical presentation. We must reveal the situational logic, as Jarvie (1972) calls it, which people express to account for their behaviour. We attempt to describe respondents' reality and elucidate the meanings and metaphors that support their understanding of the world (Crapo 1990). We do not undertake a detailed ethnographic account of Halifax; rather we employ an interpretive approach to increase our understanding of some of the problems of planning practice. We want to explore the configuration of values and meanings that surround planning activities in our society.

People express personal and professional values in their interactions. Individuals develop values through general socialization, educational training, and personal experience. Transmitted through language and other behaviour, values build on assumptions about the self and others. In a seminal paper, Alterman and Page (1973) discussed the significance of values in planning. They provided a definition of values that suits us well. A 'Value' is 'a cognitive assumption about the desirable or the undesirable to which its holder is affectively committed (whether consciously or not) and which influences his perception of the range of alternative actions or views from which he may select ...' (Alterman and Page 1973: 13). Values influence the range of choices that actors perceive they have.

An account of planning practice should reveal the values, beliefs, and meanings that actors transact through planning activities. It should inform us of the values actors affirm. An account of practice should articulate beliefs (cognitive knowledge or assumptions) about planning. It should find the meanings (intents signified) embedded within social and political structures and relationships, as well as those encountered in utterances or written texts. A successful account of planning practice should leave us with the sense that we understand why people do what they do. Even the most complete discussion of practice will not answer all of our questions, but it should convey the complexity of the queries remaining unanswered.

This study simply explores and describes one community's experience. It pieces together one small section of the puzzle we have to complete in our efforts to understand the role of planning within local democracy. The study provides a basis for subsequent comparisons with local experiences elsewhere, but it is not essentially comparative. Through such case-studies of a range of community experiences, we will eventually develop theory to account for the problems of planning practice within democratic societies.

The Function of Planning[4]

During the twentieth century, community planning has come to enjoy a particular role within the institutional processes of modern communities (Grant 1990a). Originally the dream of reform-minded philanthropists, architects, and health specialists, planning now forms part of what Horne (1986) calls the reality of public culture in industrial societies. In Canada, we have assimilated planning into our understanding of how communities should operate. Planning gives decision makers rational tools that they can use to shape and justify change in communities.

While most planners recognize the significance of values *in* planning (e.g., Alterman and Page 1973; Howe and Kaufman 1981; Moffit 1975), until recently few discussed the importance of community values and history in setting the context *for* planning. Clearly, though, planners do not practise nor create theory about planning in an intellectual or cultural vacuum. As members of the communities for which they work, planners necessarily respond to the expectations of others as they disseminate particular values.

To discern how planning came to enjoy its present function[5] in our communities, we can explore the history of those communities and the larger social, political, and economic orbits that incorporate them. Planning did not appear *sui generis* in cities across the nation. Rather, individual actors within particular social roles promoted and advocated community planning to sympathetic audiences. Key players took the steps necessary to incorporate planning into institutional structures passed on to subsequent generations. Frequently they argued that community planning represented a step towards rational and democratic control of the urban environment.

Since the early 1980s several authors have looked at the history of community planning in the context of the political economy and cultural history of nation states (e.g., Boyer 1983; Foglesong 1986; Ravetz 1986). Hence we understand that planning takes the form it does as a result of processes of cultural adaptation. National and regional levels of government adopted forms of planning in the postwar era in order to achieve vital objectives: limited and appropriate government intervention could reduce uncertainty and market unpredictability. Governments believed that planning would allow them greater control over their fate without undoing the market system upon which societies depend.

The ideas and theories implicit in planning reflect intellectual discourse not only within the profession but in the wider society. Over time we find that theories tend to converge across disciplines; theory reflects common cultural paradigms. Ideas come in and out of fashion according to historic events and cultural trends. Planners interacting with other members of their communities translate common cultural meanings into terms relevant to their practice. Thus professional discourse inevitably changes to accommodate cultural realities (Galloway and Mahayni 1977). Those ideas and theories that thrive do so because they suit the intellectual and cultural climate of contemporary society.

Planning history yields several examples of conversions to culturally acceptable theories and ideas. One of the most interesting examples involves the transformation of Ebenezer Howard's 'garden city' from a Utopian socialist system of cities to its current manifestation as the planned suburb. In his early work, Howard (1902) advocated public ownership of the land (a reasonably popular idea in the late nineteenth century) to prevent speculation and to protect the character of the garden city. The implementation of his vision in Letchworth and Welwyn Garden City, however, came about through the philanthropic efforts of a limited dividend corporation and a group of planners, such as Thomas Adams, generally unsympathetic to public ownership (Creese 1966). By the time that North American cities began adopting zoning codes, Howard (1923) retracted his commitment to public ownership. He then argued that planning regulations (which proved more acceptable to property interests than public ownership had) could protect his vision. Radical beliefs popular in the progressive 1890s became politically unpalatable in light of the anticommunist hysteria that followed the Russian Revolution. Garden city notions have not, however, lost their popularity. In fact, 'satellite cities' and 'planned communities' have become a significant part of the repertoire of ideas in our public culture.

The permutations and combinations of planning theory often mirror the waxing and waning of cultural values. Thus in the 1960s and early 1970s, as North America resounded with protest marches and demonstrations, planners gushed about the importance of citizen participation in community planning. Planners wrote dozens of books and articles about the vital importance of public involvement in planning. The recession of the early 1980s pushed 'citizen participation' out of the foreground, however, and planners turned their attention to 'strategic planning' and 'economic development.' While concern about local democracy did not disappear, increasingly it took a back seat to economic prosperity.

Community planning theory and practice assume that the residents of a region enjoy the right to influence the use and development of land within that region. In this sense, faith in 'democracy' pervades planning theory and rhetoric. In liberal democratic ideology, the people are sovereign, but governance depends on representative democracy. As the 'participation era' of the 1960s and 1970s unfolded, citizen action in planning became closely linked with participatory democracy. Few would disagree with the premise that the people should decide the future of their communities. However, when we examine practice, we find no consensus on the implications of democracy for community planning.

Early proponents of community planning in Canada, such as members of the League for Social Reconstruction (1935), saw planning as a democratizing process. Planning would provide citizens with power to shape their communities into wholesome places to live and work. It would enhance equity, encourage civic action, and change the balance of powers in a community so that collective rights take priority over individual rights.

During the 1960s and 1970s, a chorus of voices called for active citizen participation in planning (e.g., Arnstein 1969; Davidoff 1965; Friedmann 1973). Influential Canadian planners joined the chant. Lash (1977) argued for a true partnership between planner, politician, and public: his explicitly normative framework suggested that citizens in a democratic nation should participate as equal partners in shaping their own futures. Lash saw politicians and planners as servants of the people, cooperating with them in an effort to determine 'the public interest.' Political and technical decisions should reflect community concerns and needs. Planning should manifest direct local democracy where the public could participate in a 'deci-sion-forming partnership' (Fagence 1977: 4).

Acceptance of public participation as a tenet of democratic plan-ning penetrated deeply into planning theory and discourse during the 1970s, and remains evident today. As Nagel (1987) indicates, however, participation proved easy to advocate but difficult to prac-tice. Interest in public participation rose rapidly during the 1970s and fell just as precipitously during the 1980s (Berry et al. 1984: 7). Elitist democracy yielded little ground to participatory democracy in gov-ernment practice (Kornberg et al. 1982).

Our ideas about the role of public participation in planning reflect notions about the role of citizens and governments in democratic society. As Pateman (1970: 43) explains, the conventional (representa-tive government) theory of democracy, dominant in the public cul-ture of our society, contrasts sharply with the participatory theory of democracy espoused by those who advocate active citizen involve-ment. The 'problems' that arise during participation programs derive largely from the conflicting political values and expectations of the actors involved, as well as from the exigencies of bureaucratic and political processes through which we make decisions.

Critics have often argued that our society does not welcome citizen involvement in planning any more than it promotes collective or democratic action of other kinds. By providing for standardized public involvement in community planning, governments defused the radical edge of citizen action (Loney 1977). By institutionalizing public meetings and citizen committees, governments incorporated or dissipated potentially disruptive forces. Planners and politicians acknowledge the need to allow citizens a role in community decision making, but citizens often find their role frustratingly ineffective. The rhetoric of democracy has penetrated planning discourse. Everyone talks about 'democracy,' yet people do not agree about its problems or prospects. The actors in the planning drama have different ideas of what democracy means.

Can planning, as some American writers assert, restore or enhance democracy? What can we make of pronouncements such as Hoch's (1984b: 337), 'The social prerequisite for human fulfilment is demo-cratic association'? Is this armchair pontificating or empirically de-rived truth about 'human nature'? Although Americans may seek liberty or death, people can and do survive without democratic association. Planning can as readily promote tyranny as empower-ment. In assuming that planning should facilitate a particular cultural style, planning theorists risk imposing their cultural values on others. When planning theorists speak of enhancing democracy through planning, they suggest that planners can use bureaucratic offices and technical skills to create a different kind of society: the 'good society,' they aver, means one run by the people for the people. Such a vision assumes the people know best. But what if the people want to exclude certain groups from their community? We need not stretch our memories far to think of examples where people oppress others. What if the people act to destroy the environment? Again, we can find many cases where people put their own interests ahead of long-term considerations. The good democratic society requires good people: can the inhabitants of our communities achieve the ideal?

American political culture has a strong attachment to democracy. No wonder we find it pervading American planning theory. As we look at our Canadian case-study, we need to rethink the meaning and significance of democracy in planning theory and practice. Canada certainly is a democratic country. We cannot, however, assume that the meaning of democracy in civic action and community planning in Canada replicates the American experience.

Planning is a visionary discipline. It holds that humans can direct their actions to achieve given aims, but planners have no monopoly on determining those aims. Setting community goals in a democratic society necessarily involves cooperation between citizens, planners, and politicians. As we discover in our analysis of planning disputes, even after councils adopt community plans, community members may have significant disagreements about the community's aims. Actors in disputes disagree about the actions communities should take to achieve common goals. Exploring disputes lets us reveal some of the cultural meanings actors share or contest as they participate in the community planning process.

If ultimately we want to 'improve' planning in our communities, the place to begin is not with grandiloquent pronouncements about 'restoring democracy.' That simply begs further questions: what is democracy? What if the people want inequality? What if no one votes?[6] Who decides when democracy has been 'restored'?

Enhancing planning practice will take time. First, we must understand the nature of practice. What actually happens in planning activities in our communities? Why are people dissatisfied? What do community members expect of planning? Can planning give people the kind of community they want? Second, we will have to find consensus on the nature of 'good planning.' What kind of society do we want? What role can planning play in getting us there? Communities may have divergent answers to these questions: we cannot expect a simple definition of the 'good community' or of 'good planning.'

Studying Planning Practice

To understand the problems and prospects of democracy in community planning, we can look at specific examples of planning practice. How do planners, politicians, and the public interact in the process of making decisions about the community? What happens in the context of planning activities? What do participants believe that democracy requires?

In the last decade, descriptions and theories of planning practice have proliferated. Practising planners call for advice to make them more effective in their work. Academic planners attempt to clarify the nature of practice and develop a normative framework for improving performance. In ideal circumstances, practice and theory should come together in insights that enhance the prospects for democratic planning. In real life, though, the gap between the theory and practice of planning has not narrowed significantly.

To comprehend fully the nature of planning practice we need to examine the context of planning activities. Unfortunately, many of the discussions of practice we find in the planning literature give little insight into the broad cultural context in which planners operate. For instance, Schon's (1982) description of a practitioner clearly indicates 'some of what a planner knows,' but lays responsibility for problems that occur in practice squarely on the shoulders of the planner. Schon suggests that the planner has authority but no power as a 'consequence of the way he has chosen to frame his role' (1982: 358). Do planners freely determine the nature of their role in community bureaucracies? Do actors independently stage their performances? Surely community and employer expectations help to frame the roles that planners, politicians, and citizens play.

A number of planners, some influenced by neo-Marxist approaches, have discussed the nature and problems of planning practice in the context of political and bureaucratic structures (e.g., Baum 1980; Beauregard 1980; Forester 1980, 1982a, 1982b, 1986, 1989, 1992; Hoch 1984b). During the 1970s, intellectual discourse in many disciplines reflected the influence of Third World scholars struggling to understand their own colonial cultural history. Radical critiques of planning and its lack of 'true democracy' became increasingly common (e.g., Scott and Roweis 1977).

The relevance of Marxist and neo-Marxist theory for practising planners has consistently been undermined, however, not only by the powerful myths of free enterprise that guide community planning ideology in Canada and many other Western societies, but also by the often impenetrable prose and jargon that permeate Marxist rhetoric. Moreover, many of the neo-Marxist analyses prove reductionistic, suggesting that the material conditions of industrial and finance capitalism produce planning and determine its character. Hence, anything done in planning becomes evidence of the manipulations of capital. By singularly explaining everything, such analyses cannot account for differences between communities. If, for example, we want to account for the evident differences between Canadian and American communities discussed by Goldberg and Mercer (1986), we must examine cultural variables other than material conditions, since material conditions are similar in Canada and the United States.

The ideology inherent in much of the recent literature on planning practice affects the analysis presented. 'Critical theory' has proven fairly disparaging of planning practice and its lack of participatory democracy: it cannot enlighten readers about the way that planners or other participants in planning activities think about and value practice.[7] Authors such as Forester (1980, 1982a, 1986, 1989) and Hoch (1984a, 1984b) suggest that planners should engage in 'progressive' practice, enhancing opportunities for democratic action; such prescriptions betray a lack of understanding of the constraints that operate on planning practice in many communities.[8] In the wake of upheavals in eastern Europe since 1989 and the 'demise of socialism,' critical theorists espouse values repugnant to many North Americans (especially those in positions of authority).

While every profession needs normative theory, it also expects a literature that can account for the nature and problems of practice: the latter is the gap we seek to fill. The style of planning activity within a nation generally reflects the culture and history of that nation.[9] Similarly, community differences affect local styles of planning. Unidimensional analyses cannot account for differences in planning styles and choices. This is not, however, to deny the utility of materialist or critical analyses. Indeed, the contradictions of industrial and finance capitalism cause problems for communities that ripen conditions for the state to implement planning. Furthermore, the development of modern capitalism continually changes the context in which communities must plan. Nevertheless, a full account of community planning must transcend materialist analysis of political economy. It must encompass a cultural analysis of the context in which planners and citizens develop theory and practice that conform to cultural patterns of consent and dissent. In other words, problems created by economic (and other) changes necessitate planning, but community interactions and cultural values shape the parameters of acceptable planning responses.

Planning for Democracy

Planners, politicians, and citizens engage in planning activities as individuals or as members of organizations. Why do they participate in disputes? What spurs them to action? We want to understand how community organizations and bureaucracies operate because those institutions form part of the stage on which planning dramas unfold.

Detailed interviews with planners and administrators, such as those reported by Baum (1983, 1987), shed considerable light on the planner's perspective. Unfortunately, they give us less insight into how planners interact with citizens and others during planning activities. Studies of planners out of their community context can lead us, as Baum notes in the preface to his 1987 book, to blame planners, not to understand them. In an effort to explain planning practice, Baum (1987) probes the unconscious factors that shape bureaucratic behaviour. Granted, Baum teaches us a great deal about the psychology of bureaucracy, yet we are left wondering how much of the 'craziness' of the planning organizations he describes derives from culturally patterned behaviour. If we look at individual actions in the context of the expectations and performances of others, we may make greater sense of them than if we treat planners as solo performers.

Over the years, several planners, anthropologists, and sociologists have discussed planning practice in cultural context (e.g., Gans 1968; Healey 1992; Perin 1977; Ravetz 1986). Like the critical theorists, they look at the meanings communicated through planning activities. However, they expand their scope to investigate cultural elements other than political economy and bureaucratic structure. For example, Perin (1977) offers an excellent analysis of land-use practices to show that planning incorporates many beliefs and values about the family; the people making planning decisions reproduce those beliefs and values through their work. Perin explains how actors in the planning drama think about what they do. Her interpretive contextual analysis shows active individuals making choices within the constraints imposed by given social, political, and economic structures and values.

The literature on planning practice has grown extensively in the past two decades, yet we find relatively few case-studies of local planning disputes that allow us to understand the context that frames behaviour. Seldom have writers fully articulated the values, beliefs, and meanings transacted by the players in the 'planning drama.' Most of the studies of practice have focused on the planner: few have looked at relationships between planners, politicians, and citizens (e.g., Throgmorton 1992). Except for Bolan's (1980) analysis of a professional episode, few planners have examined planning activities as staged performances.

In presenting a situated example of planning practice, we attempt to look at the actors involved in planning activities, the relationships between them, the meanings they transact through planning activities, and the problems they encounter in trying to plan in a democratic society. We use dramaturgical metaphors to analyse the components of planning activities and to study the ways in which they relate to each other.

Chapter 2 explains the elements of the planning drama. First, we examine the 'stage' on which actors perform. How does the context in which planning activities occur frame performances? Second, we look at the 'actors' themselves. What are the roles and expectations of the various players? How do they portray themselves and interact with others? Third, we discuss the 'script' of the planning drama. What themes and language characterize the play? What do the actors talk about?

In the ideal play, all the actors read from the same script. They arrive at the stage at the appointed time, take their cues, and recite their lines appropriately. They understand and accept the rules. They agree on the meaning of the production. They know in advance how the play should end.

As we discover in Part 2, performances in community dramas seldom run so smoothly. Following a brief review of the regional context (Chapter 3) and the history of planning in Halifax (Chapter 4), we detail two contentious planning disputes (chapters 5 and 6). These planning disputes explore interactions between participants in the planning drama. By situating planning activities in the context of other community concerns, we illuminate cultural expectations about how the planning drama should work. We discover that planning practice reflects and reveals the dominant values, beliefs, and meanings of the community. It reproduces social and political relations in the community (Forester 1982b, 1992). Disputes form the metaphorical 'acts' and 'scenes' staged in our planning drama. They structure the planning activities we observe. They contain the meanings transacted between actors. Detailed study of disputes offers concrete insights about the nature and function of planning in our communities and, by extension, in our culture.

Part 3 explores the gap between the ideal play and the drama of everyday life in the real world. We analyse how actors set the stage, frame their performances, and script their dialogue in our case-study examples. We find that actors operate upon multiple stages, read from different scripts, fail to communicate effectively with each other, and contest fundamental values through planning activities. Arguments over values and process permeate planning disputes. In the history of any urban settlement, buildings rise and fall. Property owners apply for permission to change the use of land. Citizens lobby local government and bureaucrats for particular decisions. Actors articulate their values and beliefs as they talk about desired outcomes in the community.

Part 4 considers the nature of planning in a democratic society. Many of the problems that plague planning derive from the dilemmas of democracy in the modern world. Is it feasible to talk about improving the nature of planning practice when we lack consensus on what we hope to achieve through planning? How can we plan for the 'good society' when we cannot agree on what such a community implies?

Most of the planning literature avers the primacy of 'democracy.' Who in their right mind would argue against democracy? Even the nastiest tyrants call themselves democrats! As we explore this case-study, though, we find ourselves asking some tough questions about democracy. What exactly do people mean when they talk about democracy? The implicit consensus of mass society breaks down upon close inspection. We find that actors in the planning drama do not share a common understanding of the meaning or implications of democracy. The rhetoric of democracy can, in certain circumstances, constitute the language of exclusion and oppression.

Chapter Two

Stages, Actors, and Scripts

As actors stage their performances, they make choices about which backdrops, sets, and props to use, based upon the audiences they seek to persuade. To understand why dramas proceed as they do, we peel back the layers of context to see what the actors transact through their performances.

This chapter explains the metaphors that help us analyse community planning practice. The 'stages' are the contexts that frame planning activities. The 'actors' participate in the drama. The 'scripts' are the messages participants communicate during planning activities. We consider each in turn.

The Stage

We use the metaphor of 'stage' to explore the contexts in which community planning occurs in a democratic society. In the drama of planning, cultural structures and activities produce important venues for performances. Local planning activities nest within local, provincial, national, and international societies. Planning practice certainly reflects local values and socio-political structures, but it may also respond directly or indirectly to regional and national values and structures. Planning practice, like planning theory, occurs within a particular cultural and historic framework that accommodates national values. Unlike theory, practice also acknowledges the influence of local political structures and cultural values.

Community planning has many stages with diverse sets. The broadest stage derives from societal structures, values, and expecta-

TABLE 2.1
Examples of the influences of international, national, and provincial stages on local
activities in Nova Scotia

Influence: Level Kind	International	National	Provincial
Political structure	Nation states	Division of powers	Powers given to municipality
Ideology	Free enterprise Libertarianism	Conservative agenda	Conservative Pro-development
Policies and legislation	International treaties	Subsidies Regional development	Planning act Taxes and assessment
Economic pressures	Global economy Competition	Export economy	Economic disparity Resource depletion
Mass media	Examples of failure	Examples of practice	Coverage of disputes

tions that support community planning in industrial societies. Nes-
tled within, we find other stages on which play national themes and
values. Provincial values and structures may provide yet another
level of stages for the planning drama. A final platform, developed
through regional and local traditions and concerns, makes the stage
unique to the community under study.

Certain elements of the stage on which the drama of democracy
plays differ little from community to community. However, local
performers may move props around, change the scenery slightly, or
otherwise alter sets for their own audience. Sets change as actors
meet in different situations or scenes: for example, one scene may
feature the formal set of council chambers, while another activity
may take place outdoors in a park.

In this section, we examine the basic elements of the 'stage' for
community planning and consider some of the ways in which the
stage may differ from community to community. We consider stages
at different geographic levels: international, national, provincial, and
local. We discuss some of the diverse influences that present parts of
the background scenery for actors' performances. Table 2.1 illustrates
examples of some of the influences that affect the staging of local
activities in Nova Scotia.

To some extent, planning dramas may play on an international
'stage.' Modern industrial societies engage in a global economy and

culture in which planning and democracy constitute key concepts that are keenly debated. By and large, decision makers on the international scene accept the utility of planning for development. However, the capitalist ascendancy of the early 1990s has fully exposed the essential dilemma of planning: how much government intervention can a market economy tolerate? The idea of planning, which asserts community interests in property, confronts private rights entrenched in the principles of liberal democratic free enterprise (Foglesong 1986). The tug of war between collective and individual rights pulls planning back and forth: in the 1890s and the late 1960s, planners advocated communal interests; in the 1920s, and the 1980s individual property rights took precedence.

Among the key influences of the international stage affecting local planning performances are pervasive ideological themes. Faith in individual initiative and free enterprise drive our understanding of economic and personal success. Competitiveness has expanded from a relationship between individuals or corporations to affect economic relationships between nations and trading blocs. Around the world, governments (and their moneylenders) require citizens to compete in the global economy. Industry relocates to communities with low wages, cheap energy, and lax environmental standards. As competition for limited jobs and markets heats up, localities often adopt cutthroat measures for survival. Internationalizing industrial society has placed terrific pressure on communities. Local politicians, desperate for their communities to share prosperity, look to planning either as a tool for success or as an impediment to progress.

The postwar period brought elements of a global culture into place. Bagdikian (1987) argues that monopoly within the mass media brings people around the world a unified message. Millions tune in to watch wars and international events on the 'global' news network, CNN. Local voices find their concerns muffled in a global information system dominated by a few huge corporations. Hollywood fantasy becomes mass reality. Corporate values dominate public discourse. In the new world order, communities justly fear the loss of their sense of identity and control.

Although planning does not often generate international stories, some examples impress North American communities. In 1991, an irate citizen shot a local planning officer in the United Kingdom (with video cameras rolling); those interested in planning issues everywhere took note. The tragedy became an exemplar of 'what can happen when you fool with people's property rights.' Bad planning makes the news. During the 1990s, reporters (echoing the statements of Western politicians and economists) regularly linked the economic failure of former Soviet bloc countries with disastrous state planning. Advocates of central state intervention read the obvious message in such coverage: beware of the inherent dangers of government planning. In an atmosphere poisonous to socialist economic planning, even local community land-use planning may find itself gasping for breath.

Planning problems that become issues in other nations may alter the ways in which actors think about planning activities in their own communities. For example, American approaches to urban renewal affected community planning in many other industrial nations during the 1960s. In the 1980s, heritage conservation spread from European cities to become an important theme in many parts of the world. Actors in local disputes draw upon popular knowledge of practice elsewhere to persuade others of favoured approaches and choices. Advocates of particular styles of planning, especially international celebrities (like HRH Prince Charles), may feature in debates about appropriate decisions in communities in any number of Western societies.

Thus we see that various international structures and organizations (like global trading networks), and dominant values and beliefs (such as capitalism and liberal democracy) help set the stage on which local planning dramas play out. The influence of the international stage may differ from performance to performance: actors place their performances on the stage they feel best suits the parts they play and the messages they deliver. In some planning activities, we may see little evidence of the influence of international structures or concerns, while in other cases, the international forum may loom large to lend authority to the performances staged.

In many planning disputes, we find structures and values set by national stages. Although nation states are undergoing a period of upheaval and redefinition, they remain significant settings in which planning performances occur. Uncertainty over the future of Canada makes the national stage a slippery surface for actors. The utility of planning is contentious as governments negotiate communal and individual rights. Under the traditional balance of powers between federal and provincial levels of government, the authority to plan communities falls to the provinces. While the federal government took the lead in economic and social policy planning, the provinces generally delegated community land-use planning to municipalities.

However, during the postwar period, the federal government prod-
ded the provinces into expanding planning activities. Various national funding programs offered incentives for provinces to pass enabling
legislation for local and regional planning. Municipalities that put
plans in place could apply for regional development or urban renewal funds. Thus the national agenda of regional industrial development and urban growth spread from coast to coast.

Through the years, the provinces have usually tracked each other
in adopting legislation affecting planning. During the 1910s, for
instance, the federal government sent Thomas Adams across the
nation to help provinces draft planning legislation (M. Simpson 1985).
In later years, interprovincial cooperation accomplished the same
purpose: hence we find many similarities in provincial acts. While
regional differences occur, substantial similarity characterizes the basic
framework of planning in Canada (Cullingworth 1987; Hodge 1986).

A number of institutions, structures, and values affect the national
stage on which planning dramas play. Municipal units (cities, towns,
counties, villages) with the ability to tax and manage land create the
political and bureaucratic structures within which planning operates.
In national ideology, communities have important social, economic
and political functions; in reality, they have limited power over their
own future.

The political culture of Canada has resulted in a multi-party system with representation from the right to the centre-left of the political spectrum. Although the Progressive Conservative government in
power in the late 1980s began to erode the welfare state system,
many Canadians still favour government intervention to ameliorate
the operation of the market. Provincial elections in the early 1990s
showed the social democratic New Democratic Party with considerable strength.[1] Paradoxically, as the Eastern bloc threw off the
shackles of socialism, Canadians moved steadily to the left. With each
passing election, the Canadian voter becomes more difficult to characterize: conservative, liberal, socialist, capitalist? Less tied to particular political philosophies than in the past, voters have become unpredictable and capricious.

With the many national and international influences operating on
the average citizen, it may seem somewhat surprising that provincial
and regional structures and values remain significant in setting the
stage for planning activities. Canada is a confederation of disparate
regions: the West of new immigrants, diversity, and primary production; Ontario, the manufacturing heartland of the nation; Quebec with

French roots and its people's desire for independence; Atlantic Canada (the Maritimes and Newfoundland) with a troubled economy driven by fish, forests, and government. Planning performances in each area reflect the heritage of the people and the land.

The character of local planning also responds to regional significance in the geopolitical network of the nation. Peripheral areas use planning differently than do areas central to the locus of power. Dynamic central markets may see growth control as the watchword; peripheral regions worry about depopulation. Growing communities employ planning to manage change, while declining communities use it to promote growth and investment.

Provinces adopt legislation that enables communities to undertake particular kinds of planning activities. Legislation sets out the powers of local governments and their staff. It determines the types of political and bureaucratic structures that communities may use to stage planning performances. The law frames the role of the citizen, for example, by describing the rights that citizens have in planning matters. The dramas staged include only the scenes allowed by the laws that govern planning matters. The extent of citizen involvement in the planning process is controlled not by national values or constitutional rights (as in the United States), but by local practice and provincial-enabling legislation.

In the Canadian context, most provinces restrict the rights and powers of municipalities. Final decisions in major planning matters (from adopting a local planning strategy to approving a zoning change) rest with the provincial government. Ministers of the government retain the right to refuse local decisions. Many provinces have appointed some type of municipal board or planning appeal board to adjudicate planning disputes. Hence, locally elected politicians and residents of communities lack the power to resolve planning disputes.

Paradoxically, despite insufficient local control, most planning disputes are intensely local. They may involve choices about where to put roads, whether to save old buildings, or what density to approve. Planning issues affect and reflect concerns about local identity and sense of place. Local stages provide concrete venues of considerable significance.

Municipal government gives actors particular roles to play in the planning drama (Long 1968). Elected councillors decide whether to hire planners; they adjudicate certain planning applications. Politicians set the rules within which actors stage their dramas. They formulate the policy direction for community planning, the reporting structure within the planning bureaucracy, and the framework within which citizens can participate.

Every community has a unique history and set of traditions. One community may enjoy the legacy of a sleepy provincial town, while another prides itself on civic leadership and rapid growth. One community comprises an ethnic mosaic of new immigrants, while another boasts that most of its residents descend from original British settlers. Historical events and cultural heritage affect residents' attitudes towards planning and their conceptions of the place of planning in their lives.

Under the distribution of powers in Canada, municipalities have one significant means of realizing revenues: taxing real property. Communities' reliance on property taxes for revenues grew in the late 1980s and early 1990s as fiscal restraint hit higher levels of government. Transfers of wealth from federal and provincial governments have not kept pace with inflation. In provinces where municipalities finance welfare payments,[2] the fiscal squeeze strains resources. Local governments look to planning to help them control the costs of providing services and to increase the value of land for development. In regions with insufficient low-cost housing, governments may employ planning to promote affordability. Communities often have high and sometimes unrealistic expectations about what they can achieve through planning.

Local governments establish many sets or scenes in which planning activities can occur. Legislation formats some of the stages: for example, almost all Canadian jurisdictions require a formal public hearing where municipal council sits to adjudicate a planning application or amendment. Other kinds of planning activities and situations may include advisory committees, public meetings, public commissions, neighbourhood councils, or open houses. Within the municipal structure, local governments may establish planning departments, commissions, and committees. They may open neighbourhood planning offices or information booths. Staff create planning situations in all kinds of ways, from formal meetings in their offices to chance encounters in the community.

Informal local activities can sometimes provide sets for planning performances. For example, in the course of a neighbourhood barbecue, residents may find themselves talking about a proposed development project. Within most communities, a core of groups and individuals keep a 'watching brief' on planning issues, ready to stage planning performances as they see the need.

Staging Performances

Actors perform on many stages in the planning drama. In part those stages exist apart from the actors who play upon them: for instance, people do not challenge the legitimacy of the global market. In part, however, actors construct stages as they play their parts: for example, by talking about the global market, people give it meaning and substance.

National values and structures can filter into local practice from the regional or provincial context. Nova Scotian experience demonstrates that funding programs and legislation often incorporate national and international theory through which higher levels of government impose certain values upon local communities (Grant 1988a, 1989a). Thus, for instance, the values of rational centralization and democratic participation descended on communities through the combined fronts of 'regional economic development' programs and revised planning procedures in the late 1960s.

Local values and structures directly affect local practice. For example, if local politicians value growth, they support development projects that increase taxable revenue generated from a piece of land. Where politicians wish to provide a venue for public input into a body other than elected councils, they will likely follow local traditions and utilize familiar structures.

As we examine the local stages on which actors perform, we find they can differ in several ways. Issues vary according to community values. In some places, people worry about growth: we have too much, or we have none. Communities also diverge in structure and process, so that management style may vary: a planning department in a municipality with a strong city-manager organization operates differently than does a quasi-independent planning commission. City politics in a community where politicians run for geographically based wards differ from politics in communities with 'open' constituencies: politicians develop particular perspectives on their roles.

Depending on the heritage and local political culture of a community, population characteristics may influence the staging of planning activities. Ethnic origins and racial differences may become debating issues. During the urban renewal era, for example, black communities often suffered significant disruptions and dislocation. Socio-economic inequalities may feature prominently in arguments about the appropriateness of decisions. For instance, working-class residents may complain that intensification or relocation programs target their neighbourhoods because of their relative powerlessness.

In certain circumstances, local practice may influence national values and structures. Mass protests by citizens in major urban centres like Toronto or Vancouver may set in motion political and social processes that ultimately revise programs and approaches across the nation. Local knowledge in Halifax about protests or activities in other centres (transmitted via the mass media or other 'grapevines') may affect local action.

As we articulate the effects of cultural context on planning theory and practice, we recognize that although we can distinguish analytically between international, national, regional, and local contexts, in practice boundaries blur. When we attempt to determine the origins of specific values and beliefs, we may find we cannot say whether they are local or national. For example, Canadians generally respect private property rights, yet certain regions and communities protect such rights more assiduously than others do.

While we can postulate differences between cultural values and structures at the various levels of political organization, we must acknowledge many similarities as well. For instance, Blishen and Atkinson (1980) present data that suggest that all Canadians have essentially similar values, although regional differences affect the relative strength of those values.[3] Local communities may develop idiosyncrasies and express their values in particular ways, but they cannot isolate themselves from superordinate cultural influences: the national and international stage remain some part of the planning context. In the next section we see that although actors have a limited ability to transform the stages they play on, they have some latitude in framing their roles and scripting their performances.

The Actors

Who gets involved in planning activities and why? Three categories of actors (politicians, planners, and citizens) play key roles in the community planning process. Actors come to planning activities and disputes with divergent interests and values. They employ a variety of tactics and strategies. While individual personality undoubtedly accounts for some of the diversity we see, many differences derive from the way that actors' roles are framed for and by them.

Each of us presents a face to others as we play a social role in a given setting (Goffman 1959). Actors put on the characters they choose for themselves. Once they select a role, they must stick with the part to craft a believable character. We expect seamless performances from actors to maintain the socially constructed definition of a situation: if actors behave incongruously, we lose confidence in them or in the situation. Actors can't step out of character in the drama of everyday life: they must commit themselves to the parts they play. Actors who choose to play institutionalized roles in the planning drama affirm officially accredited societal values. Performance involves producing and reproducing particular values in prescribed settings and styles.

We firmly define significant common roles in our society. In the first few weeks of kindergarten, for example, children become 'students.' They learn to pattern their behaviour in response to the example set by 'teacher.' Gradually children internalize some of the expectations others have of them as students; later they help to socialize others into the role. The role 'student' exists before a child takes it on, but by taking it on, the child reproduces the role and passes it on to others.

Key actors in the planning drama take direction from those who have played roles before them. Some of the roles are clearly etched, spelled out in the details of legislation and bureaucratic job descriptions. Others seem less crystallized, waiting for the illumination of a new occupant to clarify the character. On the stage of particular planning activities, various actors work together to frame their own and others' roles. In the process, actors reproduce power relationships and produce social meanings in the community (Forester 1992). They affect the ways in which decisions are made and the choices of outcomes that communities can consider.

After several generations of elected responsible government, our society has framed well-accepted roles for *politicians*. We expect politicians to serve the community by making decisions in the 'public interest.' When politicians do not put the community's welfare above their own, we subject them to severe sanctions: we may refuse to re-elect them; we may prosecute them for illegal activities.

In some areas, like Nova Scotia, many people expect politicians to provide patronage rewards for their supporters. Those who help a politician get elected may believe that government largesse should come their way. Where the political culture accepts patronage, politicians serve one definition of the public interest by dispensing favours to local people. While those who oppose patronage see favouritism as 'corrupt,' its supporters view it as appropriate loyalty: they expect politicians to protect and support family and friends. Our society creates inevitable dilemmas for politicians by expecting them simultaneously to protect the interests of their local constituents and those of the wider community.[4] Politicians carefully attempt to keep all groups satisfied by playing genial conciliators and remaining noncommittal for as long as possible. Sometimes they satisfy no one.

Local planning disputes generally involve land-use decisions in which interests clash. Politicians have to decide appropriate outcomes. The responsibility of serving the community forces politicians to resolve tough disputes. Politicians frame their task as an onerous and sacred duty; the community confirms such framing by granting politicians increasing deference as disputes move towards decisions.[5]

Those who choose to become politicians must commit themselves totally to the role. They attempt to sustain an impression of authority, credibility, and empathy. Most of them 'dress for power' and are accomplished public speakers. They invoke powerful cultural values and fears (such as family, free enterprise, xenophobia) to attract workers to their campaigns and electors to the ballot-box.

Television transmission of parliamentary proceedings and popular books about corruption and patronage politics (e.g., J. Simpson 1988) have contributed to growing scepticism and distrust of politicians (Blais and Gidengil 1993). In a climate of allegation and recrimination, many people wonder whether the role is worth seeking. Compared to their colleagues in business, politicians earn relatively low pay for high-stress work. At one time, the prestige accorded politicians overcame the problems of the work. Today, however, many capable people choose to steer clear of politics.

Politicians often acquire their roles through participation in a political party. The party socializes its members for appropriate role behaviour. Candidates may attend 'schools' where they learn how to speak and act. Political organizations seek to run candidates who project the impression the party desires. The politician becomes an important symbol of the party, and hence must act appropriately for the party to succeed. At election time, party members assist candidates in the effort to persuade voters that the candidate personally represents voters' interests and values.

Throughout most of Canada, municipal politicians do not run on a 'party ticket.' Canadians maintain a polite farce of 'non-partisan' local politics. However, even where political parties do not appear on the ballot, political organizations often play a significant role in 'making' local politicians. Without a strong campaign team, usually provided clandestinely by a political party, candidates find it difficult to get elected. To retain the loyalty of party workers, politicians must maintain the party line.[6] Hence party values and strategies pervade local politics. Many local politicians see success in local government as proof of worthiness for future election to higher levels of government.

During a local dispute about the fate of a piece of land, a politician has to work out what role to play: champion of the neighbourhood group; defender of the tax base; friend of the developer; servant of the silent majority; employer of the expert planner. Various actors on the stage and behind the curtains call out cues, hoping to influence the choice. With their power to decide the outcome of the dispute, politicians become a key audience for other actors. However, politicians arguably have the most to lose from failing to convince their audience (voters and supporters) with persuasive performances.

Planners move into roles defined largely by the community. In some political jurisdictions, planners work for quasi-independent planning commissions. In others they work directly for a municipal government department. Civil servants step into a set of rights and responsibilities that they cannot easily modify; their titles and duties developed through a process that predates them. Planners join a community that may have already established a particular style of interaction for planning activities.

Within planning academia, authors have argued that planners can frame their roles in different ways. Planners can act as technical experts trained to manage the development of their communities (Hodge 1986). Following the influential work of Paul Davidoff (1965), many writers suggested that planners should become advocates for disadvantaged groups within society. Recent books and papers have faintly echoed that theme with arguments that planners should adopt a progressive or radical role, promoting values such as democracy and equity (Forester 1982a, 1989; Friedmann 1987; Howe 1992; Kiernan 1983). Interest in the study of planning practice has grown since the late 1970s. As we learn more about what planners actually do, our image of their role changes somewhat. For instance, we know that in certain contexts planners act as facilitators, mediators, and negotiators (Forester 1986). Planning schools have responded to that knowledge by adding curriculum units on communication skills and negotiating techniques to prepare graduates for the job market. The profession's preferred framing of the roles of its members, arrived at through the interactions of planners and planner-academics, affects the types of skills and theory transmitted to neophytes.

When beginning work in new positions, however, planners find they have relatively little latitude to frame their roles according to their professional expectations or individual personalities. The organizational structure of civic government preframes their role. Provincial legislation that delegates authority to municipalities limits their responsibilities. Planning practice in Canada has become decidedly bureaucratic (Cullingworth 1987; Hodge 1985, 1986) not because planners framed their roles that way, but because governments chose certain approaches. Baum (1983, 1987), Forester (1982b), and Hoch (1984b) justly criticize the bureaucratic tendencies of mainstream planning practice; they conclude that planners can 'democratize'[7] planning by altering planning styles. In practice, however, planners have other assignments. As employees of democratic governments, they carry out the will of elected officials. Planners implement political agendas. They enforce politicians' visions. In most cases, planners lack the authority, autonomy, and legitimacy to frame their own roles. 'Wicked problems' undermine their efforts and effectiveness (Kiernan 1990; Rittel and Webber 1973).

Politicians and senior civil servants look to planners for advice. They do not hesitate to transmit their wishes to employees. New planners quickly learn their place in the bureaucratic pecking order and come to understand what their employers expect. Success in an organization requires accepting the organization's goals and procedures (Baum 1983, 1987). Planners who cannot adapt to corporate values seldom last long in their positions.

The reception planners get in any community depends in part on the nature of relationships previous incumbents of positions had with other actors. Community residents, especially those active in local planning issues, develop certain expectations regarding how planners should behave. Bad experiences can cloud people's dealings with new planners who come to town.

Not surprisingly, planners sometimes find themselves torn between conflicting images of their role. On the one hand, their professional training encourages them to call themselves visionaries who help communities improve. On the other hand, they act as institutional agents, protecting their employers and their communities. The professional image of independent visionary contrasts with the cultural role assigned to the planner. In effect, whether as municipal bureaucrat or in some other employment context, the planner functions as an agent of the status quo. Much of the perceived 'gap' between theory and practice derives from this tension that planners face every day.

Planners make certain choices about positions to take in each planning dispute. They may support or oppose proposed changes, depending upon their assessment of each case. As they prepare the staging of their performances, they carefully tailor their scripts to create certain impressions. With their pivotal technical position in the drama, they seek to define the nature of situations for other actors. They follow unwritten community rules in using persuasive tactics. They must convince the audience that their only interest is 'the public interest,' and that their preferred choices are good for the community.

To win the support of politicians and citizens, planners draw on some powerful community values. As technical experts, they frequently employ 'science' and 'reason' to persuade. They cannot, however, use the same range of values, tactics, and strategies available to other actors on the stage. The politician can rail about the tax base, and the citizen can rant about crowded schools, but the planner responds politely with facts, figures, and policies.

The role of *citizen* is less well-defined than the roles of politicians and planners. It constitutes one of a subset of roles that members of 'the public' may play from time to time. In its generic form, 'citizen' refers to a native of a state or an inhabitant of a city. We usually use the term 'citizen' throughout our discussions to refer to those who take part in local government or planning activities of some type.

Many citizens participate relatively passively in planning matters: they may follow a dispute in the newspaper. Others show strong commitment to action: they may attend meetings or write articles for the local paper. Citizens come in different shapes and sizes. 'Developers' play an important role in planning activities, normally as the proponents of development projects. 'Activists' take on key roles as opponents of projects. Several categories of the public serve as potential citizens, as well as something of an audience in planning disputes. 'Residents' live in the communities in question; 'property owners' own property in the area; 'taxpayers' provide income to municipalities; 'voters' cast ballots on election day; 'the people' are sovereign; 'the silent majority' hovers as an undefined residual class of considerable ideological importance. At any point in the planning drama, these members of the public can become citizens by engaging in a performance. Actors in disputes may discuss various categories of 'the public' as suits their purposes. With each subcategory of actors, we find a slightly different claim to legitimacy.

Like 'mother,' the role of citizen carries with it powerful positive connotations that give it a highly valued and moral nature in our mythology. Our culture values individual civic action. We link good citizenship to the defence of social institutions like the family and the neighbourhood. We believe that individuals have rights and responsibilities that they should appreciate and exercise in a democratic society. A vast majority of community members, however, do not take any independent civic action. Many do not even vote. Few ever write or call their political representatives. Most never attend a planning meeting of any kind.

People decide to participate in a planning activity for a variety of motives. Some want to prevent change. Some want to control change. Some lead groups that have an interest in the development of the community. Some are drawn into the social activities of their friends or colleagues. Some seek to protect their investments. Actors who decide to take civic action because of a proposed change must quickly learn new roles as citizen activists. They may have expectations developed from their understanding of the culture. Maybe they call their elected representatives. Perhaps they walk into a community centre to talk to a staff person about what they can do. Sometimes they write a letter to the editor of the local paper. They may join a group of like-minded individuals forming to oppose the proposal.

Citizens take a greater part in framing their own roles than do the actors who play planners or politicians. Citizens have a greater variety of tactics and strategies at their disposal: they can rant wildly about corruption, or calmly recite a reasoned analysis of plan policies. They may work alone, or cooperate with others in their activities. They seek to persuade decision makers to take a particular course of action by asserting their own understanding of community values. They define the community interest as congruent with their own interests. Politicians and planners may see citizens, especially activists or developers, as minority groups working against the public interest.

Provincial legislation frames roles for citizens in the planning process; it also limits the rights of citizens to affect outcomes. Ultimately, Canadian planning law gives citizens the right to receive information and to make presentations to decision makers. Many jurisdictions constrain citizens' rights to challenge or appeal planning decisions. While politicians and planners invite citizen participation in planning matters, they need not heed citizen concerns. Planners and politicians have the power to make all decisions about the use of land. In contrast, some American jurisdictions (like California), give citizens the right through referenda to make laws about the development of their communities (Longhini 1985).

Based on his survey of planning directors, Shirvani (1985: 489) suggested that 'It should be music to citizens' ears that so many planners said citizen input was important to the setting of planning agendas.' Indeed, planners universally support public participation, in large part because of its connection to values intimately associated with democracy and popular sovereignty. In an ideological climate where salesmen use 'democracy' to pitch everything from military intervention to blue jeans, few people disparage democracy. Accordingly, knowing that planners advocate citizen involvement tells us little about citizens' influence in planning disputes.

Experience in many communities indicates that the role of citizen carries little power in and of itself. Citizens' effectiveness in attaining their ends varies markedly. In some communities, citizens regularly prevent projects from proceeding; in other communities, citizens find themselves powerless to persuade decision makers. Some politicians prove more receptive than others to concerted civic action.

We find a considerable gap between the rhetoric and the reality of citizens' roles in community planning. The popular myth of citizen control over the outcome of important decisions does not match the reality of representative government. Planning texts, political campaign speeches, and the mass media lead people to believe that citizens have power. In some communities that may hold, but the image diverges from reality in other communities. Local political networks, provincial legislative frameworks, and global corporate decisions all limit the power of citizens. The role of citizen is contextually defined. It differs from time to time, from issue to issue, from community to community. The citizens we will visit in our drama certainly have a much smaller role to play than some of them would like.

Actors and Audiences

The key actors in the planning drama stage their performances in relation to and in interaction with each other. Planners stake out the high ground of science and reason. Citizens fighting developments try to corner passion. Politicians see themselves as balancing the warring factions in search of the 'public interest.'

While all three categories of actors participate in the same play, they do not perform for the same audience. Planners play primarily to their employers: politicians and senior bureaucrats. Their ultimate success depends upon delivering a service to the community. Although they also seek to impress their fellow professionals and crave the support of community residents, they cannot survive without pleasing the bureaucratic and political structure.

Citizens perform in a kind of moral play. They want to persuade politicians that their desires represent community wishes. They may also play to the wider community audience to convince the public to pressure politicians and planners. Sometimes citizens' inability to pin down the audience they seek to persuade robs their performance of punch. Their faith in the righteousness of their cause may prevent them from managing their performances effectively.

Politicians generally play to an audience that has little overt interest in the dispute: a politician who depends on certain citizens to get elected may find their arguments persuasive, but most politicians respond to what they believe the 'silent majority' expects. Sometimes politicians play to other audiences: development interests who help finance election campaigns; planners or other staff to show 'who's boss.' Politicians carefully manage the face they present to their audiences in order to maintain their dominant position in interactions.

As we explore planning disputes in Halifax in Part 2, we will see how actors frame their roles in interactions. We look at what people say and how they portray themselves and others. We attempt to clarify their values, motives, and tactics. In examining actors' interactions, we illuminate the values and meanings people transact through planning activities: thus we reveal the 'script' of the play.

The Script

If we study the language of participants in planning activities, we find that common themes pervade the discourse. While actors do not follow firm scripts, they improvise within a narrow range of possibilities. The rhetorical devices they use and the ends they seek reflect the cultural values and meanings transacted through community planning. The language of disputes reveals the ways in which participants in community planning portray themselves and how they see others. Different categories of actors often use similar terms to convey widely divergent meanings. As we study disputes, we discover that actors use a variety of tactical strategies and rules in constructing their performances (and hence their dialogue).

Some of the critics of planning find no sense of structure or order in planning activities. Dear and Laws (1986: 249) argue that 'Planning today adds up to little more than a 'pastiche' – an unordered, unsystematic discourse.' Some advocates of planning despair over the loss of vision and commitment that characterized the early profession, but should we conclude that planning today carries no message? Perhaps planning, like other activities, conveys subtle cultural messages. For example, in their study of advertising, Leiss et al. (1990) argue that ads carry more than simply product information: advertising creates a system through which producers communicate complex social meanings to mass audiences. We suggest that actors similarly transact complex messages about social roles and values in the course of planning activities, not in an overt or direct way, but implicitly. What some call 'ritualized choreography' we say constitutes cultural situations in which people transact important social meanings. We may not find syllogistic reasoning in the logic of planning activities, but we can discover a cultural logic that orders planning discourse. Planning practice is not as crazy as it may seem.

Modern industrial societies adopted government planning as a sophisticated code[8] of rational rules to improve predictability and facilitate urban development. Legal entrenchment of planning procedures makes people believe they have agreed on the implicit ends of community planning (such as order, growth, and 'the public interest'). Planning battles, then, should merely involve *means*: how can our community best fulfil its declared desires? Planning practice, however, reveals that people contest more than means. Fundamental differences in preferred *ends* persist. Planning disputes rapidly expose debates about ends and the cultural values those ends represent. Actors argue about values and ends in planning disputes, often couching them in debates over 'means'; fights about 'ends' get so 'emotional' that those setting the stage may seek to avoid them.

If people did not care about the shape or future of communities, then no one would have invented planning. We plan because we value the spaces in which we live (Udy 1980). We plan because we appreciate the control that rational action can give us over change in our communities. Planning provides us with tools to realize valued ends and means. While some members of our communities worry that planning inhibits individual choice (another valued end and means), the widespread adoption of planning procedures in industrial societies indicates that rational control and attractive communities enjoy a high rating in the hierarchy of cultural values.

Planners have long recognized the significance of values in community planning (e.g., Alterman and Page 1973; Davidoff and Reiner 1962; Moffitt 1975). Traditionally, utilitarian values have prevailed: good planning meant efficiency, amenity, and profitability. In recent years, however, planners have sometimes argued that planning should promote other cultural values, especially democracy and equity (e.g., Forester 1982a; Howe 1992; Kiernan 1983; Klosterman 1983). Within the spectrum of players in the planning drama, we find the gamut of cultural values that dominate our society. Actors weigh their values according to their own experiences and interests, and debate the application and implication of those values in the context of planning activities.

Examining the Script

To understand the 'script' of planning dramas, we must listen to the language of participants in planning activities. In the choice of words, in the turns of phrase, in the style of argumentation that actors use, we uncover evidence about relations between actors and the meanings and values they transact. The researcher finds scripts through analysing texts (including letters, briefs, minutes, and maps) and investigating discourse fragments (usually official transcripts). We can supplement documentary evidence with interview data or recordings made during planning disputes.

Our metaphor of 'script' may not persuade those who prefer a positivist approach to empirical research. In trying to decipher the meanings and values transacted in planning activities, the researcher encounters inevitable limitations guaranteed to frustrate those who insist on strict scientific method. The data required for analysis are invariably incomplete: briefs go missing from files; some material gets destroyed. We can never know whether we have all of the 'facts,' or even what the 'facts' are. Research on scripts, even when tackled using content analysis or other systematic methods, requires interpretation and subjectivity.

Unfortunately, we seldom have clear guidelines about what material is 'relevant,' and which is not. If we situate planning activity squarely in the realm of everyday life, then an actor could potentially make a revealing remark or create a piece of documentation in almost any setting. We can never claim a comprehensive analysis. Of necessity, we limit our analysis to the kinds of materials and memories collected by participants in the drama.[9] Accordingly, we not only risk missing evidence, but we may face respondents who hide, invent, distort, or suppress information.

Any attempt to understand human behaviour in terms that have meaning for the actors involved requires that we engage in a great deal of interpretation. The anthropologist would say we seek the 'emic' or insider's perspective. The sociologist might call our approach 'phenomenological' or 'hermeneutic.' When we elucidate the script of planning activities, we try to give voice to the actors, but we may inadvertently put some of our words in their mouths. To limit observer bias, we use the actors' own words whenever possible, and attempt to employ a rigorous and systematic approach to presenting the data and analysis. Interpretation makes no claim to 'objectivity.' Instead, it asserts the legitimacy of a form of knowledge based on the subjectivity of the actors involved.

Actors script their planning activities by drawing on knowledge of the different stages they play (international, national, provincial, and local), of the other actors in the drama (planners, politicians, and citizens), and of the scripts generated by other actors. Actors can pull in a wide range of cultural values, beliefs, and meanings in framing their performances. They select from a range of rhetorical styles in delivering their lines (F.G. Bailey 1983). We might imagine a continuum of styles available to actors in our drama, depending on the relative weight participants give to reason and passion. Industrial societies award high kudos to pure rational thinking. We associate rationality or reason with science, capitalism, and progress. From the earliest days of town planning, planners have vowed their commitment to reason. However, our culture also gives qualified approval to passion. We associate passion and emotion with personal and community commitment. We view those who lack emotion as 'detached' and uncaring.[10]

In studying performances of actors in disputes, we find a delicate and shifting balance between reason and passion. Some actors gravitate towards the 'reason' end of the continuum: planners try to stake out the high ground of logic and rationality in their presentations. Other actors find themselves swept up in emotion: citizens sometimes validate their participation by passionate attachment to their home and community. Politicians are caught somewhere in the middle on this continuum, blending reason and passion to create a rhetorical style.

Actors also make choices about the type of language or terms of discourse they employ (Connolly 1974). They may choose simple codes that other actors understand without difficulty, or they may pepper their discourse with sophisticated codes (such as planning jargon) that some actors cannot translate. Both the type of language and the style of argumentation serve to frame the nature of relationships between actors in the drama.

As we study planning practice, we find that each community tends to define its problems in particular ways, reflecting local values (Cartwright 1973). Certain issues come up again and again, while others are 'dead letters.' Community concerns depend on the peculiar history, culture, and economy of a people and place. The issues raised in planning disputes frequently correspond to different takes on what Gallie (1956) refers to as 'essentially contested concepts.' Gallie explains that contested concepts involve evaluation: people argue about values of great significance to them. Contested concepts are subject to interpretation, complex in structure, and capable of modification over time. Participants in disputes may use contested concepts both aggressively to attack other positions and defensively to legitimate promoted options. Because 'there can be no general method or principle for deciding between the claims made by the different teams' (Gallie 1956: 178), debates over essentially contested concepts inevitably remain unresolved.

Several essentially contested concepts appear in planning discourse. They occur with some frequency and in divergent contexts. Participants use concepts such as 'development,' 'the public interest,' 'the character of the community,' and 'democracy' to lend moral weight and legitimacy to their arguments. Such concepts become key elements in the scripts of disputes.

Development appears often as a contested concept in planning activities. Frequently equated to growth, it also implies progress, improvement, or change. In the postwar period, national and international agencies promoted development at every opportunity. Governments adopted planning as a means or tool for development. That so many municipal departments are called 'planning and development' emphasizes the conceptual linkage between the terms. While people generally see the concept of development itself as a positive notion, some community members use the term disparagingly as they refer to the negative impacts of change on people and places. Individuals of different ideological leanings have contrasting notions of what development constitutes and how to achieve it. Their use of a common term masks contention about the means and ends of change.

Since the early days of the development of a civil service, people have argued about *the public interest*. The notion of a common good is fundamental to representative government. It implies that politicians and bureaucrats can determine the best course of action in a situation in which they must make choices: they select the option of optimum benefit. In the face of pluralistic demands, the notion of the public interest serves governments well: they may use it to defuse or undermine dissent. The proponents of 'the public interest' can attack others for pursuing 'self-interest,' 'private interest,' or 'special interests' in advocating alternative outcomes.

Planners have promoted the idea of the public interest throughout this century and appear unwilling to abandon it (Klosterman 1980). Surprisingly, planners have found little dissonance between their notion that they need a professional vision and their simultaneous commitment to serving the public interest. Indeed, the malleability of the concept of 'the public interest' allows its users to define their own concerns, wishes, and interests as the public interest.

Many arguments about planning choices contest *the character of the community*. Planners talk about healthy communities, model cities, or garden suburbs. Politicians may worry about strong tax bases and satisfied constituents. Citizens think about the people they encounter and the landscapes they see. People have widely divergent notions about the character of their community. Perceptions of community depend on many factors in people's experience including values, history, and interests. As people argue about 'character' in planning disputes, we uncover the myriad factors that affect concepts of place. We also learn that people's sense of community character is closely tied to personal identity, experience, and self-interest.

Among the most potent concepts in planning disputes is the idea of *democracy*. In the 1990s, virtually no one speaks against democracy. Everyone believes in democracy. Moreover, each of us expects democracy to result in our favoured choice. Citizens say that sovereignty resides in the people; therefore, the will of the people should prevail. Politicians explain that the people elect them to decide; the will of the politicians represents the democratic outcome. Planners may believe that their expertise gives them the tools to determine the will of the people and the needs of the community; they support democratic decision making and delegating authority to civil servants. Debates about democracy normally feature in arguments about how to make decisions and about which of several contesting views should prevail. Participants call on 'democracy' as a powerful motherhood sentiment and legitimizing strategy. Considerable passion, as well as careful reason, may flavour the articulation. All of the participants feel comfortable in calling on democracy to support their positions.

As we follow planning disputes in Halifax in Part 2, we explore the use of these contested concepts. Community residents see the character of the community and the nature of democracy as primary concerns in local land-use planning: the concepts play a major part in debates about the means and ends of planning. Development and the public interest also feature significantly in the context of the disputes we discuss. Our study of planning activities and disputes reveals that people argue about the meaning of 'planning,' 'the plan,' 'planning principles,' and 'planning theory' as they simultaneously contest the nature of the communities they inhabit and the processes those communities use to reach decisions.

Part 2

Audience,
Take Your Seats

Chapter Three

Desperately Seeking Development

In the next few chapters we look at a case-study in the drama of planning. We examine planning activities in the City of Halifax, the capital of Nova Scotia. Through the voices of actors in the play, we learn about the nature and function of planning in a community and a region desperately seeking development.

Before we turn to planning disputes in Halifax, we must first consider the larger stages on which the drama plays. As we suggested in Chapter 2, this entails exploring the broad regional and provincial context, for Halifax is the commercial capital of the Maritimes region. By international standards, Halifax is a small city with fewer than 120,000 people. However, as a regional centre, it offers many amenities: hospitals, museums, universities, and government offices.

The episodes of our metaphorical play follow in chapters 4, 5, and 6. First, we briefly review the history of planning in Halifax. Chapter 5 reveals the dispute over Market Place Plaza. The final episode, Chapter 6, uncovers the horrors of the Mitchell property case. We begin by setting the mood.

Regional Economic Context

Canada consists of a confederation of regions, each with distinct heritage and resources. Canadian politics means regional politics, with various parts of the nation fighting for a greater share of the economic pie. Successive national governments attempted to improve regional economies through manipulating policies such as railway

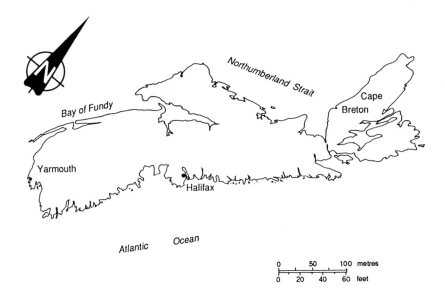

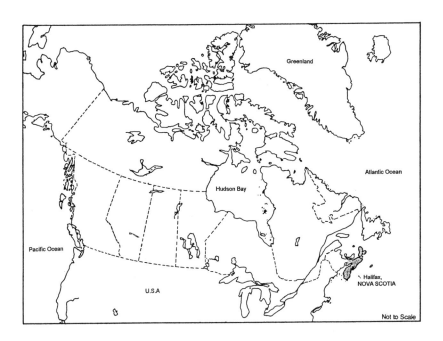

Map 3.1: Regional Context

tariffs, tax incentives, or regional planning initiatives. Despite the interventions, the Maritimes region (New Brunswick, Prince Edward Island, and Nova Scotia) remains firmly cemented in the unenviable position of a 'disadvantaged' and economically deprived area.

In the early days of settlement in Canada, the Maritimes looked set to prosper. Ports such as Halifax and Saint John bustled with trans-Atlantic trade between Britain and the Caribbean. By the time of Confederation in 1867, though, the booming days of farming, forestry, shipbuilding, and industry were numbered. As the new nation of Canada began to take shape, the centre of power and prosperity shifted westward to the Great Lakes area.

The Maritimes faced deindustrialization and declining investment as early as the 1890s (Williams 1987). Entrepreneurs found lucrative locations for investment in central and western Canada. As businesses and banks abandoned the region, emigration stripped the area of many of its skilled workers. The national government in Ottawa tried many schemes through the years to stimulate the Maritime economy. Ultimately, Ottawa believed that the Maritimes could prosper as a mining and manufacturing area with appropriate opportunities. Unfortunately, instead of turning a 'hopeless basket case' into a prosperous industrial centre, the national government fostered dependency and underdevelopment (Surette 1988: 30).

During the 1950s and 1960s, Ottawa poured money into programs to redress inadequacies in infrastructure: roads, bridges, and wharves improved (Howland 1957; Savoie 1986). While transfers of payments raised average incomes in the region, they did not generate the economic prosperity that people craved. By the late 1960s, the national government heavily promoted regional planning as a way to stimulate growth and development. Programs based on the 'growth centre' or 'growth pole' philosophy provided funding to the region. According to the theory, viable urban centres grow more quickly and generate more wealth than other kinds of settlements. Concentrating investment in these centres would provide 'trickle down' benefits to the rest of the region.[1]

Regional planning came to Nova Scotia through federal initiatives to promote growth centres. Ottawa designated the Halifax–Dartmouth metropolitan area a regional centre. In 1969 the region received $2 million to begin regional planning. The Metropolitan Area Planning Committee (later Commission) began its work clearly intending to use land-use planning as a means of achieving regional economic development.

Ultimately, regional planning failed in Nova Scotia (Grant 1989a). As the twentieth century draws to a close, the province remains economically disadvantaged, as are other Maritime provinces. Capital and labour continue to head westward (or out of the country entirely), encouraged by national policies that promote 'people prosperity' rather than 'place prosperity.'[2] Regions and places overlooked by modern capitalism struggle along without the resources to alter their peripheral status.

The economy of the Maritimes remains heavily dependent on transfers of wealth from the central government. 'Equalization' payments to support provincial programs and income assistance to individuals have propped up the regional economy. However, in the last decade the national government has limited growth in transfer payments. Cutbacks to development programs, military expenditures, and social program funding all hit the Maritime economy hard. Economic hardship contributes to a cultural climate of scarcity, fear, and desperation.

Socio-historic Context

As one of the areas first colonized in Canada, Nova Scotia has had over two centuries to develop its distinctive character. If we examine its particular history and the composition of the people who inhabit the province, we begin to reveal the cultural context in which Nova Scotians live their lives and participate in planning activities.

Nova Scotia became a British colony after years of war and dispute with the French. Its original people, the Micmac, sparsely inhabited the region. In 1755, the British expelled early French settlers, the Acadians[3]. Through the eighteenth and nineteenth centuries, immigrants from the British Isles moved to Nova Scotia to take land grants or to find work. Loyalists came north from America during the American Revolution and the War of 1812. Blacks seeking freedom and land migrated from the United States and Jamaica. Germans settled the Lunenburg County area, but few settlers came from other European countries. By the 1980s, some 72 per cent of the population indicated they descended from British stock (Beck 1988).

Following the clearance of peasants from clan lands in the early nineteenth century, some 50,000 Scots migrated to Nova Scotia to make a new life (Prebble 1963). These migrants had a significant impact on the province. Their traditions influenced art: Scottish dancing and bagpipe playing remain popular in the province. Their attitudes towards authority (the deference and fatalism that led their ancestors to accept the orders of the lairds to leave their homelands) retain some legacy of the past (Friedenberg 1980).

While some British colonies rejected the yoke of imperial rule, most Nova Scotians accepted the authority of the Crown. When the American colonies rebelled against British rule, Nova Scotia did not join the revolt (in part because of the substantial British military presence, no doubt). Like the other Canadian colonies, Nova Scotia received thousands of Loyalist immigrants in the wake of the revolution. The Loyalists affirmed an already strong commitment to the Crown.

Britain's wish to disengage from its North American colonies contributed to the confederation of four provinces in 1867: Ontario, Quebec, New Brunswick, and Nova Scotia joined to form Canada. Despite its participation in this experiment, Nova Scotia had reservations about independence. While Nova Scotia had an elected General Assembly as early as 1758, local self-government came quite late. For many years, fear of revolution and chaos dampened enthusiasm for local 'democracy' in the province. Unlike their counterparts in other parts of North America, Nova Scotians showed little interest in local self-government. Halifax incorporated in 1841, with the franchise extended to 800 voters. Aside from two other towns that sought local control, most Nova Scotia municipalities only moved to self-government after the province mandated it in 1879 (Beck 1973).

When talk turned to confederation in the 1860s, Nova Scotia held an election on the issue. Although the majority voted against becoming a province of 'Canada,' Nova Scotia's leaders ultimately signed the agreement. For some years many Nova Scotians felt betrayed. Debates raged about whether Nova Scotia should remain in Canada. Some Nova Scotians continue to believe that confederation caused the problems the Maritimes currently face: central Canada sucked resources and opportunities away from the region. Given the outcome of the election on Confederation, we can understand Nova Scotians' scepticism of politicians and perhaps even of democracy.

Several commentators on the political culture of Nova Scotia suggest that the 1850s and 1860s constituted a formative period in the shaping of political values (Beck 1973; Simpson 1988). In his monumental study of patronage politics in Canada, Simpson argues that 'in the 1980s Nova Scotia's political culture was fundamentally the same as in the 1860s ...' (1988: 172). Nova Scotians remain conservative, fatalistic, deferential, and cynical. They expect politicians to use government largesse to reward friends and punish enemies: such is the history of patronage in the province (Simpson 1988). They believe that citizens have little power to effect the kinds of changes they desire in their lives (Brym 1979). They see politicians as suspect.[4]

In rural parts of the province, people have traditionally engaged in work that responds to values of independence and self-sufficiency. While they accept a sense of social hierarchy that tolerates structured inequality and engenders deference, they also have strong ideas about private property. Unlike parts of the country that entered confederation after the 1860s, Nova Scotia has very little Crown land. Accordingly, the province has developed legislation in a context in which private property rights take precedence: the province itself has relatively little real interest in property.

Workers in Nova Scotia have never developed strong solidarity and influenced government policy in a major way. The deindustrialization of the province since the 1920s has certainly undermined labour interests. Unions have proved strongest in Cape Breton, the northeastern region of the province. In the early decades of this century, as labour dissent enveloped the nation, strikes occurred with some frequency in the mines and other industrial areas. However, the provincial government moved quickly to repress strikes through police and military intervention. During this century the legislature has consistently passed bills to weaken trade unions and to prevent them from organizing workers. When the government announced a freeze on the wages of public sector workers in 1991 (through a bill that put collective agreements into legal limbo), Nova Scotians accepted the action as necessary in times of fiscal restraint.[5] Few commentators asked whether suspending the rights of workers is appropriate in a democratic society. The Nova Scotia government echoes the political mantra of conservatives everywhere: we have to make the climate good for business. If limiting the rights of workers and unions improves economic fortunes, Nova Scotians will likely approve.[6]

Attempts to promote planning in Nova Scotia may run headlong into an unsupportive culture of social and political values and structures. Politicians want to allocate government resources according to traditional styles, not by 'rational' bureaucratic procedures. Giving planners the authority they need to implement policies means transferring some power away from politicians. That has met with resistance in some quarters, especially in rural areas. People who value their independence do not want planners telling them what they can and cannot do on their land.

After the regional planning experiment ended in Halifax, the city did not give up on planning entirely. Community leaders came to accept that planning could provide the tools that communities need if they want to promote economic development and growth. Hence Halifax continued planning through its own mechanisms, but shaped its function and character to suit community expectations.

Legislative Context[7]

A brief review of planning legislation explains how the province frames local planning practice. Legislation generally reflects cultural values and beliefs: for example, planning acts in Nova Scotia have consistently promoted the rights of private property owners. Laws also establish the social and political structures within which local practice must operate. Legislation defines the roles allocated to citizens and planners, and limits the effective meaning of 'community planning' in Canada to regulating the use of land.

Nova Scotia was among the first Canadian provinces to adopt planning legislation with its Town Planning Act of 1912 (Nova Scotia 1912).[8] By 1915 it had redrafted its law (Nova Scotia 1915) to reflect the bureaucratic model of planning espoused by Thomas Adams and the Commission for Conservation (M. Simpson 1985). Under these early acts, citizens had limited roles to play in planning activities. Unless people owned property, they had few rights under the legislation. Preventing unwanted actions or ensuring desired actions required intensive lobbying of the local planning board or town council.

Nova Scotian municipalities did not hire staff planners to develop and implement their town planning schemes. Various business groups had an interest in town planning from time to time and might commission schemes. Local boards were to implement the schemes. Despite the initial enthusiasm for town planning, however, in fact little planning ever reached the implementation stage.

Following the explosion of an ammunition ship in Halifax Harbour in 1917, Halifax participated in a town planning experiment. In order to facilitate the redevelopment of the Richmond district of the city, the provincial and other levels of governments set aside funds and passed the necessary laws to allow Thomas Adams to test some of his ideas (Armstrong 1959). The resultant 'Hydrostone' project remains a planning landmark in the area.

The 1939 Town Planning Act (Nova Scotia 1939) constituted a

major revision to the legislation and a commitment to promote town planning in Nova Scotia. The legislation encouraged municipalities to hire expert planning staff and to appoint town planning boards to prepare plans. Like its predecessors, the act assumed that citizens had limited interest in the planning process. Councils had the power to settle disputes, and citizens had no recourse to appeal to higher authorities. The act did not treat citizens as partners in the planning process. Instead, it presumed that planning required the expertise and judgment of professionals and knowledgeable lay persons.

Under the legislation, many communities drew up master plans or zoning schemes. The City of Halifax adopted a planning scheme in 1945 and later hired staff planners. The 1945 plan remained in effect for more than thirty years, but had relatively little influence. Federal funding initiatives for slum clearance and urban renewal did, however, lead to the demolition of areas of the downtown and to a growing interest in the idea of town planning.

In 1969, the province totally revised its planning legislation (Lang 1972; Nova Scotia 1969). The 1969 Planning Act reflected different assumptions about the nature of planning and the role of citizens and planners in the process. Formulated in a national and international climate of intense citizen action and economic growth, the act responded to the need that provincial civil servants perceived for provincial coordination and public involvement through regional planning. Under the new rules, citizen planning boards gave way to professional planning staff. Planning became a modern tool for regional development. Citizens had greater rights to information and participation in the planning process. Implementation of the plan involved the cooperation of planning staff and councils.

Although Halifax had some planning staff before 1969, the new act gave Council the push it needed to work on a new plan. Many politicians remained sceptical about planning during the 1960s. However, because the legislation required that all municipalities adopt development plans, Halifax began work on a new master plan in the early 1970s.

Municipal politicians perceived the 1969 act as exceedingly 'liberal' in the rights it gave citizens to appeal Council and staff decisions. Cities like Halifax had many decisions appealed. Developers complained that the appeal process delayed their projects unfairly and limited their property rights. Municipalities protested that the provincially appointed Planning Appeal Board unfairly overturned the decisions of democratically elected representatives of the people.

Citizens active in planning matters said that the act did not give them clear enough rights to participate in planning and to influence decisions.

In 1983 the province passed yet another Planning Act (Nova Scotia 1983), this one reflecting the conservative national climate in ascendance. The act constrained citizens' rights to appeal and gave councils greater latitude to make decisions on land-use matters without challenge. Councils received considerable discretionary power to set planning policy and determine how community members might influence decisions.

Despite the act's mandated 'public participation programs,' in many ways it limited opportunities for participation while extending the professional planner's scope for action. The act increased the authority of planners by giving them power to implement plans with limited interference from councils or citizens. The law presumes that citizens should give their input to councils as municipal governments set policy, or in circumstances when councils have room for discretionary action. Citizens exercise whatever authority they might have in lobbying councils to adopt policies or reject applications for changes in policies. In the normal operation of municipal government, implementation of the plan lies with expert planning staff whose actions must respond to policies officially adopted by councils.

The dates of new planning acts do not mark firm lines between periods in which attitudes and styles totally differ. Nonetheless, they indicate benchmarks by which we note the end or beginnings of rather different approaches to planning and to the role of planners and community members in the planning process. Early legislation in Nova Scotia reflected the optimism of the Progressive era: faith that scientific management could cure the ills of urban life. As Utopian hope waned during the depressions of the 1920s and 1930s, Nova Scotians abandoned planning.

In 1939, the province may have responded to the perceived success of central state planning in promoting industrial development in other nations. The legislation seemed inspired by trust in the wisdom of local elites who, guided by trained professionals, sought to develop urban centres.

By the late 1960s, North American societies responded to massive societal changes that shifted cultural values towards 'participatory democracy': 'Legislators wanted to respond to demands for greater public participation in decisions about the shape of Nova Scotian communities, but traditional practices and established power relationships die hard. The 1969 act offered not a warm embrace but instead a cautious handshake to those who asked for a role in decision making' (Grant 1988a: 262). While the role of the citizen expanded, so did the role of the planner. Without trained staff, municipalities would find it difficult to undertake full-blown planning. The act marked the final acceptance of planner as expert and regional and community land use planning as the recipe for economic development and growth.

Revisions to the legislation in 1983 reflected the resurgence of conservative values following the rapid decline of 'radicalism' in the 1970s. The 1983 Planning Act clarified the division of labour within municipal planning and the structures and processes for reaching decisions. Citizens could advise council on policy development and discretionary matters. Council fixed policies and made judgments. Planners implemented plans. The act reinforced the dominant political, economic, and social structure in Nova Scotia, while establishing a stable climate for the development of land.

We see, then, that changes to planning legislation in Nova Scotia followed the rise and fall of societal trends within the nation and the province. As social pressure for citizen action grew within North America in the late 1960s, Nova Scotia responded with legislation that defined a greater role for citizens in local planning. Simultaneously, the 1969 act affirmed the leading role of provincial governments in promoting economic development through land-use planning. With the decline in citizen action from the early 1970s and negative local reaction to regional planning, the provincial government began reviewing planning legislation. Following the growing conservatism in industrial nations, the province adopted legislation (in 1983) that protected the rights of property owners above all else. It created supportive conditions in which communities could plan for development.

Local Action in Regional Context

Local planning activities and disputes occur within structures and contexts created in part by provincial legislation, in part by national or regional programs, and in part by community heritage and traditions. Both national and regional contexts help to frame or set the stage for actions taken by actors in local communities.

In the next chapter, we briefly explore the history of land-use planning and land-use disputes in mainland Halifax. We see that local events reflect national trends in certain situations, while people also respond to regional values and traditions. For example, although the 1969 act reflected national and international pressures from citizen action (such as the antiwar protests in the United States), we find the first major citizen initiatives occurring in Halifax in the early 1970s. Halifax operates on a slight time-lag: the protests come to Boston and Toronto first.

Regional traditions and values may put a quick end to actions that proved successful elsewhere. For example, provincially appointed agencies like the Municipal Board and the Nova Scotia courts have consistently limited citizens' abilities to challenge municipal decisions. Existing social and political structures offer citizens who contest established power and privileges little lasting influence. The stages upon which actors perform and the scripts they deliver are set in a mood of desperation and powerlessness. As we will see in the episodes that follow, the relentless pursuit of prosperity is an underlying theme in the drama of democracy in Halifax. As people argue about the character of their community and the nature of planning in a democratic society, at least they all agree on the desperate need for 'development.'

Chapter Four

Planning Issues in Peninsular Halifax

In this chapter, we briefly review planning issues in Halifax during the postwar period.[1] We examine the way that Halifax planners, politicians, and citizens think about planning and about each other. We begin to sense how the actors play their parts in the planning drama. We pay special attention to actors' perceptions of each other's roles and characteristics, and their thoughts about the function and nature of planning. What did they say about their own concerns? What did they see as the interests of others? How did they define the purpose of planning? What did they think about the plan? Fortunately, many of the actors wrote or spoke clearly and forcefully about what they expected from the planning process and its participants. Through this chapter and the next, we examine some of the documents published in the context of planning activities. Along with interview notes, these documents provide the data for our analysis of the drama.

To supplement published and collected documents, and to gain greater insight into the concerns of actors who participated in planning activities, we conducted a series of interviews with planners, politicians, and citizens in Halifax.[2] While the passage of time may have fogged some recollections about events that happened long ago, actors' values come through clearly in their comments. As we analyse what people write and say about planning, we begin to expose the cultural drama involved.

Halifax in the Postwar Period

After the end of the Second World War many Western industrialized nations began massive reconstruction efforts to rebuild their communities. The Canadian government spent money to encourage industrialization and development. One of its key programs, the National Housing Act of 1956, provided funds for communities to remove blighted areas and replace them with new growth. Halifax qualified under the program and received assistance to hire Gordon Stephenson of the University of Toronto to undertake a redevelopment study (Stephenson 1957).

While the national mood reflected optimism and faith in progress, Nova Scotia faced continued economic decline. Central Halifax showed obvious signs of decay: run-down houses and vacant buildings. City officials who asked Stephenson for advice apparently accepted the growing consensus that planning offered tools to promote orderly development and economic prosperity.

Nova Scotia's local chapter of the Community Planning Association of Canada (CPAC) added its voice to those encouraging community planning (B33; B41).[3] CPAC argued that citizens should cooperate in the planning process by listening to planners talk, joining planning associations, and going to meetings about planning. One pamphlet advised:

> City planning is not a magic cure-all but, with whole hearted citizen co-operation, it can go a long way towards making our urban areas beautiful, economical and safe environments for ourselves and our children (B33: 2).

> It is essential for the citizens of our city or town to debate the Development Plan fully, to understand it and, when it has been adopted, to work towards making it a positive reality ... More active participation is needed now, both by private enterprise and by individual citizens to put our Development Plan into immediate effect (B33: 7).

Following Stephenson's report (1957), Halifax declared a portion of the city below Citadel Hill as the 'Central Redevelopment Area' (CRA) and hired staff to work on a redevelopment plan. The redevelopment project stimulated the City to take planning more seriously than ever before. The impractical 'master plans' of previous years gave way to project development around the CRA.

Between 1958 and 1963, the City cleared several blocks of run-down tenement housing that once provided low-cost homes for many

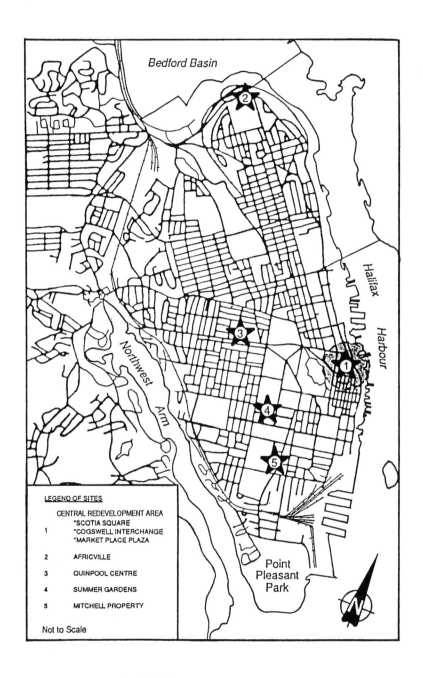

Map. 4.1   Peninsular Halifax

of Halifax's poor. Some of the displaced moved to new public housing in the far north end, but many had to find their own lodgings.

News clippings on the redevelopment show little evidence of
community opposition to the massive project as the clearing proceeded. Respondents could not remember any protests, as a former alderman recalled.

> A: 'See things were moving, cities were booming and it looked like
> Halifax was being left behind. That easy money. That easy federal
> money for urban renewal was there and I think they just grabbed it
> and ran. It was the thing at the time: jobs, money and – you know.
> Not a lot of protest at that particular time.'

Urged to act on urban problems by the federal government, Council
saw redevelopment as appropriate to the City's interests. Most Haligonians seemed to view the project as obliterating an obnoxious and
embarrassing slum. Neither politicians nor planners took account of
the people who lived in the area. A Council member from the time
remembered: 'There was no objection to clearing – they were all
tenement properties. People weren't considered all that valuable in
those days. There wasn't much welfare. We certainly weren't a welfare state.'

In the 1950s and early 1960s, evidently, Haligonians saw the problems of the city in physical terms: run-down buildings that had to go.
They presumed that the residents of the buildings would thrive
elsewhere. Not everyone agreed, but the efforts of a few property
owners and residents to resist expropriation and relocation made no
headway.

Newspaper clippings from the early 1960s indicated business
concern because the site sat vacant for a few years before redevelopment began.[4] One former mayor called the slum clearance scheme 'ill-
fated' and pointed to the need for more public housing for the poor
(B35B). Generally, though, the community accepted the project as a
sign of progress and improvement.

> A: But you know, it was the old bulldozer syndrome, where they
> were ripping down – 'big was better, bigger was best.' A lot of peo-
> ple got caught up in urban renewal – a lot of federal money around
> for tearing down areas which were dilapidated. In some cases they
> were slums, but along with the slums there was a lot of worthwhile
> buildings and areas that could have been saved. But you know you

hate to judge ... but ... it was wrong ... People right at the time didn't know what to do with the centre of town ... It was the wrong approach, but if you look at what was available at the time, it would have taken a real visionary to have changed it. He or she would never have had the support. So I'm not going to condemn it, even though I don't like it and it's wrong.

As this Council member indicated, the project worked in its time, though subsequent generations condemned the wholesale destruction. The alderman rejects judging the actions of the past by today's values and standards.

After several years of delay, Council approved 'Scotia Square,' a proposal submitted by a group of Nova Scotian investors (Collier 1974). Construction began in the late 1960s on the complex that included three office towers, a hotel,[5] and a shopping centre. Multistorey apartment buildings rose later. Staff recommended a major highway route along the waterfront, but began to acknowledge public concern about unanticipated issues relating to the heritage value of properties that the highway would obliterate (B35D; B35E).

No development project in the postwar period matched the CRA in its scope or implications for the downtown area. Despite its impact on the city, however, slum clearance generated no public protest. Evidently, those interested in planning in Halifax reached something of a working consensus on a model for development. While Council members may have had their reservations, they decided to give planning a try.

A: The prevailing ethic of Council was free enterprise and planning was just an interference keeping people from doing what they wanted with their property ...

At least 75 per cent of the Council were not pro-planning; mind you, they might have been pro-development, but they weren't pro-planning in any longer sense.

Q: Did they see planning as a means to an end?[6]

They accepted planners because other cities had them and this was supposed to be the thing to do. The common position I recall some of those members taking was 'so the planners are saying what they think the public interest is, and the developers are saying what they think the business interest is, and we should somehow find some

Scotia Square

middle ground between the two,' as though they were not a part of the public side. You know, they were mediators between the private developers and the staff.

We see, then, that while politicians remained sceptical about planning, they were ready to experiment with planning to get access to federal funds and to try to promote development. As players on a national stage, they feared that Halifax could fall behind other communities. If other cities used planning, then Halifax should do so as well.

The few citizens knowledgeable about planning in the postwar period, many of them activists in the Community Planning Association, supported the Stephenson report. They argued that Halifax needed to hire expert planners who would use planning to generate growth and ensure order. Although most citizens could not expect an active role in the planning process (in fact, some could be displaced by it), they could provide valuable moral support for experts and politicians.

The destruction of a black settlement at Africville, on the northern end of the Halifax peninsula, similarly generated little protest during the mid-1960s (Clairmont and Magill 1971, 1987). The model of urban development that dominated the period and nurtured the spread of planning harboured no sentiment for tradition and self-reliance. It sought a future of steel, concrete, and glass where planners might provide the surgical tools to remove cancerous growths and restore urban health.

In these early years, it seems that citizens and planners agreed that planners had the skills and the vision necessary to help developers transform Halifax into a dynamic metropolis. Imported experts brought with them the gospel of 'redevelopment.' Planning provided tools for municipal progress. Slum clearance paved the way for radical social and economic transformation by creating a *tabula rasa*, the prerequisite for progress. Science and technology would provide additional tools that would shape Halifax into a modern, high-rise city, able to compete with any other.

As the 1970s approached, however, quiescence began to give way to the turbulence of the 'participation era.' The historic consensus that obliterated Africville and constructed Scotia Square fell apart under new pressures and new values.

The 'Participation Era': The 1970s

By the end of the sixties, a mood of protest suffused North American societies. In Halifax, some community residents began questioning planning decisions. Heritage groups lobbied to protect waterfront buildings. Citizen activists came to recognize the potentially destructive aspects of community planning undertaken without adequate public input; increasingly they demanded a role for citizens in the planning process. The early activists represented an eclectic mix of 'hippies,' young professionals, and others committed to a new social and political agenda.

The 1969 Planning Act supported the changing atmosphere. The law made planning mandatory and provided new opportunities for citizens to participate in planning matters. The legislation extended the province's power in land-use matters and imposed regional planning on the city. Not ready to concede any authority to the province, Halifax stonewalled on implementing regional planning and for many years stalled on preparing a municipal plan.

The decade began with a bang as the province funded 'Halifax Encounter Week' in early 1970. Organized by the Voluntary Planning Board,[7] the Encounter brought a panel of experts (most from outside of Canada) to the city to stimulate the community to change. For five days the panel dissected Haligonian values. They found a society 'dedicated to underachievement' (Hartnett 1970: 17), with a massive inferiority complex. Hundreds of people attended nightly 'town hall' meetings. Thousands watched the proceedings on television. Halifax had never seen a spectacle like it. People who may never before have thought about planning issues spoke out and insisted on their right to participate in the development of their community. Citizen action and participatory democracy received a real boost.

After Encounter, the province sought to channel citizen action into productive avenues. Through the regional planning process, it encouraged the formation of MOVEment for Citizens Voice and Action (known as MOVE), a coalition of citizens' groups interested in everything from welfare rights to community planning (Gall 1974). With a grant from the province, MOVE hired staff and began research and lobbying on various issues.

A major land-use dispute in Halifax arose in the early 1970s over Harbour Drive and the Cogswell Street Interchange. According to the engineers' plans, Harbour Drive would traverse the peninsula along the waterfront, providing rapid traffic flow through the downtown. To accommodate it, the City would have to expropriate and tear down several old warehouses and buildings. The Cogswell Street Interchange, taking up more than 10 acres of valuable downtown land, would link Scotia Square with Harbour Drive.

Harbour Drive, through a series of battles, became a rallying point for several interest groups. Heritage groups wanted to preserve and restore the historic waterfront buildings in the downtown core. MOVE staff decided to fight Harbour Drive north because it would disrupt residential neighbourhoods. After several intense public meetings and organized lobbying from activists, Council decided to cancel the downtown portion of Harbour Drive and assist a developer to restore the waterfront area for commercial use.

A former Council member recalled the context of the times when

Cogswell Interchange

Haligonians felt pressure from events occurring in other Canadian cities:

A: The developments of Vancouver, Toronto – I could smell them breathing down my neck from Toronto. With Marathon – big developers, Trizec, the Bronfmans, and I've forgotten the big combination there – mostly Toronto and Montreal. Of course we were running into the problem with the Council in Toronto – it had started to generate with the Spadina Expressway – the objections to that. I met David Crombie the night after he became mayor ... But we chatted about where we were going and where he was going. And it was out of that Toronto scene, I think, that development, the free running of developers was slowed down. And they reflected on us. Now the mob, of course, were the ones who were blamed for stopping the development in Halifax. And the mob was [names three aldermen].

Clearly, activists protesting Harbour Drive looked to citizen protests elsewhere for inspiration. Documents and interviews alike show that protestors hoped to repeat the Spadina Expressway experience. One citizen activist described the context: 'Well, certainly in Harbour

Drive North we were without any hesitation, using Spadina as an example – using arguments or modifying arguments that were being put forward in Toronto or Jane Jacobs's book to apply to Halifax.'

We should recognize, then, that events reported in the national media and decisions made at the national level became important elements of the context in which Haligonians participated in land-use disputes. Four hundred people came out to public meetings in part because they saw Harbour Drive as a critical issue, but also because the mood of the times supported mass citizen action.

Interest in planning issues may have peaked in Halifax in January 1973 when the director of planning presented 'The Master Plan!' to Council. The 1969 Planning Act required municipalities to prepare a municipal development plan. 'The Master Plan!', fewer than twenty pages in length, was the City's first response. A Council member, who presented that document to the public, remembered:

A: We had our first meeting at Queen Elizabeth High School. There must have been a thousand people, and they had a thousand ropes, and they were going to hang me because everybody wanted us to come in with a set plan – you know, here's your city – this is green, this is the building – but we didn't. We came in and said, 'You know you have to develop what kind of city you want and that takes dialogue' – it takes talk, it takes principles, it takes policy – not specifics. It has to be broad general policy and then you work down. Well, they didn't understand that. What a meeting! Geez, they were wild. Speaker after speaker – we were crazy. Why did we call the meeting when we didn't do anything? You know, etc.

The reaction truly surprised Council, according to a planner:

P: Council, I think, attempted or intended to adopt [the document] as a kind of primitive statement of what a plan should be, if not a plan itself, and sent it to public hearing. ... I think the response – at least I've always been given to understand that the response from the public caught Council quite unawares. That there had been a real change in the level of interest which had eluded them. And that what people were saying was not so much what was good or bad about the plan, but that they wanted a plan that they would be consulted about.

Citizens, it appeared, wanted planning. Furthermore, they demanded a role in it. Planning activities had become situations for significant community action.

Estimates of the number of residents present at the public meeting vary from 500 to 1,200, but no one denies that citizens gave 'The Master Plan!' a hostile reception. National events and provincial initiatives had built up expectations about the importance of planning and about the significance of citizen involvement.

A CPAC brief (D10) explained why citizens viewed 'The Master Plan!' with alarm. CPAC saw the plan as vague and ambiguous, resulting from an inappropriate planning process. Citizens wanted to participate in the framing of plans, not to react to them.

Why did so many people take an interest in the plan? One of the citizens active in planning in Halifax explained:

C: I think ... that fighting City Hall was certainly a country-wide issue. And I think Trudeau's thing about 'participatory democracy,' the Company of Young Canadians – the various kinds of organizations that were funded to try to facilitate people into taking part in decisions that affected their lives – I think that cut right across the board, that people wanted to have some say about what kind of a neighbourhood they lived in, about what happened to their city. I think that the Heritage Trust played an important role in educating and alerting people to the possible destruction of the historic buildings on the waterfront ... And I think that generally people were just ripe to have their say and get organized around it.

A planner concurred:

P: Oh I think it was probably several things. Clearly some sense – there was a lot of different discussion going on at all different levels, there was a lot of regional plan work being done ... There was some new development beginning to happen. Scotia Square had come along in '68 and there was some sense that things were beginning to change ... I remember very clearly the discussions I had with ... some people here about the effect of Scotia Square. And the effect was dramatic, that finally something was beginning to shake and change. It was tremendously exciting. It was tremendously positive, and I think once that settled in, that there was some possibility for some change and some growth and some new direction, I think people got very interested in it and wanted to not just have that happen around them – to protect their interest, to foster their interest, to keep their neighbourhoods.

And it was very stylish. It happened to come at a time when it was very much a part of the ether that people get involved in planning. It was in Toronto, it was in Montreal ... It was very much a part of the times that people wanted to be involved. I don't think it was by any means peculiar to Halifax. And all of those things happening at once just generated more momentum.

The planner explicitly acknowledges that local planning in certain ways reflected events and trends elsewhere in the nation. Participation and involvement in planning issues was in the air.

As citizen protests grew, politicians and planners grew weary. The *Toronto Daily Star* cited the mayor as saying that MOVE opposed everything, but did not really represent the people of Halifax (B33B). For interest groups, the issue of representation is always a vulnerable point. One of the MOVE activists explained:

C: I think [MOVE] actually did a reasonably good job of representing that broad collection of views. And for a period of time, I suspect MOVE was taken moderately seriously as a reasonable sort of representation of whatever opinions were out there. I don't think MOVE failed because it lost the credibility. I think MOVE failed because there just wasn't a staff any more, and it needed a staff to stay together ... And one of the ways you put an organization like that down is to say, 'Well, it's not representative, they're self-appointed, etc.' But it's my impression that MOVE didn't do a bad job at all.

How do unelected interest groups establish credibility for their opinions and positions? Many of them felt that they spoke for the public, yet they had no way to legitimate their claim. Those who disagreed with a group's position could simply assert that the group did not represent the public.

Elected politicians and city planners support an elitist model of representative democracy, while citizen protestors advocate participatory democracy. The two models of democracy provide actors with fodder for debate about appropriate decisions and processes. For example, citizen activists argued that citizens should participate fully in framing the plan; by contrast, planning staff opposed appointing a planning advisory committee, preferring other kinds of citizen involvement that would not create new decision making structures (B26).

At the same time as the city debated whether to adopt the plan, citizens fought to protect views from the highest point in the city, the Citadel fortress. As Halifax developed during the late 1960s, high-rise structures replaced the original low-rise skyline. The once panoramic vista of the harbour gave way to snippets of view between buildings. Some citizens worried that eventually they would not see the water from the hill. They organized and lobbied to protect the remaining views, and eventually convinced Council to pass view-planes legislation in 1974 (Pacey 1979).

Increasingly, land-use disputes reflected different images people had of the character of the city. Those opposing development projects argued for low-rise buildings, heritage preservation, and neighbourhood protection. Those advocating development projects called for growth, increased tax revenues, progress. The pro-development lobby saw their opponents as backward-thinking. The antidevelopment lobby viewed developers as greedy monsters.

Disputes engaged citizen action in several parts of the city. For instance, in the Quinpool Road area, some residents fought to prevent development of a shopping centre and apartment complex. Individuals successfully appealed some development projects that the City approved along the waterfront. It seemed clear that the level of interest in planning issues and concern about planning decisions had never been higher. Relations between Council, planning staff, and citizens grew tense.

A former Council member reflected on the behaviour of citizen activists and planners:

> A: ... The newspaper reported the battles, from a slightly biased point of view towards developers, I think. And developers were representing one or two per cent of the population. And people that you would call 'green' today, representing one or two per cent of the population. And other than that, nobody gave a damn! But Council's normal reaction, with the exception of a few of us, was 'We want the buildings, we want the revenue, and you green people who come from Australia or New Zealand, but certainly don't come from Canada, don't bug us!' That was a lot of the reaction.
>
> And I must admit that, you know, I wasn't overly impressed by some of the people making presentations. There were two or three people at every public hearing; you could anticipate them using up three-quarters of the time. I can't blame them, in retrospect ... Halifax is a very old-fashioned, down-to-earth, north-end uneducated town – it's changed a lot in the last thirty years ...

Historic properties

> Well, the planners kept pretty well ... to themselves. They didn't
> speak out to the public, they spoke only to Council or to staff at staff
> meetings. There was a lot of animosity towards them. They weren't
> accepted as having any realistic view of life. You know, 'if it's good
> for New York, it's good for us,' sort of thing. Everybody was shocked
> when New York went broke!

We see that the politician attributed much of the protest to people
who 'come from away,' the ultimate put-down in heritage-conscious
Nova Scotia. Perhaps, the politician implies, native-born Haligonians
do not participate in planning issues or complain about Council
actions. The respondent's comments show that politicians saw their
new planners as idealistic visionaries, not as pragmatic municipal
employees. Because the planners came to Halifax from other provinces, they didn't understand local concerns. Council felt planners

sought to impose limits on development that politicians desired. In the alderman's comments, New York appears on the same international stage as Halifax, offering both good and bad examples.

The tentative consensus (imposed by federal funding programs) that planning offered tools for development had given way in the 1970s to the idea that planning potentially constrained opportunities for development. Citizens advocated planning to protect their neighbourhoods and their heritage, while Council sought urban development; at times, those objectives conflicted. Within the municipal bureaucracy, the Planning Department had a small staff,[8] but the Development Department grew steadily larger.

'Planning' proved a hot issue in the 1974 municipal election in Halifax. With the election of a new pro-planning Council and a new planning staff in control, the city finally set about a full-blown planning process. Citizens, politicians, and staff worked together to develop a municipal development plan that all could claim as theirs. The process used in regional planning became the model. Whereas politicians and planners at the turn of the decade saw themselves as the ones with the responsibility to plan, by mid-decade all parties saw citizen input as a vital part of the process. Like other communities through North America, Halifax accepted citizens into the planning process – not as full partners, perhaps, but as legitimate participants.

A staff report in September 1977 outlined the Planning Department's commitment to public consultation.

> Public participation in planning has its roots in our society's commitment to a process of democratic government. The basic theme it articulates is the right of citizens to be involved in decisions which affect their lifestyles ... What is required is a process which provides opportunities for public input at an early stage in the decision-making process. In this way, the City of Halifax can develop a capacity for effective consultation with the public, and create a climate conducive to discussion, negotiation, and sound public decision-making (B27: 1).

After four years of work, the City of Halifax adopted its Municipal Development Plan (MDP) in 1978. Citizens devoted many hours of committee work preparing the plan. However, whereas hundreds of Haligonians turned out for planning meetings in the early 1970s, turnout for the final meetings on the MDP proved disappointing (A1). Still, those who saw the plan adopted felt confident that finally Council had some policies in place to shape decisions.

A planner explains staff's impressions of the plan and the process that developed it.

P: We had a lot of discussion going at that point about how to redirect [change]. We came to ... a very clear understanding in the meetings and in public that we wanted development, we wanted certain kinds of development. We wanted growth, but we wanted it to go in certain ways ... And for the first time, ... we had ... aldermen making ... choices. I mean staff wasn't making those choices. And what happened ... was that we transferred ownership at this point – this was not a staff plan, it was everybody's plan. Staff had a big stake in it, obviously. The public had a big stake in it, obviously, and the Council or the MDP committee, mostly Council, had a big stake in making the choices – and so everybody owned a chunk of it. That was an almost unique experience. Some other cities have done it, but I don't think that they did it to quite the extent that we did it.

The planner perceives that planning in Halifax in the 1970s involved cooperation between the parties in Lash's (1977) three-sided triangle: politician, planner, and public. 'Everybody owned a chunk' of the final plan. As we discover in the case-study disputes described below, the perception that politicians, planners, and the public worked together to frame the plan gave the plan immense legitimacy in the eyes of citizens.

In the discourse fragment above, the planner also demonstrates a commitment to development: 'we wanted development.' Although the process involved an interchange with politicians and public, the planners attempted to set the agenda. By the time that Halifax adopted its first practical land-use plan, planners accepted that planning offered tools for development. The impractical idealists of the early seventies had been replaced with pragmatists who shared politicians' commitment to development and growth.

One of the first tests of the 1978 MDP came in 1979 over a high-rise project on Brunswick Street, Market Place Plaza (described in the next chapter). While disputants often argued over what 'good planning' might mean for a site, in this instance they had before them agreed policies to guide their decision. As a detailed analysis of the case demonstrates, however, having the MDP in place did not end land-use disputes. Instead, the MDP became a significant new weapon in the arsenal of the various factions.

Politicians and planners felt firmly convinced by the late 1970s that they had made every effort to involve citizens in the planning process. Citizens served on planning committees, attended public meetings, and appeared before Council to state their views. Yet outside observers sometimes felt that Haligonians didn't get the same level of input that citizens elsewhere might expect. In commenting on the waterfront development project underway in the late 1970s, Swain says of the level of public involvement achieved, 'Such a cursory process would have been decried as undemocratic by active citizen groups in most other cities' (1979: 278). Groups like CPAC organized some events to try to convince the Waterfront Development Corporation to solicit more public involvement, but had limited success. The tide of intense citizen action had already ebbed.

With an MDP and a waterfront plan in hand, both developed with citizen input, staff felt they had a strong sense of direction for the future. Citizens who arrived to protest projects that met the development intent of the plans faced an occasionally hostile reception. With citizen input institutionalized in the planning process through committees and policies, and with fewer citizens showing up at Council meetings to protest projects, those who continued to oppose development proposals increasingly found themselves treated as antidevelopment cranks. Citizen disillusionment grew.

> C: I think that originally people got involved in planning because they saw it maybe as a tool by which they could have some influence over what happened in their city. Because it didn't work out that way in a lot of cases, people were turned off to it. They don't see it that way any more. They've become cynical and more issue-oriented.
>
> There were so many battles that we fought where it was realized that ... we were part of developing the policies that were in those plans. We knew what we meant. We knew what those policies meant. We knew what people were asking for. But then ... the planners could interpret them in a completely different way and go to court and swear to it – and if that didn't work, then they would just change it. I think it was really difficult for people to continue having any great faith in the city planning process to change.

In sum, then, during the period in which the 1969 Planning Act operated, the influence of municipal planning in Halifax gradually increased. Citizen action in community planning peaked during the early 1970s and became institutionalized through the plan preparation process in the mid-1970s.

The comments of various Council members show that politicians prior to the 1974 election strongly supported urban development and put up with planning because it provided a means to federal funds for local development. Various land use disputes during the early 1970s revealed growing value conflicts between those who promoted 'development projects' and those who opposed them. The 1974 Council accepted planning both as a means and an end in itself: as a way to regulate and encourage the 'right kind' of development, and to limit the extent of conflict over land use.

To enforce its approach to planning and development, council hired and fired planning and development staff. Over the years, the planning function bounced about within the administrative structure, sometimes coming under the authority of the Development Department (as during the CRA project), and later gaining its independence as a Planning Department. By the mid-1970s, Council employed planning staff who saw planning as a tool for development, who could work towards implementing Council's vision, and who would involve citizens in the process.

Hence, during the mid to late 1970s, a new consensus on the role of planning developed. Politicians, planners, and citizens worked together to create an MDP that would set out a vision of Halifax for the future. Plan policies would guide future decisions. Council would judge proposed projects against approved policies.

Unfortunately, that consensus lasted only briefly, for the MDP did *not* prevent land-use disputes from arising. Policies offered latitude for interpretation. By the end of the period, planners and citizen activists saw planning through distinctly different lenses. Planners saw the plan and zoning by-law as providing tools for implementing development, for sorting out the good projects from the bad. Citizens who had worked with planners and politicians to write the plan expected that they had fashioned a shield to protect their community from unwanted change.

Perhaps divergent values led citizen activists and planners in these different directions. Citizens advocated low-rise, small-scale development projects. They spoke of family, tradition, and heritage. They hoped for a society free from the growing alienation of mass society. They wanted full participation in decision making at the local level. By the end of the 1970s, their disillusionment with their inability to affect the course of development left them frustrated. Their relations with staff suffered.

C: We felt quite possessive about that plan. I mean [we] organized a whole lot of meetings ... where we had workshops on every manner of things and displays. People came in and drafted policies and came out with new policies, and really kept working on it. And then the planners just took it away and made it into that big bureaucratic document that it is to this day – really quite unwieldy.

And there was another thing too that was going on. The planners were, it seemed to us, spending an awful lot of time with the developers. It always seemed that they were making the case for the developers, always trying to find a way to make a case for the developers to City Council. And a couple of times they got caught out – they used to socialize together ... I remember during one planning appeal, we complained to the chairman because one of the planners and the developer went to lunch together and I thought that was highly improper. The planner was there representing all citizens, and [the Board] agreed ... Those are pretty tough things to deal with. ... It is hard to sustain an interest in the planning process if what you say doesn't get taken into account, and if nothing seems to change anyway.

Citizens saw the planners as making the planning process less accessible. Rumours spread about planners socializing with developers. Citizens came to see themselves as increasingly ineffective – 'on the other side' opposed to the interests of planners and politicians.

Planners, well entrenched in the municipal bureaucracy, espoused professional values that promoted regulated development. They recognized that their employers, the Council, wanted growth and progress without public outcry. They knew that developers needed clear rules so that they could invest with confidence. Planners felt that citizens had a right to participate in advising Council, but that final authority in government must rest with elected politicians.

In the years to come, changes to planning legislation would clarify the role of the citizen and the role of the planner in local land-use planning. Increasingly, planning practice entrenched the professional values of the planner along with the political values of City Council.

The Conservative 1980s

Staff reports in the early 1980s show that planners saw citizen participation as an unavoidable part of the planning process.

Citizen participation appears to be here to stay, as it is clear that with or without established procedures citizens will make themselves heard ...

If citizen participation is to be an asset to municipal decision-making rather than a fact-of-life to be grudgingly tolerated, it must be broadly-based and well-publicized, as well as simple and understandable (Heseltine 1982: 1, 2).

References to 'democracy,' which punctuated earlier reports on participation, had given way to nuances of concern by this time. The tone of the staff report, with words like 'grudgingly tolerated,' alludes to staff's desire to improve citizen participation.

Neighbourhood, or detailed area planning, had begun in several parts of the city, with citizen committees doing much of the work. It appears that the intensity of land-use disputes in the downtown area decreased following the failed appeal on Market Place Plaza. Instead of fighting what they came to see as hopeless battles over projects, citizens put their energies into developing plans to protect their neighbourhoods with strong policies. Also, with tighter economic times, developers proposed few major development projects for the downtown. Then in 1983, the province passed a new planning act limiting citizens' rights to appeal Council decisions.

Various interest groups continued to organize and lobby on behalf of their concerns, however. When a developer appealed Council's refusal to grant a development agreement for a high-rise near the Citadel in 1983, Heritage Trust hired a lawyer and gained standing to help the City successfully defend itself. Later, Heritage Trust applied for a rezoning to control the height of buildings along Brunswick Street. In 1974 Council had passed a motion asking staff for height controls. Ten years later, after concerted citizen action, Council finally adopted height controls across from the Citadel.

One of the most contentious cases of the 1980s involved a dispute about the appropriate designation and use of a parcel of land that was kitty-corner to the Halifax Public Gardens, at Spring Garden Road and Summer Street. Dalhousie University sold the property to a consortium of doctors and professionals for development as high-rise condominiums. An eclectic collection of gardens enthusiasts and heritage advocates banded together to oppose the proposal, fearing that it would threaten the Gardens and the heritage streetscape around the park perimeter. Over two years and tens of thousands of dollars later, the Friends of the Public Gardens conceded defeat as Council approved Summer Gardens.

If
City Council
won't plan,
plan to change
the Council

Political button, Friends of the Public Gardens

The battle over Summer Gardens severely strained relations between planning staff and citizens opposing the plan amendment. One
of the Friends remembered:

> **C:** Now part of [the antagonism] may have been that some of the
> people in the Friends did indeed treat [planners] as morons. That
> may have queered it in lots of ways ... I always had the sense that
> [planners] were on somebody else's side, and that the only reason we
> got any support at all was because we had enough legal expertise ...
> to make them wary about just dismissing us. We had people who
> knew what the law was, what our rights were, what their responsi-
> bilities were in certain respects so that they at least gave some atten-
> tion to it. But it was everything benign, certainly not active.

Citizens didn't see planners as helping the people but as siding with
developers. The respondent acknowledges, however, that citizens
may have contributed to the growing alienation between citizens and
planners by being disrespectful and antagonistic.

Planning staff supported the plan amendment.

> **P:** Now, in the case of Summer Gardens, ... we recommended that
> [Council] entertain a plan amendment because, in our view, the origi-
> nal existing policy was wrong ... Nothing was ever looked at. What's
> its proper use? What's the right use to make of this property? ...
> What we said to Council was, 'Look, your first condition is that
> you've never made a proper policy choice about what the future of
> this land should be. Should you reconsider the plan? Yeah, you
> should reconsider the plan.'

Having said that, then your next step is to start the process ... I accept the fact that the public sort of says, 'Well, this is what's proposed to us. And is it legitimate?' Yeah, it's legitimate. Is it the right thing to do? That's what this process is all about – it's to find that out, to look at the pros and cons of that.

Very often the public takes an argument like Summer Gardens as if it were an empirical argument – as if it were something you could prove with positive statements that it's right or wrong. It's a normative argument, and [planners] can't inject ... opinions into a normative argument.

The planner sees citizens as having trouble making a vital distinction between 'fact' and 'opinion.' Planners, the respondent says, deal with facts. Citizens and politicians deal with opinions and values.

Clearly, planning disputes deal with normative matters. Citizens want to use planning tools to enforce their values about the townscape. Planners, however, refuse to participate in normative debate in the context of particular disputes. They enforce the values embedded in the plan and its by-laws. Where a normative choice has to be made, planners accept the verdict of Council. Citizens interpret as problematic the unwillingness of planners to support the values that citizens articulate. 'The planners don't listen to the people.' 'Planners don't keep up with new theories in planning.' 'The planners always push high-rise development.'

Planners may not recognize the extent to which their practice reflects their own values, yet their comments indicate that they see development as highly desirable. While many citizens characterize Scotia Square as a 'monstrosity,' a planner calls it 'positive.'

As government employees, planners believe they implement the municipality's corporate agenda. 'Our agenda is to have a system, a process, that has criteria and works ... I think we've worked very hard not to impose our values ... You can't always do that, but I think we do a fairly decent job of it.' To do their jobs successfully, planners internalize the values of their employers while simultaneously characterizing themselves as objective technicians.

Under the 1983 Planning Act, few community groups in Halifax chose to fight decisions through to appeal to the Municipal Board.[9] The ordeal of some appellants who had court costs held against them, and the heavy expenditures associated with fighting Council decisions discouraged citizen action beyond the final public hearing. Some citizens decided to direct their activity to the political arena instead.[10]

Another planning dispute in the south end raised some of the same issues as the Friends had voiced. The experience of the parties to the Mitchell property dispute, presented in detail in Chapter 6, serves as an interesting example of the nature of disputes in the late 1980s. Citizens organized and lobbied intensely to prevent a development in their neighbourhood, but took no further action once Council decided against them.

Under the 1983 act, we find the roles of the various players in the planning game firmly defined. Citizens have a right to seek information and to speak out. Planners advise Council and implement the plan. Both citizens and planners have only as much influence as Council gives them.

We note, however, that citizens active in planning matters in the late 1980s (and early 1990s) feel frustrated by their assigned role. They're no longer willing to spend the hours fighting a lost cause.

> C: I think people have gotten into survival. There's no support – the resources aren't there for people. Maybe I'm cynical, but I feel it's unfair to ask people to be involved in something where your involvement is not going to make much difference, nor is it going to affect or improve your lot in life. Maybe it's because there hasn't been a lot of development pressure. I think as that changes, people will probably (if they see things that are likely to come under the wrecking ball, or if they see major changes in their neighbourhoods) ... get involved again.

Many citizens voiced great doubts about their ability to influence decisions and their willingness to persist in fighting for their image of the city. They don't feel that planners or politicians listen to them. Their powerlessness to influence outcomes undermines their faith in the efficacy of democracy. Planners, though, indicated that they welcome input.

> P: [Citizens should get involved] to defend their interests, to make their views known ... Don't pull their punches. I mean the whole thing. I guess I have a very un-Canadian attitude about some of these things. I think a good row is the only way to sort out some of these issues. I don't know why it needs to be friendly. It's nice when it is, but ...
>
> I think the public is terribly badly served when the Council won't do anything until [people] come out and tell them what to do. I think

it's extremely important that the Council make decisions, make good decisions, make informed decisions, and that they be in charge of making them. I think it's extremely important that the public make its views felt in that. I think it's extremely important that both of them get staff advice which is independent, which is hopefully dispassionate. If they're happy with it – if one of them is happy with it, if both of them are happy with it – that's great. It's nice ... but if everybody hates it, that's fine too. They've got to get the advice. They've got to understand what it is they're trading off, what the implications of their decisions are. Because most of their decisions ... really aren't clearly right or clearly wrong. They just have upsides and downsides which are different. They have good consequences and bad consequences.

While planner respondents welcome participation, clearly they do not respect politicians (or other planners) who let the people 'tell them what to do.' Citizens should attempt to direct, but politicians should not be directed. This apparent contradiction occurred frequently in planners' remarks. They can live with the paradox.

Some of the planning staff have worked for the City many years and know their jobs well. They have a clear idea of their function: they are employees. They run projects through the policy environment of the plan and advise Council of what falls out. They are not attempting to create some ideal vision of the city, but are helping to clarify issues before Council makes decisions.

Citizens may have rather different expectations of planners, however.

C: I find that planners are like anybody: once they get there and stay there too long, they become pretty entrenched. They take the path of least resistance: 'This is how we do it, and this is how we will always do it' ...

It's awful that the planners don't go away on refresher courses, or get a sabbatical and try something different. They probably don't get any new ideas. I think one role that they should have is keeping themselves apprised of what's new, of what's changing professionally in the field.

I guess the other role that they should play is just to be open in the same way to everybody. A lot of people who are used to working their way through bureaucracies are okay – someone like me going in to ask for something would probably be a lot more successful than my neighbour, who never darkened the door of the Planning Department before. They wouldn't try to pull something over on me.

Then when it gets into the planning process, I just feel that their role should be facilitators, to look for the best resources they can find, to look for a good process, and listen to people.

This respondent had clear ideas about the appropriate role of the planner. The planner should listen to and be accessible to the people. In other words, the planner should facilitate the citizen's influence on planning. At the same time, however, the respondent wants planners to bring vision and new ideas into the process. There seems something of a contradiction in these two modes: planner as expert visionary, and planner as facilitator of the ideas of others. Perhaps citizens hope that if planners went looking for new ideas and the latest planning theory, then planners would promote the visions that citizens share.

Another citizen voiced similar sentiments about planners, but had little good to say about politicians either.

C: From public officials, we expect publicly accountable behaviour. From my point of view, that meant really and truly looking at what was proposed. [In one dispute, citizens raised] objections ... of real concern on a number of kinds of levels and it seemed incumbent on [the planners], to protect my interests as a citizen here, to look into matters, to look into things and as much as possible to check it out ...

What I was mainly appalled about ultimately, was that public bodies both accountable ones (that is to say elected) and bureaucrats (the Planning Department) could seemingly perceive that something as major as this was okay without being careful about it ...

[Politicians] probably don't trust [the planners], but I quite clearly don't trust the politicians. They manipulated the process. The bureaucrats (the planners) – and I don't use that term in a pejorative sense, as a bureaucrat myself, so don't take it that way – as the civil servants (to put it in a more positive way, perhaps) – it was harder to tell with them. I certainly didn't have the feeling that there was much leadership provided to Council by them ... Or if there was leadership, it certainly had nothing to do with the process that they seemed to agree to, of public interaction in the process – of the public having some kind of input or the public having some place or role to play in the resolution of this. I never had the feeling that they subscribed to that except in the most lip-service kind of way.

Obviously, the respondent does not trust either planners or politicians to look after the community's interests: planners' analyses are superficial and value-driven, and their approach generally careless. Not only does the citizen question the motivations of staff, but even their technical expertise.

Citizens have come to expect that the planner's role should include providing direction in 'good planning.' Planners should advise the community on the best choices possible in developing land. When citizens' views of 'best choice' and planners' advice on suitable options differ, then citizens may feel betrayed. They may believe that planners and politicians do not take planning seriously.

> C: I don't think that planning is important to the politicians or the bureaucrats at City Hall. You never hear it as an election issue ... I never read [in the papers] that the aldermen are waving around the plan and saying 'this decision is a violation of the City plan.'
>
> ... It's difficult to imagine that there's a lot of interest in what the plan says or doesn't say, or what it should be doing for the city ... The plan is a document to guide the city's direction and growth, and the process should be kicked in whenever they want to change that document. But I don't think they ever relate their decision-making process or their budgeting process or anything else to the plan. There's just all kinds of ad hoc decisions ...
>
> Q: Why do you think they have a plan?
>
> They probably don't even know they have a plan. They have it because they're required to have it. They went through the process when the Planning Act was – well, they got rid of the clause in the old planning act that said 'thou shalt plan' – I think that when they had the province on their back forcing them to plan or with the ability to step in and plan for them, then they got involved in planning. But I don't think the province cares [today] whether or not a municipality has a plan.
>
> This government got elected on an antiplanning platform, so I don't think there's generally any support for planning. The federal government wiped out the Ministry of State for Urban Affairs – CMHC[11] doesn't require any planning for its funding any more. It doesn't have any funding any more outside of social housing – and even for that, all you have to do is submit a landscape plan. So there isn't at any level much demand or support for planning.

We see, then, that citizens may feel that planners and politicians either ignore the plan, or thwart its intents. Some no longer believe that the city, the province, or the federal government take planning seriously.

To planners, planning functions as a set of policies and tools to help politicians make choices.

> P: I do think that what they miss often, what many people miss, sometimes even Council itself, is that the plan ... was never intended to make Council's decisions for it. It was to help it make consistent and sound decisions by directing it through a number of considerations which would be similar in each case, whereby they could keep constant those things which should be kept constant, and could address the differences.

As far as planning staff and Council are concerned, planning has fulfilled its intended function. It provides a process and a framework for the City to make decisions about the use of land. It allows staff to craft development in the desired shape. It focuses Council and citizen attention on the key policy issues, while allowing staff the latitude to do their technical jobs.

From Overview to Specifics

This brief overview of the history of planning in peninsular Halifax in the postwar period gives a general indication of some of the issues the community faced. We discussed how Halifax politicians gradually came to accept planning: first as an inconvenience imposed by Ottawa along with urban renewal funding, later as a useful framework within which to make difficult land-use decisions.

In the early years of planning in Halifax, politicians looked warily upon planners. During the early 1970s, as provincial legislation dragged Halifax into planning, politicians began to see the usefulness of planners. Citizen action at that time helped convince Council to take planners and planning seriously.

Citizens participated actively during the preparation of the Municipal Development Plan and various secondary plans throughout Halifax. In the mid-1970s, they felt that they were partners in the process. However, once the city officially adopted the plans, citizens felt they no longer had the power to affect land-use decisions. They felt increasingly excluded from the process.

The next chapters explore two case-study disputes from the 1970s and 1980s. From the comments of various actors in the disputes, we gain clearer insight into the nature of community planning in Halifax. We see how the actors describe themselves and others, and how they frame their performances. We discover that they have divergent views of the purpose of planning and attribute different meanings to it. We watch actors playing to a variety of audiences and reading from a number of scripts.

The disputes demonstrate that participants operate from distinct frames of reference. Actors do not necessarily share the same values: for instance, while some participants view heritage as primary, others advocate economic development. Different actors do not regard urban spaces as the same kinds of places: for example, where some participants in disputes focus on the use value of land, others discuss the exchange value of land (Logan and Molotch 1987). Because the various actors in these disputes do not share basic values and operating assumptions, they find it impossible to reach any kind of consensus on items in dispute, processes for decision making, or appropriate outcomes. They 'speak past' each other. They fail to understand each other's motivations and actions.

While most of the active participants in the planning drama are white, middle-class men, some characteristics differentiate the categories of actors. Citizen activists tend to be articulate, well-educated professionals who are politically or socially committed; some twenty to forty people constitute the 'core activists,' with other citizens coming and going according to the issues. The small number of developers in Nova Scotia are generally locals with good political connections (and sometimes aspirations); major national and international interests have paid relatively little attention to Halifax. Politicians often come from the business or professional community, have long-term roots in the province, and have strong connections to one of the main political parties. The City of Halifax employs approximately a dozen planners, most of them trained in planning schools in Ontario.[12] The conflict between actors derives in part from their divergent backgrounds and different interests.

The case-studies that follow offer examples of land-use planning disputes in context: acts in our drama. We see that planning disputes become one venue in which people debate significant cultural values and beliefs about urban form and the role of citizens and planners in making land-use decisions. As actors interact during their performances, they produce and reproduce social relations. The script of the drama shows value debate in process. In studying these disputes, we come to understand how communication sometimes fails because people articulate essentially different meanings while using a common language.

The first episode we discuss in detail in Chapter 5 portrays the dispute over Market Place Plaza,[13] a multistorey commercial development near the historic Citadel fortress. Market Place Plaza generated community action as a city-wide issue in 1979 and 1980. A broad coalition of groups and individuals worked together to fight the project, taking their case through to appeal.

The second case, described in Chapter 6, features the dispute over the fate of the Mitchell property. During the late 1980s, the owners of this 2-acre parcel in a residential area of the south end of the city proposed by-law amendments to allow multistorey residential development. In this case, residents of the neighbourhood, assisted by some members of the wider community, worked 'within the system' to try to influence Council's choice.

The case-studies differ along a number of dimensions. First of all, they took place under different legislation. Market Place Plaza occurred with the 1969 Planning Act in effect; the Mitchell property dispute came under the 1983 act. Second, although both involve proposals for multistorey buildings, Market Place Plaza provided commercial space, while the Mitchell case concerned residential development. Third, Market Place Plaza is in the downtown commercial core, while the Mitchell property is in a medium-density residential area in the south end. Despite the differences, however, we find substantial similarities in characters, plots, and outcomes.

Chapter Five

Market Place Plaza

In early 1979, a local developer[1] came to city staff with a proposal for a high-rise office development on the corner of Brunswick Street and George Street (see Map 5.1). With its glass sheathing, 'Time Square' would reflect the image of the Old Town Clock, which had kept the hour for Haligonians since the nineteenth century. Halifax faced the first major test of its newly adopted Municipal Development Plan. A major dispute ensued.

Act One

City staff argued that the proposed building would strengthen the Central Business District (CBD). As the staff report noted,

> The MDP wishes to encourage mixed use development in the CBD. This building does not meet that goal since it does not include residential uses or different intensities of retail and office use. However, on a site this size, the development of three types or intensities of uses is difficult and may not be economically feasible (D17: 2).[2]

Drawing on CBD policies, staff consistently supported the developer's plan to build a multistorey office tower. In coming to a position, staff determined that some policies evidently had limited significance: a housing component in the mix could be waived because it was not 'economically feasible.'

Hundreds of people attended the public hearing to let Council know that they disliked Time Square. Having fought through the

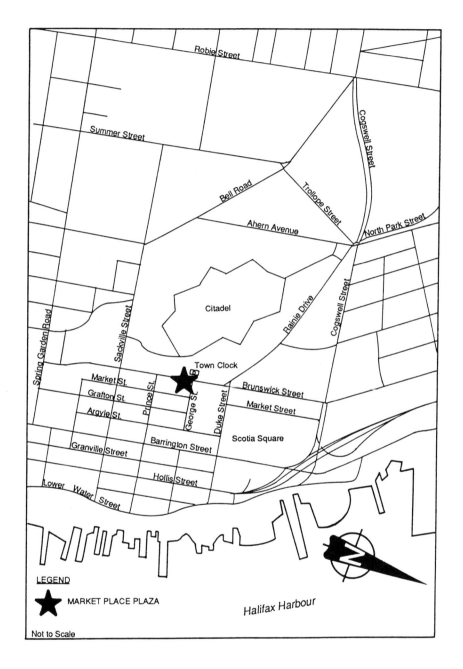

Map 5.1   Market Place Plaza

1970s to protect views from the Citadel and to develop municipal planning policies, many activists came out to see if the new regulations would work. One citizen remembered:

C: It was a fifteen-storey glass monster proposed. The staff report on it didn't even mention the effect the building would have on the view, and it was *not* because they didn't know - I'd pointed that out in my report, but they suppressed my written submission which showed it. Well, when the case came to public hearing, people just rose up and marched to Council.

Briefs, such as that of the Community Planning Association of Canada (CPAC), show that opponents feared that the kind of project proposed threatened the character of the city.

Actions such as the Views By-laws and the historic renovation projects have generated immense positive publicity for the City. The expectation has built up in the minds of the people of Halifax that these policies will be acted upon ...
    The Citadel and Brunswick Street are what imparts to Halifax its sense of place. This is what we will lose (D18: 1, 5).

The presentations reflect a strong commitment to preserving heritage: both natural and architectural. They indicate the extent to which planning had come to represent the hope of protection from unwanted change. CPAC challenged Council to act on the policies.
    Before making its decision, Council sought legal advice from the City solicitor: for the first time, Council faced a major land-use dispute under a Municipal Development Plan. Aldermen acted cautiously. The solicitor's advice couldn't have helped them much:

The problem for Council is that there are few proposals which could clearly be termed inconsistent with the Plan. The style of the Plan is such that most proposals will be consistent with some policies and inconsistent with others ... Council, then, must not only decide whether a proposal is consistent with the Plan, but must also decide whether approval or refusal would best carry out the intent of the Plan (D19).

The solicitor identified the key difficulty with the plan. With its vague terms like 'complementary,' the plan did not provide the tools to resolve the inevitable disputes that arose. As it came to pass, the plan simply offered a new language and context in which to continue old battles.

Despite staff's recommendation that the project proceed, Council turned down Time Square. For a while, the opponents of the project may have thought that their image of the city had won the day.

> The glittering capital centre of Atlantic Canada that [the developer] imagines Time Square would reflect doesn't exist. Halifax, knowing it's not anti-development to have your own sense of class, is not putting on such Uppity-Canadian airs ... Shamefully inadequate city staff analysis of the proposal ... recommended the building be approved (Zierler 1979: 10).

Zierler's remarks reveal the snobbery that sometimes characterizes identity-formation in the Maritimes region. In large part the 'sense of character' Haligonian opponents wanted to preserve excludes distinctive features of 'Upper Canadian' cities.[3] If Toronto and Montreal reflect glitzy images in high-rise towers, some Haligonians prefer that Halifax retain its traditional modesty.

The final quote from Zierler's article presents a theme frequently found in the comments of opponents of development projects. Staff analysis, as indicated in the staff report and in public presentations, may be open to criticism. In this case, Zierler asserts without specificity, that she finds the staff analysis 'shamefully inadequate.' As the case proceeded, some such criticisms became more explicit.

In a feature article, a local magazine presented the developer's perspective on the case.

> [The developer] ... is vowing holy vengeance on environmentalists, history buffs and little old ladies who recite poetry in public ...
>
> He had put his lawyer ... to work dredging through the minutiae of municipal law to make sure every ordinance and regulation and policy city council had dreamed up would be met.
>
> At the public hearing to discuss Time Square, 400 people showed up to tell him in no uncertain terms he had made a dreadful mistake ... They countered his slick slide show with homey poetry readings. They matched his invocation of the Municipal Development Plan's call for economic development in the downtown core with an equally compelling admonition from the same document to preserve the city's heritage ...

'The heritage people, God bless them, have won a lot of victories,'
[he] says bitterly, 'but what they don't understand is that if they
succeed in stopping developments like mine, they're just going to
end up pulling down the whole table on top of themselves.'
... 'People are going to realize that unless we get some new developments downtown, they're going to end up paying more and more
residential taxes' (D22: 29,30, 31).

The developer does not see the opponents of his project as representing the general public view. In evident sympathy, the reporter
portrays the project's critics as 'little old ladies' and 'irate citizens.'
Clearly the developer believes in development, although he sees the
ordinances and regulations as 'dreamed up' to frustrate him. The
final comments in the quotation allude to an important symbol in the
battle for Council's votes: taxes. That theme recurred in the months
that followed as the developer brought forward a new proposal:
Market Place Plaza.

Act Two

An internal report indicated that staff planners supported the second
contract zoning[4] proposal as they had the first: 'The developer has
obviously made a serious attempt, in my view, to respond to public
criticism of his previous proposal; our judgement must be whether
he has been successful. My opinion is that the design of the present
proposal is acceptable ...' (D23D).

Plan policies gave staff considerable room for interpretation. The
staff report suggests an implicit hierarchy of policies in the plan
whereby some policies have greater significance than others. While
citizens had found fourteen relevant policies, staff saw only two key
items.

We also see in the memo the transformation of personal taste into
professional opinion. The vagueness of the policies requires interpretation. In this case, the planner (trained originally as an architect)
indicates a certain understanding of 'complementarity.' The planner
judges a 'sympathetic' approach 'more honest' and 'aesthetically
preferable':

There are two ways in which this kind of complementarity may be
achieved:

(a) by replicating historic architectural forms, materials and textures; in effect by building a false 'old' building. Only in very rare occasions is this approach successful ...

(b) by building a totally modern structure which attempts to harmonize with the character of existing buildings or streetscapes through a sympathetic architectural design. This approach, which the designer of the proposed development has adopted, is generally felt by architects and urban designers to be the more honest and, if it is done well, the more aesthetically preferable of the two (D23D: 2).

Planners saw their value judgments as essentially technical assessments. Some also attempted to turn citizen opposition into technical points. For example, when asked what citizens saw as the issues in contention, one of the city planners interviewed responded by defining the concerns in terms of height and distance: 'It was really the relation of the building to Citadel Hill ... The discussions raised a number of questions about how a building there should relate to its surroundings – should it replicate existing structures or be unique?' A prominent opponent of the project wrote to Council to challenge staff's findings and interpretations, alleging 'many serious omissions and inaccuracies' in the staff report (D24B). Certainly citizens were ready to argue technical details with staff, but only as a means to defend their vision of the community. As one of the opponents explained in an interview:

C: The second version was still too big, in my view - Market Place Plaza. It offered a bad backdrop for the clock ... But it really damages the view. And you know, one Canada Day after it was built, we were sitting on Citadel Hill at night for the fireworks display over George's Island. There on the roof of that building was [the developer] and with him were [City staff] and [a planner] - they're all big buddies, you know.

Clearly, citizens who opposed the project came to see the planners as 'part of the problem.' Planners did not apply plan policies in the way that opponents read the policies. Planners said some policies were not relevant. They seemed to side with the developer, instead of with 'the people.' Rumours about planners fraternising with developers abounded.

Clock Tower, Citadel Hill

The considerable animosity that developed between planners and citizens comes through in internal staff memos and citizen files. One planner wrote to another regarding a citizen's letter sent to Council:

> This section contains a number of highly subjective statements, in the guise of arguments or self-evident truths, and are consequently difficult to respond to.
>
> ... Taking the two perspective sketches ... , it is just false to say that the new building 'dominates' the Town Clock – what it does do is fill in the background, but that's all.
>
> It is straining the meaning of 'complementary' to use it to suggest that new buildings should be finished in the same materials as the

old. A 'complementary' design does not copy or imitate what is already there.

The rest of [the] paragraph betrays a dislike of contemporary architecture, and a reverence for all things historic, which is almost pathological in its intensity, and with which there is really no point of contact. Building methods and materials *have* changed, new buildings *are* usually bigger than old, and *don't* have arched windows, slim cupolas, etc. The best we can aim for are new building designs which capture *some* of the main rhythms and proportions of the traditional street architecture of downtown Halifax, and that's what the 'articulation' achieves. We cannot duplicate the past, or create replicas. There is no more to be said (D23B: 1, 2).

In this vigorous defence of the staff position, the planner refutes the opponent's claims. The choice of words like 'pathological' to characterize the opponent's values reveals the great rift in values and opinions here. The planner sees his own views as rational, logical, and definitive while viewing the opposition as subjective and emotional. He cannot see the value judgments in his own assessment. Here the expert's logic, which views modern architectural styles as acceptable, becomes 'truth' while the citizen's arguments in favour of other architectural styles are 'false,' 'subjective,' or mere 'opinion.'

Despite their best efforts to maintain their professional cool, planners do react to public criticisms. When asked during an interview how staff respond when citizens oppose a project, a planner said:

P: That depends on how the citizens act. Probably defensively ... Certain types of personalities tend to grate on you sometimes. It isn't always pretty. But our job is here to serve. We listen, we get opinions, and we point out the policies of the plan. In as much as the plan allows for interpretations, we make interpretations, but they have to be based on the policies in the plan.

Ultimately, the elected body has to make the decision, based on policy ... It just isn't very useful to come in and say 'you're destroying the city.' It isn't constructive.

The critical element is the people you're dealing with. Some people can deal with policy, some can't. If [development lawyer X] or [lawyer Y] come in here with a development, you know it will be based on policy in the plan. But someone will attack this development that's in the north end based on a woman losing access to sun. I have to respect people's capabilities and know that people not trained in planning or law will argue their case differently.

The planners see themselves as objectively and rationally reviewing plan policies and applying them to the proposed development, while opponents argue on emotional grounds. Although planners have to 'respect' differences in the way that people treat them, they feel more comfortable dealing with those who understand the policy environment within which they operate. They can identify with those who speak the language that they understand, and who present their cases in the same style as would a planner.

In public responses to the project opponents' criticisms, staff revealed no emotion and gave no ground. Within the Planning Department, however, planners defended and explained their actions in strong language, as an internal memo demonstrates:

> It has been the explicit strategy of the Plan to permit as-of-right limits to be exceeded wherever and whenever appropriate. The purpose of limits, particularly in the Central Business District where the limits are especially conservative, is to gain control over the elements of land use and design which could cause major problems in the future of the CBD. The thinking of this Department in the past and in our current research has never been that the as-of-right limit be considered as anything like an absolute limit on development. ... This Department is preparing some commentary on the costs and benefits of development ... Unless we deal with such difficult and not terribly tangible concepts ... the distinction between short-term costs and benefits and long-term costs and benefits, between private costs and social costs and private benefits and social benefits will become tantamount to the medieval scholastic discussion of the number of angels that can dance on the head of a pin (D24D: 2, 3).

The language offers an illuminating glimpse of the planner's perspective on the issues. The planner sees the plan as helping the City guide development. The plan is not rigid. It works with the market rather than controlling the market. It functions to promote construction. It does not require full cost accounting.

> The decision that the developer seeks requires serious Council consideration of a number of matters. In some contexts, and in some areas of the City, market considerations are relevant. The CBD is not

such an area. It is the area where our conscious policy is to give the market as much free rein as possible.

The strategy we have chosen throughout the Municipal Development Plan, which is often missed by groups on both sides of the argument of whether or not the regulation of development is good or bad, is that we *have* chosen to leave certain kinds of decisions to the market ... The Plan does not substitute government judgement for private judgement *except* in such cases where the externalities created by the private developer are to the detriment of the public good ... The statement that the proposed building seriously contravenes two important heritage policies is simply a fallacy ... The two historic buildings should be preserved ... However, the CBD portion of Brunswick Street is not now and never will be an historic streetscape ... A living, breathing, thriving Central Business District is not created by recreating images of the past any more than it is enhanced by destroying valuable heritage buildings (D24D: 3, 4).

Obviously, the planner had a different understanding of the heritage policies than did some of the project's opponents. For the planner, 'recreating images of the past' does nothing to stimulate the Central Business District. This focus on economic development and growth in the CBD clearly seemed central for the planners. Because the developer takes the economic risk, planners accept the developer's judgment that a project can succeed and will prove beneficial to the city.

A copy of the staff memo in the files of one of the groups that opposed the project indicated citizen reactions to the arguments. Someone had written 'What policy number?' beside the planner's claim that the 'Policy is to give the market as much free rein as possible.' Certainly citizens who thought that plan policies should have offered predictability and stability bristled when they saw the department's eagerness to waive regulations 'whenever appropriate.'

As Council moved towards a public hearing on the second proposal, letters, and briefs from Haligonians began arriving at City Hall. They reveal some of the values contested and indicate an undercurrent of hostility towards developers. One citizen wrote: 'It has become evident that the developer holds in contempt the desires and concerns of the citizens at large, and considers his own ambitions more important than the long term interests and unique spirit of the city. He also appears to be motivated by a desire to thwart the popular will' (D26).

Another said:

> I am most upset to learn that there is yet another developer trying to stick his foot in the door; the door being the view of Halifax harbour, and the foot being very large indeed. How much longer do we as citizens have to protest and fight for what we want. Hasn't it been clearly stated that the view from the Citadel is not to be destroyed? Why isn't there some kind of permanent policy about this, so that we will stop being harassed by individuals who are more interested in making a buck than in the welfare and enjoyment of the citizens (D25)

Such letters reflect the belief that winning land use concessions from municipalities allows developers to improve the exchange value of their properties. These citizens perceived that developers reap their profits at the cost of the use values and common enjoyment of the community at large. After years of battles to protect the views around the Citadel, many citizens saw the project as an 'end run' around the new rules. They expected Council to stand up to the challenge. The passionate 'fighting words' in the letters represent one extreme in the range of opposition.

Organized groups[5] who opposed the project took a moderate and reasoned approach in their written and verbal presentations to Council. They understood that to succeed in 'the game' (and potentially influence Council), they had to play by certain rules. They had to cite plan policies, present perspective drawings and slides of the impact of the building on the view-planes, and challenge the expert advice offered by planning staff.

Many at the public hearing spoke of the significance of the Old Town Clock, the Citadel, and the views. Speakers held that Council should judge the project in terms of its sensitivity to elements around the site. They offered their interpretations of 'complementary,' and argued about the need for height controls on Brunswick Street. The project's opponents revealed their strong commitment to preserving heritage and their concern for the 'character' of the community.

Some of the presentations and written submissions questioned advice and evidence given by staff.

> [The planner] suggests that, previously, citizens fought only for view-planes. This is not true. Citizens fought for, and Council agreed to, viewplanes *plus* a height control on Brunswick Street.

[The planner] states that setback calculations are 'absolutely irrelevant' ... These concerns (shadow, wind, etc.) are all discussed in the policies of the MDP and hence, are relevant.

He says that to require conformity to setback regulations is the 'farthest thing from our minds' and that 'to do so would be a design disaster.' These are unusual comments in view of the MDP policies and the fact that his own Department have recommended new setback regulations in the 'Planning Criteria Statement for the Brunswick Street Area' to further control design (D28B).

Citizens refute specific remarks and opinions offered in the staff reports on the basis of accuracy and completeness.

Opponents occasionally went so far as to question the competence of staff to make certain predictions. A university economist dismissed the economic analysis of the project provided by staff:

... without a detailed analysis, in most cases it is impossible to say whether a particular project will generate a surplus or deficit. It would seem to me that the City should take the steps necessary to include a careful fiscal appraisal of major development projects as part of its on-going planning process. ... For ... the reasons cited, I would suggest to you that the prediction of revenue to the City generated by the Market Place Plaza project is much more complicated than one would be led to believe from the Staff Report (D29: 1, 2).

Because they could not understand or accept the advice coming from planning staff, some opponents came to doubt the integrity of staff to represent the public interest fairly and openly.

Staff are reading into those sections [of the plan] a degree of flexibility far beyond anything envisaged by the majority of citizens who laboured over the years, in both official and unofficial capacities, to develop legislation to protect those resources in order that they may be enjoyed by the generations that will succeed us. ...

In conclusion, I must record my further concern that the Staff Report in question was apparently released on the day following the public hearing ... Without this reflection of the thinking of City Staff it may well be said that the evidence was not all in or available to the many concerned citizens who endeavoured in conscience to outline their own positions, or those of the societies or agencies they represented, with regard to the proposed development (D33: 2).

Evidently, some of the opponents perceived staff as frustrating the democratic process by which planning *should have* allowed citizens to create the type of community they envisaged. In practice, planning did not result in the automatic refusal of 'undesirable' projects. Rather than encouraging 'appropriate redevelopment,' as the opponents saw things, planners appeared to conspire with development interests by indicating their support for a proposal that did not satisfy the policies as written. The opponents grew angrier as they realized they could not convince planners and Council that the project should not proceed.

Not all organized citizen groups opposed the staff recommendation. In fact, some urged Council to approve the project. The Halifax Homeowners, supporting the interests of property owners, appeared with a former alderman as spokesperson: 'We the Halifax Homeowners Association, whose every member pays to belong to the association, and also pays municipal taxes for the privilege of living here, ask this Council to consider our concern when we see development needlessly being turned away, with the consequent loss of revenue' (D27A: 1). Business development will reduce property taxes and hence can benefit the entire community. The Homeowners accepted the staff report's findings and made no reference to specific policies in the plan. Above all, they valued the economic benefits of downtown development. For them, potential growth and prosperity made the project desirable.

In a letter to Council, a prominent member of the local business community affirmed the value of heritage while defending the project in a general sense as contributing to the 'health' of the downtown.

> ... as a founding and continuing member of Heritage Trust, I cannot associate myself with the position that it takes toward this application.
>
> While due respect must be given to historical resources such as the Citadel and the Town Clock, as much regard surely must also be given to creating a vital and healthy central business district (D27B).

Perhaps this sentiment encapsulates the dogma of the local public culture: you can respect heritage, but don't prevent development.

Many project opponents grew sensitive to allegations that they resisted development. In Halifax, labelling someone 'antidevelopment' is a derisive epithet. The 'pro-development' lobbyists portray the 'antis' as opposing prosperity or wallowing in a sentimental past.

Newspaper reports of the meeting indicate the tightrope opponents walked as they tried not to seem to oppose development:

> City council first listened to supporters of the project at Wednesday's public hearing and there were few compared to the number of individuals who opposed it.
>
> ... Like the Heritage Trust of Nova Scotia, many groups said they are not against development 'per se' on Brunswick Street.
>
> ... Parks Canada warned that any massive structure in the location proposed would alter the character of Halifax and virtually destroy the character of the Citadel.
>
> ... Other groups submitted petitions ... A survey of 500 city residents ... found that 483 people responded yes when asked whether they felt the proposed building is too high (D32).

Press coverage indicated that the opponents made many appeals to process, appropriate development, heritage, and popularity. They urged Council to follow a proper planning process: first make policies, then stick to them. They assured Council that the opponents did not oppose development per se, only this particular proposal that threatened the city's heritage and character. They demonstrated the intensity of public opinion on the issue by the volume of signatures on the petitions presented to Council.

Such arguments reflect the values that motivated many citizens to oppose this project. The opponents' image of the 'good Halifax' builds on the historic past and heritage of the city. For them, Halifax is a small-scale, low-rise, intimate community. Its significant buildings are Victorian or Georgian, faced in wood, brick, or stone. The Citadel provides its focus, its veritable *raison d'être*. The view of the harbour reminds Haligonians of their inheritance and how easily they can lose it.

Many of the people who opposed Market Place Plaza 'bought into' planning because they believed it would give them the tools they needed to protect their image of the city. Planning policies to protect heritage and to ensure the complementarity of new structures should, they expected, have meant an end to the battles over particular development projects. When the battles continued, citizens looked for someone to blame and found the planners a handy target.

Before Council adopted the plan in 1978, aldermen had to answer directly for decisions they might make about projects perceived to threaten public resources. Once planners became arbiters of plan policies, however, much of the heat passed from Council to the planners. Not only did project opponents have to worry about an overly cosy relationship between aldermen and developers, but now they saw that the experts they expected to protect the plan seemed primarily interested in promoting development. Many citizens felt betrayed.

After Council adopted the Municipal Development Plan, disputes about the 'image of the city' continued, although they were rephrased in terms of disagreements about the meaning of plan policies. The language of the plan provided fertile ground to germinate new resentments. As the project opponents criticized staff for inadequate or erroneous analysis, they explicitly rejected a view that saw growth as positive. Rebuffing arguments that they regarded as naive and romantic, planners implicitly rejected a view that celebrated continuity and tradition.

Act Three

For the planners, this first major project under the plan raised a significant concern about the credibility of planning.

> **P:** We saw, and I think they saw, some very important issues on the table. One was the credibility of this discretionary development agreement[6] process. The developers had been just very wild about this notion that you could only build 45 feet and after that you had this wide-open, crazy development agreement process – where it looked like there were no rules. And we were saying, yes, there are rules; there are rules that you've got to follow. You've got to follow a very careful line, you've got to get credibility on both sides. You've got to listen to your public, but you've got to follow the rules too ... you can pay all kinds of attention to the ... very activist-oriented constituencies, but you're trying to develop. I mean your whole plan says you want to develop, you don't want to turn off the tap either. You want to direct it ... the plan is about ... trying to get things to go where you want them to go and to do what you want them to do ...
> ... the City's point of view was having to have a credible Council process - that when Council got what it wanted, it would then defend its decisions, so that there would be some developer confidence.

This planner, then, wanted the development community to see the planning process as credible and predictable. Council must approve the project because the proposal satisfied plan policies. This first major test of the plan in the CBD challenged the planners to demonstrate that planning could work, that it could channel development in desired directions. Unless developers gained confidence in what the plan would give them, they might abandon Halifax.

At the same time, the planner suggests that the public might want Council to circumvent rules. While Council must listen to the public, it must decide according to the rules of the plan. In that context, we might ask, what is the function of public involvement?

City Council finally approved Market Place Plaza. Perhaps Council members found some of the emotionally-charged pro-development editorial comments in the local paper persuasive.

In recent weeks Halifax council has turned down a number of projects which would have greatly increased city tax revenues because of problems which were either non-existent or overblown.

... The frustrating thing is that the opposition to these projects is not a popular movement as perceived by most people through the coverage in the media. It is an elitist movement led by a few people who care little about the tax base of the city.

If these people cared that much about the beautiful town clock (and it is) they would don overalls and scrape and paint the clock which is suffering from a great deal of wear and tear. One would suggest that our heritage would be much better preserved by such an action than by stopping the creative use of an empty lot across the street ...

One thing is certain. And that is that city councils must consider the overall best interests of the community in making development decisions not just the views of a few outspoken members who have the time and energy to attend public hearings. Our own Halifax council has not always been successful in doing just this and it has been the general population that has suffered as a result (D37).

Maybe Council saw the opponents as 'elitists' with time to spare to paint the Town Clock. Perhaps aldermen weighed the advantages and disadvantages of the proposal and decided that, on balance, it served the 'overall best interests' of the city. They must have believed that the protest did not extend beyond those present in the public hearing chamber, and that the project could make a positive contribution both to the economic base and to the image of the city. They must have agreed with staff that the proposal met the policies of the plan.

Several of the opponents went on to appeal the decision to the

Planning Appeal Board and the courts. Despite the cost and effort involved, they felt strongly enough about their case that they hired a lawyer and fought for many more months.

Notice of Appeal
The grounds of our appeal are:
- The decision cannot reasonably be said to carry out the intent of the Halifax Municipal Development Plan ...
- The decision is inconsistent with previous motions and policies of Halifax City Council;
- The decision is inconsistent with good planning principles;
- The decision cannot be said to reflect input from the public at public meetings and hearings ... (D39).

At appeal, the rules for making decisions change and the local context plays a reduced role in the outcome. After reviewing the evidence, the Planning Appeal Board upheld Council's decision.

Certain ironies developed in the course of the appeal, which did not go unnoticed by one of the appellants.

C: I think one of the things that saved us - we were all fairly new at this – was having ... TO hot shots like [famous planner-architect] come down, who were very confident, very authoritative, and who were on our side. And I think it's regrettable that we needed to import someone to make a difference. It's typical! The irony of that is exactly what we were fighting against: lack of Halifax-based design. The architects of the building tended to come from TO. The image of the Halifax landscapes and sites themselves were, I think, pretty well ignored and anything that came from Upper Canada got approval from City staff, or anything that looked like it came from Upper Canada.

As they fought to uphold an image of Halifax that differed from the image of urban(e) Upper Canada, the opponents had to import experts from the very cities they disliked. Citizen opinions alone could not reverse the decision once planning rules came into effect.

C: One of the things that has always bothered me is that it seemed to me that discussions of human scale were ... treated as sort of romantic, naive ... even worse than the aesthetic qualities of a building ... You can get experts on both sides to testify to anything, but the real human issues get lost ... and it seems to me that that sort of thing never counted enough in any of our planning. What it feels like to stand with a ten-storey building knocking the wind out of you and with no architectural detail all the way up - just this blob ... those things are so personal and human it is difficult to talk about them and to be effective about them without sounding like you're the kind who likes to smell roses all day or something.

The process of the appeal laid bare the nature of 'acceptable' evidence, and limited the contribution that non-experts could make to interpretations. The citizens who participated felt powerless to influence the outcome. Moreover, their desire to affect the decision and their emotional commitment to a particular outcome made them suspect among those whose views differed.

Citizens believed that 'democracy' meant participation, but they felt that politicians and planners had no wish to hear them. While the appellants sensed that their actions created animosity from planners, the planners interviewed denied such reactions. One urban planner had no complaints about the generous appeal provisions of the 1969 Planning Act, yet his use of the phrase 'anybody off the wall' may reveal some concern about frivolous appeals.

P: The biggest problem was the delays. We tend to write plans not for appeals but for planning, but then when you go to appeal, you have to explain and defend. We want to be well documented so that we can explain everything. The appeals taught us to get our stuff documented. We learned to be prepared ...

Under the old Planning Act, anybody off the wall could give an appeal. [Market Place Plaza] really shut that down before the act was changed because the Planning Appeal Board allowed the developer costs when they dismissed the appeal.[7] I don't think the developer ever took those costs, but he could have. So that decision indicated that appeals had to be well grounded, not frivolous. I'm not suggesting the appeal there was frivolous by any means, but it made groups nervous.

The project's opponents finished the case with a bitter taste in their mouths. Their loss was expensive, both in financial and emotional terms. As one citizen said:

C: But that was a massive appeal. There were about ten appellants. It became a numbers game with expert witnesses. I still feel the decision was wrong. We found forty-four errors of fact in the Planning Appeal Board's ruling, so then we went to the Supreme Court of Nova Scotia to try to get the ruling overturned on a technicality ... When we got [the developer's agent] on the stand to ask about the errors, we basically asked 'Were you stupid or corrupt?' and he said 'Stupid,' but I'm not sure I accept that. During the trial, the developer had lunch with the judge ... our lawyer was outraged. It just about killed him to see that. The whole thing was so corrupt. When I was on the stand, the judge used intimidation tactics to try to unnerve me. He asked me where I lived, and said 'That's not near the Citadel.' A lot of people would have been cowed by the nasty questions and personal remarks. I found it personally intimidating, and some of his remarks were kind of [chauvinistic], you know? We felt he was biased, the old bugger.

The anger is palpable in the citizen's choice of words: 'stupid,' 'corrupt,' 'old bugger.' The citizen cannot accept the process or the outcome as legitimate.

C: The only way you can win against those odds is to have *very* heavy citizen opposition to a project. You need time to gear that up. And because we had just fought off Time Square, people were tired and we didn't have time to gear up against the second proposal.

... In the decision, you can see how they twisted things. I remember [one planner] on the stand saying that he didn't think it mattered if there were eighty storey buildings around the Citadel. Imagine!

[A citizen] looked at all the staff reports at one time and found that all of them favoured big developments. There's something wrong there - not all developments can be good.

Citizens who helped to put the 1978 MDP in place believed that it would guarantee 'good' development for Halifax. They expected low-rise development along Brunswick Street. When Market Place Plaza survived all the tests, they felt betrayed by a corrupt system. In the process, they lost respect for planners.

Planners, however, felt vindicated by the final outcome. Council considered all of the factors, including public lobbying, and made a decision according to the plan. The Appeal Board and the courts upheld the decision. The plan worked and the project went ahead. The plan would promote development. One of the planners explained:

Market Place Plaza

P: The plan was intended ... to help Council to make decisions. It was not intended to make decisions for them ... It set out as clearly as it could a series of things we want and ways we wanted to do them, recognizing that we will always have competing aspirations for things and that those have to be balanced and decisions made in a much finer context than you can ever anticipate in a plan ... And what you want is a process wherein Council considers those lists of things and makes the best decision they can with the best information they can get at the time. And so we have a process that requires them to look at the kind of shopping list of the qualities that we want ... There are some of those that we absolutely must have, and then there are some of those that we should ask for, and then there are some of those that we might want – they're given a range of discretion even in their wording. And we have a process which I've always described as being a kind of three-legged stool where they get hopefully independent and dispassionate staff advice, where they get the policy environment of the plan (which is fairly rigid in some areas and not very rigid in others), and they get public discussion – either a public meeting, or a public hearing, or a combination of the two. Then they have to sit in the middle of that and balance what the plan says they should have and the consequences of doing or not doing certain things ... and the public welfare or the public good that they're either going to generate or harm as they've heard it from the people that are affected by it. But they still have to make a decision.

The planner explicitly defines planning as a rational process for decision making. He acknowledges that it may not produce popularity, but implies that it is necessary in a democratic society.

P: I don't think there's any obligation that we [should] all like each other in that process, that we [should] all be supportive of each other. I mean it's very nice when it happens, but I've never seen any obligation as to why staff should only recommend to Council that which the public wants, or that Council should pay undue attention to a squeaky wheel. And they really have an obligation to try to make good decisions. As long as they hear all sides of an issue, that's never bothered me whether we've won or lost, and I think that's true of any of the staff around here. They will hear things from the public that I'm not supposed to pay attention to, and the public will hear things from me that they may not like to hear, or they may love to hear. And that poor bunch of elected people there have to ... make up their minds.

Market Place plaza proved to the planners that planning could work. The MDP provided the policies and procedures that Council could use to hear all the evidence and make a decision. Through planning, politicians would hear the voices of the people, the rules of the plan, and 'dispassionate' staff advice. As is appropriate in a representative democracy, the elected Council would consider the facts and make a decision. Planning had become part of the democratic process of making decisions about the use of land in Halifax.

Chapter Six

Mitchell Property

In the fall of 1986, rumours began to circulate that one of the few remaining estates in the city would soon come on the market for development. Residents of the south end worried that redevelopment would eliminate the unusual 'Italianate'-style mansion owned by the Mitchell family for over eighty years. A citizen's letter to the editor indicated the concern: 'This very beautiful house was built in 1870 ... It qualifies for designation as a heritage property, but this status was refused by its present owner ... In addition to its own architectural value, the house is an integral part of the Victorian streetscape of Tower Road' (C2). The dispute would continue for two years.

Act One

By early 1987, the estate of the late Colonel Mitchell approached Council for a plan amendment to allow development agreements[1] on the site. While the zoning allowed high-density[2] development, a height regulation in the land-use by-law would not permit buildings higher than 35 ft.[3] Staff quickly rejected the application.

> A request for an amendment to the Municipal Planning Strategy should be based on a substantial change in circumstances. Staff does not believe that there has been any such change in the case of the subject properties, or in the area immediately surrounding. In fact, staff has some reason to believe that the present designations and zoning have brought a large measure of stability to the area and that any attempt to introduce changes at this point would be strongly

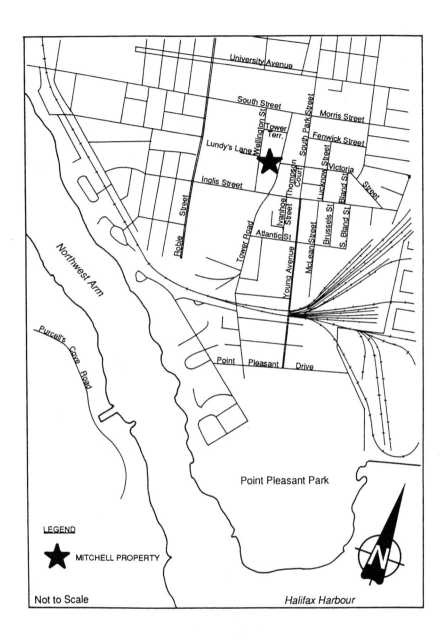

Map 6.1   Mitchell Property

resisted by the community. The planning strategy appears to be successfully achieving its intent, and staff is not aware of any sufficiently
weighty community justification for considering an amendment at
this time.

As a final point, Council is advised that Policy 1.1.1.3 (MPS, Section V) would allow Council to amend the 35 ft. height limit in the
Land Use bylaw without amending the planning strategy. The applicant has been made aware of this option, but has chosen not to pursue it (C4A: 2).

Staff would not support a plan change to accommodate development
of the site because existing plan policies had stabilized the area and
met the community's wishes. At the same time, however, staff advised Council to consider a land-use (zoning) by-law amendment to
raise allowable heights on the site.

Area residents, who feared that redevelopment of the site would
mean the loss of the ornate old house or its replacement by a high-rise
condominium project, took heart at the staff's speedy rejection of the
application. The local press reported on citizens' efforts to organize.

> It's shaping up like another ... battle between heritage-minded resi-
> dents, city council and a developer ...
>
> 'It's ludicrous that the owner can say "Sorry, I don't want my
> property designated as a heritage property," ' said ... a South End
> resident who is concerned about the house being torn down.
>
> 'Just about all the neighbours are opposed (to the property being
> developed),' said [another resident], ... who held a neighbourhood
> meeting ... Thursday night and formed a group to stop a high-rise
> development (C6).

The journalist leads us to conclude that certain values direct the
opposition. The opponents sought to preserve heritage and to prevent
high-rise development. They believed they spoke with one voice for
their neighbours.

Letters to the local newspaper indicated that some citizens were
worried about the effectiveness of planning tools to protect their
neighbourhood.

> Will the zoning, and as a consequence, the character of the neigh-
> bourhood be changed? Residents of the neighbourhood are waiting
> with bated breath to see what their fate will be ...

> Life can be a 'cliff hanger' – can one predict the future continuity
> of the milieu he chooses to live in by checking the city zoning desig-
> nation or is zoning an arbitrary categorization that can be dispensed
> with at will (C7B)?

This resident links the character of the neighbourhood with the
zoning regime in place. The phrasing implies that without the plan,
chaos could replace order and continuity in the urban environment.

When Council defeated the request in April 1987, most of the
opponents felt jubilant: 'This decision seems to be a very good one
for all concerned,' [a resident] said. 'As far as we're concerned, the
issue is settled ... We're just saying this is the law of the land, which
is the municipal development act' (C7A).

The citizen commended staff for upholding the plan and regarded
the issue as settled. Not all of the opponents were convinced though,
as a letter to the editor in May 1987 revealed.

> The fate of the neighbours of the Mitchell property on Tower Road is
> still a big question mark. The city planning department feels that
> high-rise buildings in this area of heritage homes is inappropriate;
> however the executors of the ... Estate apparently don't agree. The
> latest 'scuttlebutt' is that they are again going to submit a plan by a
> developer for a high-rise building (C11).

This citizen probably did not see the original staff report that suggested that staff *preferred* an increase in the height limits on the site.
He continued,

> Residents in traditional neighbourhoods such as mine are always at a
> disadvantage ... The neighbourhood is a spontaneous assortment of
> families going about their lives while developers are organized, fo-
> cused, and motivated by money.
>   They systematically and relentlessly pursue their goals with repeti-
> tive assaults on any legislation or opposition to their ends ... The
> development team has sophisticated advisers and techniques – the
> neighbourhood is in disarray. The professionals versus the amateurs
> – on the one side, the profit motive, on the other, fear. It somehow
> does not seem like an equal match (C11).

The citizen's comments reveal a commitment to a 'traditional' (low-
rise) neighbourhood, full of families intent on their own business.

Save the Mitchell House

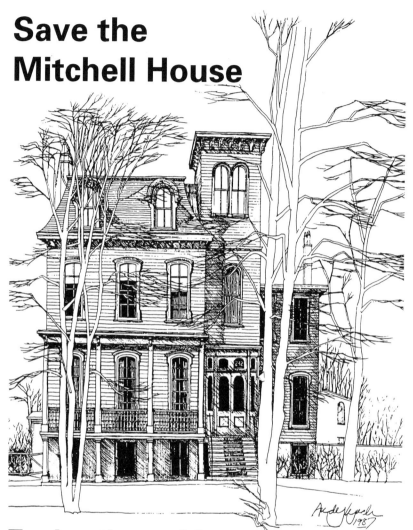

To sign the petition, contact:

Save the Mitchell House poster. Drawing by Andy Lynch

A group of residents and heritage buffs rapidly formed Concerned Citizens for the Mitchell Property. They began organizing to try to save the old house. Some members tried unsuccessfully to purchase the property from the estate for redevelopment in a low-rise heritage style.

> Fifteen citizens, including several waving placards, stood in front of the Mitchell property on Tower Road at 7 a.m. today to protest the pending demolition of a Victorian mansion on the site ...
>
> 'I think it's a very difficult and sad situation we find ourselves in because we may not have legal recourse to stop this,' [the alderman] said Wednesday ...
>
> [A citizen] who lives across the street from the Mitchell home, which has been vacant for the last 18 months, said citizens in the area are shocked by the disregard the owners are showing for 'such an important part of our past.'
>
> 'We're not opposed to development,' she said. 'It was inevitable the property would be developed.'
>
> She said her group had hoped any development of the site would be done in a manner sensitive to the style of the house, 'the last Italianate-Victorian house in Halifax.'
>
> She said Halifax will have little to differentiate itself from any other city in North America if it continues to rip down such buildings (C19B).

The citizen's last remark indicates the extent to which heritage resources become characteristic markers of Halifax for some people. The project's opponents feared that destroying landscapes and buildings would transform Halifax into an undesirable and undifferentiated North American city.

Citizens fighting for the house blamed both the estate and Council for wasting the community's heritage resources. They believed that they enjoyed wide community support in opposing high-rise development (although the journalist pointedly enumerates 'fifteen'). Their efforts did not receive universal support, however. An unsigned report in one of the local papers used subtly negative language to describe the situation.

> A demolition permit, issued for the 117–year-old Mitchell house on Tower Road, is causing some public concern. The home has not been designated heritage by the city but, according to a couple of dozen citizens protesting its impending removal, it has many values.

Heritage streetscape, Tower Road

Ward 1 Alderman ... is among those concerned. 'Council is reluctant to designate a property "heritage" against the owner's wishes.
All we can do is try to have the owner appreciate what is there.'

Several offers have been made to purchase the house and/or the
property, according to ... a leader of the protest group (C13B).

This piece undermines the effectiveness of the 'protest group' in
several ways. The editorial writer says there's 'some' public concern,
implying not much: just a 'couple of dozen citizens.' Council had not
designated the home a heritage property. Then, in a classic strategy,
the author used the voice of the alderman who fought to *save* the
building to defend Council's reluctance to designate it; the tactic
thoroughly undermined the alderman's opposition to demolition.

At the eleventh hour, the mayor managed to convince the estate to
delay demolition for thirty days while negotiations proceeded to try
to save the house. The spokesperson for the owners indicated there
was considerable anger about the fuss people were making over an
'ugly' house: '[The owner] last night said his family has been shabbi-
ly treated over an ugly house which nobody used to care about ...
"Don't let them fool you. The people who get involved in this will
do anything they can to stop any and all development. They're
bored"' (C19A). The estate saw their opponents as 'bored' and out
to stop development. Relations with citizens steadily soured as negotiations proceeded between developers and planners.

Meanwhile, the Concerned Citizens doubled their efforts to try to
gain support for their cause.

Supporters of the Save the Mitchell House program hope to assemble
a 3,000–signature petition prior to Christmas as a demonstration of
interest in saving the 117–year-old house on Tower Road in south
end Halifax.

'The petition is not controversial,' said citizens' group spokesman
... 'We just want people to show they care' (C14).

By this time, relations between the owners of the estate and the
citizens opposing its redevelopment had reached a low point. Citizen
representatives trod lightly to avoid further alienation. Opponents
realized clearly that they had to demonstrate to Council their wide
public support. One citizen explained how the group proceeded.

C: We got the petition ... and then we moved into a new phase because someone who had not been a member of the group came up with a suggestion that we should be pro-active on this. It was no good appealing to people not to destroy the house – we should propose that we do something with the house ourselves. So we came up with the idea of a museum of Victorian Halifax. And we actually tried to negotiate with the owners of the property, with the estate, to purchase the house. We felt that we could raise 2 or 3 million dollars, whatever it would take, to buy the house, restore it, and put a museum in place, and we were going around government agencies, the museum system, looking for support for that ...

Anyway, we had this meeting with the executors and we told them what we wanted to do, and they seemed quite friendly, but of course nothing ever came of it. We never heard from them again. Or we could never get them to set a price on it.

Often during land-use disputes, those who favour the development label those who oppose the project 'naysayers.' In this case, the opponents determined to avoid such name-calling by offering viable development alternatives. Their ambitious plan to purchase the building reflects their acceptance of many of the 'rules of the game' of those who play for high stakes in improving the exchange value of land. To the 'traditional' opponents' tool kit of petitions and heritage arguments, the Concerned Citizens added fund-raising for a museum.

The strategy employed by the Concerned Citizens reflects the group's membership. In addition to some of the familiar faces in the fight for heritage in Halifax, several 'new' people joined the fray. As in any local issue, some people who live near a project get involved. The local residents in this case moved in powerful circles. Most lived in expensive heritage homes and worked as business people or professionals. They believed that waving placards would not achieve their ends.

The thirty-day reprieve on demolition of the property passed without resolution of the impasse. By late April 1987, time ran out.

[A] spokesman ... said last night the group has been told by a demolition crew member that the 118–year-old Tower Road, Halifax, home will face the wrecking ball at 6:30 a.m.

... If it is torn down, it will be a particularly bitter loss for the lobby group ...

The group hoped to raise enough money to buy the house, and

convert it into a museum. That plan was scuttled when the family refused to sub-divide the land.

The group responded with a new idea: it had 3,000 pamphlets printed, and prepared for a letter-writing campaign and corporate support to save the house.

'We were just about to start a big blitz, to enlist public support in a big way, but I guess they forestalled that,' said [a spokesperson] (C24).

Organizers experienced a profound sense of bitterness and loss as the house fell.

There was a pile of rubble yesterday where a piece of Halifax's history used to stand ...

As dawn broke, frustrated protestors watched the property they fought to save being reduced to rubble.

... One anonymous passer-by who lived in the area when she was a child thought differently. 'It was an eyesore – the site looks better now with the pile of rubble on it. And worse, the old colonel's dog used to chase me every time I passed the house. So good riddance ...' she said.

... [A] member of the work crew said structural work to allow for demolition had been going on since the December reprieve.

'You know what I think?' said [the worker]. 'For all the antiques, if I had them, they'd be in the garbage. And for every tree I see, they'd be cut down. What's the good of them?'

'Why have one house taking up five acres of land when they can put a dozen in. It's stupid, you know' (C26).

In order to balance his report on the 'frustrated protestors,' the journalist found ordinary citizens critical of the building and grounds. Their comments reflected some of the other values and beliefs expressed during the dispute. Throughout the discussions, the estate had maintained that the building was old, dysfunctional, and decrepit. The heirs saw no historic merit in the structure.

The worker who acknowledged that structural work for demolition began in December made the Concerned Citizens feel totally misled. (The estate had never admitted its unwillingness to preserve the house.) But the worker also returns to the important subthemes of jobs and development, if only implicitly. He would tear down buildings and trees with his backhoe to make way for housing.

Mitchell property after house removed

Citizens who opposed the demolition felt demeaned.

C: When I came to Halifax ... , I was enchanted by the city, by the
streetscapes, by the just beautiful architecture and the trees, and the
way in which it was still a really habitable Victorian and Georgian
city. And I just cared about it. And actually that house in particular I
thought was absolutely beautiful. And the day that house went,
something broke in me, although I still go on with this kind of work
because ... I feel it's my duty. I don't really care any more. I just
broke inside when that house went because I could not conceive of a
city which would allow that to happen ... And I guess that was when
I began to feel 'What's the point?' I still do it, but I'll never do it with
the passion that I did it before. I guess everybody has their own
cause, and this is mine.

While some accepted the loss stoically, others truly grieved.
    In an opinion page editorial, one citizen alleged that the destruc-
tion of the house threatened the character of the city.

The list [of heritage buildings lost] will grow, on and on and on over
time until we eventually look like a poor man's shadow of Calgary or
Mississauga.
    Perhaps that is not surprising. We have constantly chosen, espe-
cially in Halifax, to hire our planning staff and many of our architectural consultants out of Upper Canada. One of our prominent developers has, without fail, always used Bloor Street advice, and it shows
in the present vision of the future being erected on the Halifax waterfront for an old and historic Halifax law firm.
    How can a Mississauga planner give advice to Council if he or she
has never seen, let alone lived in, a 118–year old house?
    ... Europeans know the value of heritage and how to work with it.
They are also willing to work with it and capitalize on it.
    To Upper Canadians born in the wilderness of suburbia, it is a
curiosity to be confined to the historic ghetto or sacrificed to the
aluminum and glass visions of tomorrow.
    ... Tourists come to Halifax and Nova Scotia because it is different.
Remove the difference, and the reason to come takes people to Quebec City, or La Vieux Ville de Montreal, or to St John's or St Pierre et
Miquelon, Amsterdam or Riga ... Halifax and Dartmouth will recede
into the bland vision of our planners and politicians and will be
properly ignored (C28).

This writer links the loss of the Mitchell house and the entire issue of planning in Halifax to a broader cultural context. Like many of those who value heritage, he alludes to the special character of European cities. Like those who disdain modernism, he refers to 'Calgary and Mississauga' derisively. The writer values the historic *difference* of Halifax, and defines the city's character by that heritage.

This writer goes further than many other opponents, however, in laying responsibility for Halifax's diffident attitude towards heritage at the feet of its planners as well as its politicians. As he suggests, most of the planners 'come from away.' Worse still, they hail from 'Upper Canada,' the region held responsible for numerous Maritime problems. These planners have, he implies, no sense of history or vision.

Act Two

For a year after the demolition of the house, little happened on the site. Concerned Citizens went into hiatus, but some of its members continued to check with planners to find out if the estate had submitted a new application. The estate, anxious to sell the property, began to talk with staff about a height amendment, as staff initially recommended. A new application became public in May 1989.

> [Executors are] hoping council will raise the maximum 35 foot height ceiling to levels as high as 90 feet, making way for a development as tall as a nine-storey building ...
>
> 'It's a very major change from the original 35-ft height. And the existing rules are, I think, appropriate for the residential area. I wouldn't like to see any changes,, [said one resident] ...
>
> But city development officers, who worked with [the estate] for six months on the application, say the proposal meets all the rules...
>
> 'What he is trying to do is increase the height in the centre of the property mainly to allow that 250 persons per acre (the current allowed density) – and translate it into a taller building,' said [a planner] of the city's development and planning office.
>
> 'But then again, without seeing the staff report, it's very difficult to visualize it.'
>
> The *Daily News* couldn't get a copy of the report yesterday, even though a white notice was tacked to a tree on the estate, saying more information is available to the interested public ... 'There are some anti-development types who are probably against anything,' [the

estate spokesperson] said ... 'This is a very modest request that meets the intent of the municipal development plan' (C30).

Staff recommended that Council increase the height allowed from 35 ft throughout the site to graduated increases of 55 ft to 90 ft at the centre of the site. The reporter reveals a fair bit of irony in this piece. Staff say the public needs to see the staff report to understand, but reporters couldn't get copies of the staff report. Staff say the proposal 'meets all the rules,' but then propose to change one of the rules.

Citizens who opposed a high-rise on the site grew angry with planners. They argued the existing regulations sufficed. They felt that staff had lied to them when seeming to deny that planners had met with the estate.

> C: I guess we were party to all the communications between the Planning Department and the Council. We didn't always agree with what they proposed, of course, because it was obvious throughout that the planners ... were looking for a way in which the existing planning regulations could be bent for that site to allow maximum development ... We are not against development, but we think that compatible development and development which is sometimes not on a very large scale is better in the long run for the city, but we don't really feel that the city planners take that into consideration. We also find that there's a very strange mind-set in the City Planning Department or the City Development Department that heritage is something that has been classified as 'heritage'. It's designated. It's been through the process. If it's absolutely beautiful and unique, but it doesn't have a designation, it doesn't exist.

Bureaucrats, the citizen suggests, can only see issues as black or white. Either the property has an official heritage designation or it is not a heritage property. Citizens who value heritage reject such classification schemes as myopic. Citizens opposing changes to a site have a different idea of what 'good development' means for a site.

Some of the planners who worked on the case concurred with the developer's argument that residents opposed any development.

> P: They didn't want anything. They didn't want anything over 35 ft. And I think the developer was prepared to meet them half way there as well ... They definitely did not want anything, and that's not fair.

> A few people who live right here cannot rule the roost. I don't want
> to get too deep in this because the battle is over and done with. You
> know, I don't have any wounds.[4]

Planners feel that some residents will oppose any change in their
communities. To succeed in their roles, planners must insulate themselves from the ire of the public. Plan policies protect planners. Said
one planner, 'I'm not especially concerned with what the area residents have to say, the reason being that I have the plan there. Okay,
I know what I'm trying to do in accordance with that plan. Things
are so antidevelopment and ultraconservative now in certain areas of
this city and I know it doesn't matter what it is going to be, there is
gonna be opposition. So you just kind of try and block that out.'
Planners operate according to the rules. They focus on what they
believe the plan allows. They determine to live through criticism and
opposition without taking it personally.

As discussion proceeded, critics of Council and staff found new
points to condemn. The process of decision making and the rights of
the public became issues, as a local editorial noted.

> Once again Halifax City Hall has demonstrated its weak vision of
> grass roots democracy.
>
> Earlier this year, council ended its policy of releasing relevant staff
> reports and other documents two or three days in advance of public
> meetings ... With the documents safely out of public view until the
> last moment, they need not worry about being embarrassed by citi-
> zens or reporters ...
>
> After six months [of negotiations between staff and developers],
> the public will see the application two hours before it comes up.
>
> The romantics among us like to think of civic politics as the root of
> democracy, but this action is barely worthy of a banana republic
> (C29AA).

The writer draws on our strong cultural attachment to 'democracy'
to chastise Council and staff for withholding information.

Staff reports suggested that the height change would give the
developer design flexibility necessary for good development: '... staff
is convinced that the most effective approach to development rests
with the proposed height precincts. Given that the subject proposal
maintains a more rigorous approach to development, it must be
viewed in a way that is clearly consistent with the overall intent of

the MPS' (D2: 4, 5). Staff believe that the plan promotes 'efficiency' and 'flexibility,' and that relaxing zoning limits on heights complies with the intent of the plan. On a high-density site, staff interprets 'appropriate development' (never fully defined in the plan) to mean high rise.

Opponents of the project added city staff to the list of those they had to battle.

Angry residents said they've been stonewalled by Halifax city staff, who have made it all but impossible to get information on the proposed changes ...

The fact that information was given to the developer, but not to the neighbours shows favouritism on the part of city staff, [a resident] charged.

Neighbours say the proposed development is too high and would be out of character with the historic, family-oriented neighbourhood (D32).

Citizens saw the planners operating as allies of the owners and developers of the property. Yet, they made clear, they expect planners to act as neutral keepers of the public interest.

To rally support to continue the fight, Concerned Citizens for the Mitchell Property called a public meeting.

The gloves came off Monday night ... [as about] 75 residents attended a public meeting to discuss [removing height restrictions] ...

City staff were also accused at the meeting of not co-operating with residents in the area concerned about the kind of development that takes place on the site ...

'I am told that [two members of Concerned Citizens] are at the centre of this activist group,' [the estate spokesperson] said. 'Their attacks seem so unwarranted to us that you have to wonder if their failed attempts to purchase the property ... have embittered them. I question whose interests they are serving' ...

[A resident], representing the Ward 1 Residents Association, said an amendment to the height restriction would wipe out the public input that city council solicited when developing the city's Generalized Future Land Use Map ...

'We see no legitimate reason to make changes to these policies,' she said. 'There is no other objective other than to guarantee the owner an immediate increase in its value' (C33).

In the context of this informal meeting, ad hominem attacks and accusations flew. The estate's spokesperson questioned the motives and self-interest of the project's opponents. The proposal's critics attacked the 'greed' of the estate and the advice given by staff. All of the participants saw themselves as representing the greater community interest.

The city's Planning Advisory Committee (PAC) held two public meetings on the amendment. At the first meeting in July 1989, planning staff tried to explain their advice to sixty citizens eager to understand.[5]

> *Citizen 1*: What I would like to ask is if the 35-ft height restriction that is now on the property is changed. If this was to be approved, what's to stop the owner from sitting on the property for another five to ten years and then asking for the height restrictions to be changed yet again? Could that be stopped?

> *Planner*: ... If it were to change to what's being proposed here, I would hope the owner of the property would be satisfied because this is as far as staff would be willing to take it. It doesn't mean he can't come back and make another application. That application would be up to City Council to deal with ...

> *Citizen 1*: But up until now, we have been assured that although we couldn't prevent the property from being developed to its maximum capacity, we were protected in the height to which it could be developed. But that now has crumbled and the height is going higher and higher. What's to stop that 90-ft wedge from moving closer and closer to the street?

> *Planner*: It's not crumbling – it hasn't crumbled yet ... I want to make it clear that I'm not trying to denounce or paint a bad picture of how the property can be developed now. From staff's point of view, there is simply no doubt that the proposed height precincts have equal validity under the Plan (C36: 6, 7).

The planner does not deny that advice involves interpreting the plan. 'This is as far as staff would be willing to take it,' but the owner can ask for more. Furthermore, the planner argues, 90 ft is as valid a height as 35 ft. By contrast, the citizen indicates that she thought that planning regulations should protect communities from unwanted changes.

Citizen 2: ... Many of us won't like having another big block of population centred in that particular location ...

Planner: ... Given that distance of 150 ft and given the fact that we're dealing with 90 ft – or ten or eleven storeys, not thirty storeys – 90 ft back in on the site, from the staff point of view, we have a hard time seeing that as an undue impact as far as land use is concerned.

... Some of what I'm dealing with tonight is very technical.

... Our office is always available and anyone who wants to go over any of these points, by all means come and see us. It's very difficult to deal with some of these points at a public meeting. It is much easier to sit down with a pencil and paper and we're certainly available for that. There is lots of time before the next public meeting (C36: 9, 14).

The second citizen's remarks indicate a common concern of those who oppose high-rise developments: large buildings could bring strange new people into the neighbourhood. The planner sidesteps the citizen's fear, though, and tells citizens that the issues are 'technical' and 'difficult.' The emotional content is never addressed.

In defending staff advice on height, a planner respondent repeatedly referred to 'the fact(s)' in a carefully reasoned statement.

P: The fact is that ... taller buildings are part of the south end – that's part of the character. People are prepared to live with that. So if people have and will continue to live side by side with these enormous apartment buildings right on the property line, how can it be that a building set back 90 ft from the street line be any worse? In fact, there's no way you can consider it to be in the same ballpark – and this is what we were trying to point out to Council. And in fact, this is what we said to Council. Look [pointing to map with high rises marked in black figures], ... within a block or two of the Mitchell property, here are a series of apartment buildings ... which all meet or exceed the height of what's being proposed on the Mitchell property ... All of these buildings are right on the street line. All of these buildings lay immediately adjacent to several families. None of them have the amount of open space and trees. None of them are separated from other properties by three streets. What we're saying is these buildings have not ... been to the detriment of the neighbouring buildings, the neighbouring properties ... And what we're saying is that if these buildings hadn't been to the detriment of the south end, then how in God's name can that spell disaster for the south end? ... But again, we're not pulling all of this out of thin air. We're working with the municipal plan that has a set of criteria – and that's what we had to judge it by, and it was decided to go with that.

This difference in perspective between planners and citizens underlies many similar disputes in Halifax. The planner may have a tendency to see the city in 'plan view' from above. Indeed, planners often referred to maps of sites during interviews to orient themselves. From plan view, the Mitchell property lies in a neighbourhood dotted with high-rise blocks among low-rise developments. Filling in one more 'dot' on the map does not significantly alter the pattern.

Ordinarily, residents do not conceive of the city from plan view. For the residents of the neighbourhood, the view from street level seems most significant. They walk or drive past the site, rarely looking at maps except to find places they don't know. They see the site as part of a streetscape dominated (in linear feet) by 'family-style,' low-rise buildings. High-rise buildings present tangible risks: wind tunnels, rapid population growth, unpredictable neighbours, and questionable design. As a citizen remarked, 'Yes, there are a lot of high-rises in the area, but most of them were there before the plan came in. The question is how many you can take before a place stops being a neighbourhood. I really wonder whether this neighbourhood will still be here in thirty years.'

By contrast, planners see themselves as working with the community the way it is: a composite of low-rise and high-rise structures, of owners and renters, of neighbourhoods within districts. Residents have a different preferred image of the community: a low-rise, residential, family neighbourhood. What planners see as dots on a map residents see as intrusions into an idealized townscape.

Although the planner tried valiantly to convince those present of staff openness and willingness to listen, some speakers at the meetings attacked planners for seeming to side with the developers.

> *Citizen 3*: I can't figure out who is making the proposal here. You seem to be putting the proposal forward. Is the developer asking for the 90 ft and you're saying that there are controls on this land and therefore you're only willing to support a proposal of this kind (C36: 16)?

Under the procedures used in public hearings in Halifax, planners present the details of proposals to the public. It may seem to citizens that the planner is speaking for developers. Planners, though, see themselves as responding to applications.

Planner: All that staff are being asked to do is recommend to Council on whether or not it is appropriate to poke a hole up through this 35-ft height in the fashion that is shown here. After we had analysed it, all the indications are that it is ...

Unidentified speaker: I guess my concern is that a lot of time has been spent by staff for the developer. There are quite a few people here right now who probably don't support that proposal. Is there someone on staff who would take the opposite view and come up with an alternate proposal which could then be negotiated with the developer? That would be more equitable for both parties concerned.

Planner: That issue can be taken up with the director of Development and Planning. I don't mean that in a disrespectful way. I'm not the only person on staff who has dealt with this. Four other planners have dealt with it – the director and the city manager as well. This isn't just one planner coming before you. This has been dealt with thoroughly, as are all major applications. We spend a lot of time with developers in dealing with properties of this magnitude (C36: 18, 19).

As planners review the policies in the plan that deal with particular properties, they come to some conclusion as to whether the changes requested 'meet the intent' of the plan. Superiors review their work, and ultimately the department produces a common staff report. Hence others in the municipal organization validate the planner's work and opinions.

When a citizen asked the planner whether staff could advocate other views, the planner suggested that the citizen talk to the director. The existing bureaucratic structure cannot readily accommodate divergent views. Citizens find it frustrating that staff whose salaries come from public taxes cannot respond to the range of community views.

If planners support applications for zoning changes, as the planner did in this situation, citizens may suspect collusion with developers. Clearly, developers apply for zoning changes to enhance the exchange value of property. Zoning has become a central mechanism in setting the value of land. Sometimes citizens conclude that planners 'work for' the developers because, by the nature of the process, planners end up explaining (and defending) proposals before citizens.

> C: At the public meetings [the planner] seemed to be doing the marketing for the estate. I could hardly believe it. After some twenty-five or thirty people spoke their minds against the project, [the planner] got up and rebutted them point by point. It was as if he was working for the estate, not for us. There was an appalling lack of democratic process. It's amazing the ease with which they blatantly disregarded the plan after all of the work that went into it ... It's not the role of the city to take sides in disputes like this. I don't mind losing a battle fair and square, but I question the moral right of the planner to come down on one side like that. The planners are working for all of us, not just some of us.

Most planners react strongly to such charges. They see themselves as protecting the city and its corporate interests. They feel that their work supports the public interest. Their job, especially in Development Control, is to ensure that Halifax gets good development. They do not bring 'bad' proposals forward.

> P: Well, we certainly come across as being in league with the developers, that's for sure, but ... it goes back to the fact that it's the strength of your municipal plan. I've got absolutely no respect for a developer or a planner that just plays games and looks for a safe way out. You read your plans and if they are very liberal and leave a lot of opportunities for contract development or rezoning or whatever else, you are going to see a lot of applications go to Council with a favourable recommendation and in that regard, staff comes across as being pro-development, and people begin to say, 'oh, well, staff is pro-development and they are in cahoots with this developer.' And all of a sudden, there is this animosity.

Planners see themselves as doing their jobs: sifting a development proposal through the policies of the plan and seeing which ones make it through. Because they act as municipal agents, they must protect the City's interests. They cannot reveal confidential discussions with developers for fear of creating a poor investment climate. Hence they cannot adequately explain or defend themselves before irate residents.

Agents of the developer supported the planners' integrity:

D: You hear from a lot of citizens groups that they are distrustful of City staff, but that's without justification, frankly ... I think it's unfair for people to say that city staff are pro-development. The public doesn't see all the cases where staff say no at an early level, where they say, 'Go ahead, but we'll recommend against it.' Most of the requests end there. Staff really acts as a watchdog on behalf of the public in those cases.

At public meetings when I hear people go after the staff, I'm amazed at their patience, their restraint, and their willingness to try to explain things to people. It's not an easy job that they have. Sometimes people aren't familiar with the terms or with the process, and they just aren't making good points, but the planners listen. It's unfair sometimes the way that residents treat staff.

The minutes of public meetings attest to the thick skin planners must develop. While many citizens choose their words carefully and deal with substantive issues, others become accusatory or abusive. As the planners say, it's all part of the job: you have to be able to let criticism roll off you or it can crush you.

Some planners paint a slightly rumpled portrait of their own performance in dealing with developers and citizens.

P: So I see planners as often facilitating what communities want, what neighbourhoods want, but ... because I end up on the development control side, it often seems like in presenting a development proposal for approval, for rezoning or for a development agreement, [there is] a lot of explaining what the policies say. I really haven't had much public input. I get the application, I look at the policies ... but when it comes time to present it at a public hearing, I'm already sold on it. And so I'm almost, in some sense, in situations where I've presented, I feel almost like a consultant for the developer, like I'm pitching it, and I'm trying to convince the public that really if it's not necessarily good for your neighbourhood, it is consistent with the policies that have already been adopted. And sometimes I'll end up recommending approval because it's consistent with the policies, even though I don't think it's a good development.

In this quote, the respondent acknowledges the potential discomfort of the planner involved in implementing the plan. Because she only takes forward those applications she supports, the planner can sometimes feel like a salesman. Because he must operate by the policies in the plan, the planner may sometimes have to recommend projects he dislikes.

An alderman offered a perspective on planning and planners.

A: The problem is that the planners are not loved. Like most bureaucrats, they're distrusted. People are no different than you and I – we all distrust bureaucrats. Citizens against a project see them as the enemy. I'd probably feel the same way if I were in their shoes ... You have to recognize that planning issues are *very* political. They always end up at Council. If you separate the planner's and the politician's jobs, you have a problem. Ultimately, the planners have to get their changes through, so they have to understand the politicians – there's nothing wrong with that, but they can get to be too political and that creates problems for citizens. Planners here in Halifax tend to be very self-serving – they look out for themselves. And I'm their biggest critic.

A planner who does not work for the City agreed that Halifax planners can begin to worry too much about their own success rating. As a result, they may not bother to listen to complaints from citizens.

O: I think that the Planning Department got involved in that kind of psychology as well. Not just in terms of being pro-development or pro-growth, which may be good or bad, depending on the specifics of it, but much more dependent on approval – you know, the kind of 'approval rate.' You can kind of imagine that there's a score sheet somewhere where someone is keeping score of the number of times our recommendation gets approved by Council as a measure of success, of performance of the Planning Department and planners. Once you get into that kind of mentality, you start losing some perspective on what it is that you believe in or what kind of society you're working towards, the kind of unfettered advice that you might offer ... And you start thinking, ... 'Well, we're part of the system, and part of our role is to read the nuances of which way the political wind is blowing and make sure that we're going with it as opposed to against it.' And the measure of effectiveness is how many of your recommendations actually get approved. And one way to make sure they actually get approved is to make sure that they're going the same way as the winds are blowing.

The respondent's depiction is damning. As a trained planner, the respondent clearly expects urban planners to offer 'objective advice.' Instead, the respondent believes Halifax planners limit their options because of a concern with the tally sheet of their performance.

Several respondents suggested that the Development and Planning Department seemed overly political, eager to please Council.[6] Planners denied tailoring their advice to Council; they explained that since Council's vision already sets the policies in the plan, inevitably only those projects that Council will likely support survive when sifted through plan policies. Over time, the values of political leaders, embedded in the plan through approval procedures, become second nature to the planners who implement the plan.

So many people wanted to speak their minds on the fate of the Mitchell property that the PAC held a second public meeting in September 1989. Citizens prepared new defence strategies for the fight.

> *Citizen 4:* ... Since our last meeting, many of us have had the opportunity to listen to Prince Charles describe what happens to cities when planning is not controlled. On many occasions he stated that we have these wonderful laws in place and why is it that we outrageously abandon them (C38: 2).

Over the years many celebrities have become experts on planning matters, and some planning gurus have become celebrities. In this quote, the citizen uses a celebrity, Prince Charles, to advocate a particular approach to planning. At other times in both documents and interviews, citizens referred to the writings of Jane Jacobs to explain why low-rise, high-density settlements 'work best.'

> *Citizen 5:* I would just like to comment very briefly on this whole question of City planning, I think anybody who has read Jane Jacobs's *Life and Death of Great American Cities* knows about the whole principle of eyes on the street, the whole idea that high-rises very often become slums very much faster than low-rises and the best way you can foster community and the retention of existing neighbourhoods is to build something low where people can interact ... (C38).

Most planners have read Jacobs's work and heard Prince Charles's pronouncements, but they do not quote them. Indeed, they may react negatively to such theory.

> P: Well, on one level, planners react with scorn and ridicule when they hear somebody stand up and quoting somebody ... But in some senses, there's a sort of incapacity to actually respond to it ... like with any field, what gets down to popular culture and popular reading isn't where the current state of the field is often, and so when people stand up and quote somebody like Jane Jacobs or something, you know planners ... usually [think], 'Well, it's not even worth debating because that's only like one aspect – that's one voice about what planning can be about.'

Do planners keep up to date with developments in planning theory and practice? Perhaps not enough. Martin et al (1988), reporting on a survey of Canadian planners, found that planners did not report reading a great volume of recent material. The most influential works came from the 1960s and 1970s and included Jacobs's best seller.[7]

> P: I know when I was in [my previous job] that I was too busy to read anything. And that, you know, was one of my ongoing kind of problems there, and it was a criticism that I had – and ... that the councillors had – that they felt too much of the advice they were getting from the planners was personal opinion and wasn't informed professional opinion. And I probably would say that's true with all planners, especially the longer they've been practising. You get a little more distant from recent thinking. And while some things are passed around in a circulating file ... usually it's just like a title and a table of contents and nobody ever goes back to read it.

Much of the implicit theory that guides practice, it appears, derives less from the research literature within the field than from interactive exchanges between planners in the course of their daily work.[8] Certainly planners made no effort during the meetings to respond to the challenges citizens presented. Instead of discussing theory, they focused on the specifics of the plan and proposal before them.

During the PAC meeting, citizens tried desperately to come to grips with the technical details of the plan. The planner invites trust in his response.

> Citizen 6: I understood that 35 ft can be finished off to be 45 ft. Does that mean that 90 ft can be finished off at 100 ft?

> Planner: Yes, that's right ... No secrets here – 35 ft gets you 45; 45 ft

gets you possibly 65; and 90 ft, possibly 100 ... The reality is that under the R-3 controls, developers build to the maximum density and they do it in a way that is economical for them (C38: 4, 5).

Thirty-five will get you forty-five? Under the south end plan, builders could get up to another 10 ft of height without violating the height limits.[9] Citizens tried to figure out what that meant while the planner went on to talk about development economics. The appeal to openness and honesty got lost in the sophisticated code of the technical message.

> *Planner:* ... I have dealt with this property in different capacities in the last couple of years and to tell you honestly, most of the people who have looked at the site have tried to develop it in a condominium fashion and tried to get a good development ... If you try to increase the size of the unit, you're so squashed down on the property when you're limited to four storeys. The bigger the units are, the fewer you get ... At the 35-ft height limit, given reality as it is, you end up with a rental type of apartment building if you try to achieve that maximum density (C38: 5, 6).

In practice, the planner says, developers go for the maximum they can build at the least cost. Developers will not build attractive low-rise, medium-density townhouses if they have high-density zoning. To get good quality development (condominiums), the City has to give the developer latitude to go up to preserve the amenities of the site, Jane Jacobs and Prince Charles not withstanding.

> *Citizen 7:* Studies have been done which indicate fairly clearly that the higher people live away from the street, the less is their involvement with the community ... So I'd just like to state that as an opinion of why I would value something close to the street, hopefully aesthetically pleasing but not isolated and alienating from the neighbourhood in which I live (C38: 6, 7).

Citizens speaking out against high-rise buildings articulate a fear of 'alienation.' They don't want faceless residents in their community; they want neighbours. The planner tried to convince them that with greater height the developer could sell larger condominium units to a higher class of people. Staff concurs with residents' desire for owners rather than renters on this property: all of the parties value home ownership. Unlike the optimistic citizens, the planner does not expect the developer to opt for producing fewer units than the density allows on the site. Residents made it known that they didn't want *any* kind of apartments if they could get townhouses.

The intent of the plan remained elusive through the dispute. People talked about it and used it to defend opinions, but they did not define it. What does it mean to respect heritage or to have high-density residential? Why can zoning regulations once deemed appropriate suddenly become inappropriate? Is 90 ft a 'moderate' height? Citizens felt frustrated when they got inadequate answers to such questions. Some began to ask, 'Is planning a charade?'

Planners believe that any form of development that doesn't explicitly violate the provisions of the plan may be appropriate. Staff have the responsibility to advise Council on requests that come from the development community. They aren't asked for their personal evaluation of whether a project is 'good'; they only decide whether the plan allows it.

Citizens see planning differently. They expect the plan to protect and defend a certain vision or image of the city, usually the present landscape. As a document crafted with extensive public input, the plan has almost a sacred status for some citizens.

> *Citizen 5*: Through all of the '70s the Municipal Development Plan, the Detailed Area Plan and the subsequent revision of the plan, citizens of the area have been involved.
>
> There were thousands of citizen hours involved. Basically what came out of this was a declaration on the part of the people who live in the area of the kind of development they wanted to see.
>
> ... As I said, the Ward I Residents Association has consistently supported and still supports the citizen process which developed these policies and the policies themselves as an expression of the wishes of the residents for their property and our neighbourhood. We see no legitimate reason to make any changes to these policies at this time (C38: 17, 18).

For this speaker, the plan expresses the will of the people. It embodies the public interest. It stands for order, democracy, and fairness. Public participation in plan preparation gives the plan special status in the community.

Some of the speakers at the meeting expressed their growing frustration with planning.

Citizen 8: I'm a little bit confused because I often hear of Halifax being a planning-oriented city. We have a planning-oriented Council. We have experts who are hired as employees of the City who are planners, but I've come to feel as a resident that maybe the City isn't too sympathetic when it comes to planning. We have the developers and the property owners and we all know what they want, and then we have the rest of us. Sometimes no one appears to really care what we appear to want (C38: 23).

Several speakers wondered why the developer couldn't make a profit by building within existing regulations

Planner: It might very well be possible ... I am not about to get into the developer's financial situation on the site. If City Council wants to, it can. It's not in the plan for me to ask if this increases the value of the property, does it create a more viable solution. I think it creates more viable solutions than what exists right now, but in terms of dollars and cents, the plan does not ask me to get into that (C38: 24).

As the planner makes clear to the citizen in this exchange, staff cannot comment on whether the zoning change improves the profitability of development: the plan has no policies on profit.[10] Although citizens may see profit as the primary motivation for the requested amendment, planners do not treat land value as a planning issue. The plan seeks to facilitate development, respect heritage, and encourage compatible infill (housing between existing units), *not* to restrict private profit. The plan regulates the use of land, but owners retain the right to develop. Planning does not change the nature of the political economy.

Regulations that citizens see as protective amulets for neighbourhood character are regarded by planners as flexible tools to promote development. Citizens often repeat plan policies and hold up planning documents as magical charms to safeguard communities from change. Planners view policies as tools to fashion good development projects.

Act Three

Citizens preparing the 1982 south end planning strategy favoured low-rise development. Colonel Mitchell had complained to planning staff at that time about the proposed height limit on his property, but was reassured by a staff report that he still had potential to develop. Said a developer, 'Well, any reasonable person would read that staff report and understand that staff was saying they would allow contract development on the site with provisions to increase the height beyond the 35 ft in the schedule. That recommendation was approved by Council.' Unfortunately, staff made an error that the owners discovered when they tried to sell the property. Staff knew that one of the planners had misread the plan and misled Colonel Mitchell. Would the City honour its earlier apparent approval? One of the members of the estate's team explains their initial strategy. 'My thought at first was that since this was a goof-up at City Hall, we should appeal to them to rectify the problem. We had some discussions with City staff, but they were not prepared to acknowledge that they had made an error – they just couldn't admit it.' Staff urged the owners to apply for the height change, but the estate decided to ask for the development agreement it thought the City had promised.

> D: It seems that there may have been something of a hidden agenda in all of this, though I'm not sure. Staff had been hammered quite a bit at the Municipal Board and from the public about the number of contract developments they had approved. Council had decided that it wanted to limit the number of contract developments it went into, so that may have been part of it.

Council turned down the development agreement, and eventually the planners got the application they originally requested. According to a developer, 'The estate became pretty frustrated with the lack of a sale of the property, so when [one of the estate's agents] was in the Planning Department on other business ... , one of the staff came up to him and said, 'Why don't you apply for an amendment to the height precinct map? Staff will support you on this.' Evidently, staff wanted to see the property developed. They saw it as a 'gorgeous property.' According to representatives of the estate, staff worked hard to get the height proposal through.

When the Planning Advisory Committee reviewed the case following its two public meetings, it recommended that Council reject the height precinct amendment. Its report to Council read, in part:

> ... Some members expressed the view that allowing increased height on this site would not necessarily lead to better or more appropriate development than would be possible under the present 35 foot height limit.

It was felt that the type of development that would result would
not be in keeping with or sensitive to the surrounding street-oriented
neighbourhood which includes a registered Heritage Streetscape on
Tower Road directly across from the property (C42).

On 4 October 1989, Halifax Council held a public hearing. In addition to the old arguments, a few new tactics appeared at the eleventh
hour. For example, the estate presented a petition signed by 255
people supporting the application.

> D: [The] tide seemed to be turning. Funny things were going on.
> Maybe the public opposition was too shrill. Maybe Council began to
> recognize that an injustice had been done to the [the family]. Budget
> restraint and higher taxes were beginning to loom large too. Also, the
> high-density, low-rise concept was proving not to be a panacea ... the
> people in opposition to the change rested on their laurels after the
> PAC recommended against the change ... Well, the [family] grew up
> in that area, in the south end and they know people there ... They
> went door to door in the area and asked people to sign a petition.
> They were rarely refused – people signed it.
>   We aren't talking about a [massive high rise] ... This is more like a
> Garden Park or Carlisle – eight or nine stories, unobjectionable. It
> will blend in with the surroundings ... Right now there seems to be
> this thing among planners about having things at street level – that's
> gaining in popularity. But there's also another approach of setting
> buildings back in a garden setting – that's okay too.

The owner's agent acknowledges that approving the change means
making a choice about values: it means seeing the high building in
a garden setting as unobjectionable or 'okay.'
    The hearing showed that both sides could play the popularity
game. Developers and owners have learned to use the petition as do
their opponents. Hence all parties can claim 'the people' favour their
cause.
    Many respondents revealed their concerns about planning in a
democratic society. Citizen activists believe that democracy means
listening to citizens who speak up.

> C: I really think that democratic principles were violated in this case.
> That bothered me more than anything. Democracy is not ideal, but
> it's better than anything else. There have to be checks and balances in

the system, but I feel they won't be there until we get a stronger Council to give direction to staff ... If the staff in Planning were told, 'This will not be condoned in future,' then they wouldn't be as arrogant. But they've been allowed to do as they please, and Council ignores them. We really need those checks and balances because if a group has ultimate power, then it won't use it wisely. We have to protect democracy.

Developers think that democracy entails respect for individual rights and delegated authority.

D: I get angry when I hear the opponents of a project say, 'If this is a democracy, then elected representatives have to listen to us the people and refuse this.' That's hogwash. A democracy has to respect and represent the rights of individuals too. We have to balance the rights of the individual and the community – that's what democracy has to mean.

A council member indicated that democracy implies the fair application of laws and procedures for resolving differences, adjudicating rights, and determining outcomes.

A: But here we're democratic. We say that if a man owns property, he's entitled to do something with it. That's the code of the West. He can make a request. But that's where the system falls apart from the citizen's view because the ordinary citizen is unprotected. When he buys a piece of property, he has no guarantee that his neighbourhood won't change. I'd like to stop that. It's time that we had some security. We still need to have some flexibility, mind you, but too much has to be stopped.

Thus, while many of the actors talk about 'democracy' and appeal to it as a value, clearly they mean different things.

In the due course of democratic municipal process, Council approved the height change in October 1989. The next day's paper reported:

[One alderman] said many aldermen struggled over the reams of information on the issue before deciding how to cast their votes.

'It was a tough decision,' he said. 'We listened to the planning department. The turning point was the strong staff recommendation.

They were quizzed, badgered, you name it. But they had the answers' ... (C45).

One of the aldermen explained the decision in an interview:

A: You see, when different people looked at that lot, they saw differ-ent things. Some saw trees, some saw an interesting house, others saw a run-down house and prime real estate. But what really galled me was that one of the people who stood up and exhorted against allowing greater height on the site actually lived in a twelfth floor apartment overlooking the site. That's hypocrisy. The people who saw the site as a nice house, beautiful trees wanted it to stay the same. They either wanted nothing there or individual homes. They didn't really want anything. The guy who owned the land was with-in his rights, but the opponents hung on every straw.

The alderman ends with a key point: the rights of the property own-er. If a property owner has evidence that the City has acknowledged her rights to develop her property in a particular way, and if plan-ning staff assures Council that what is requested is good planning, then Council should approve. If, at the same time, Council can save trees and open space, that too is a public good. Some of the neigh-bours, the alderman explains, 'Were against it for the wrong reasons.' The Council member revealed a strong commitment to home owner-ship: the land owner has the right to build; the twelfth floor apart-ment dweller (renter) has no right to comment. A Marxist would no doubt find the politician's remarks illuminating.

The dispute left a bitter after taste, as a developer acknowledged:

D: This was really an excellent example of what can go wrong in a development case. Things got so technical that even an educated layman couldn't decide what was happening. The public interest isn't served in a situation like that. We're left with no knowledge of what will ultimately go on the site. I'm not sure if what results isn't push-ing for design through zoning by-law, and that isn't good. You can't legislate everything.

A citizen respondent offered her perspective on the effect the dispute had on residents:

C: [This case] developed strangely politically because it was a somewhat different group in nature ... : fewer academics, fewer people from away, ... a couple of people with quite a lot of clout in the local business community ... It was primarily a group from the neighbourhood ...

[The Concerned Citizens] felt extremely embittered. They were furious with the Planning Department. The Planning Department played stupid games ... Like I said, this was an extremely personal one.

But I think the group felt really, really sorry by the Planning Department's behaviour, betrayed by Council, frustrated by the lack of broad public support, and really sour on the whole thing ... I don't think most of these people will [bounce back and stay involved].

The dispute may have further weakened support for planning. A member of the Halifax Planning Advisory Committee noted:

The Planning Department keeps saying, 'This is in the plan, and the plan policy says that we want to increase density on the peninsula as a way of making better use of resources. That policy was formulated over a long period of time with public involvement. Now rezoning pieces of the inner city ... works against that policy.' The politicians and the citizens keep telling the Planning Department that they don't really care what the policy says, that in fact they didn't understand what they were buying into when they approved that policy ... The politicians are listening to the screams of people on that street and they aren't concerned about the policy at all. They're much more concerned about what they see on the ground. A lot of people have grown very suspicious of planning generally, and of what it is that 'the plan' itself is going to do for them. The plan is vague enough that people take different sections of it and quote it in different ways. But a lot of residents of the peninsula are saying that they aren't happy with a lot of things that are in the plan. They certainly didn't understand that they were buying into redevelopment of the peninsula in the way that it's happening.

Public expectations of what planning should deliver differed significantly from the realities citizens experienced.

Part 3

The Reviews Are In

Chapter Seven

Staging Planning Activities

The world as it is offers a context within which human action becomes meaningful (Kraushaar 1988). Articulating that context of action helps us understand the problems and nature of planning practice. Analysing the context of planning disputes in Halifax allows us to account for some of the problems that participants identified and for the outcomes that resulted.

If we had no disputes about the use of land in our communities, we would have little need for planning. Planning activities provide the stage upon which we transact certain cultural meanings and argue about the application of cultural values to our townscapes. In pluralistic democratic societies, planning venues provide opportunities for debate about 'the public interest.' Hence, community planning has become fully integrated into local political structures, processes, and values.

In this chapter we analyse the staging of planning activities in Halifax. The cultural context in which planning activities occur involves structures and values from both within and outside of the community. The drama of local disputes takes place on a series of stages representing embedded cultural contexts.

International and National Context

In our analysis of planning disputes in Halifax, we find that many levels of context contribute to the stage or stages on which actors perform in the drama of local democracy. Planning activities show that international and national structures and values can influence planning theory and practice.

Planning theory, often imported into Canada from American or European sources, reflects the international context in which it develops. The political economy of industrial capitalism frames much of modern planning theory, although authors may not explicitly acknowledge it. Some planning theory owes a debt to Utopian socialism, while other theorists draw on nostalgic images of verdant rural landscapes, homey small towns, or vital urban communities. The values that permeate much of the planning theory drawn into local debates originate in the international context of American or European cultures.

National and international cultural values help set the stage for local planning activities; indeed, we find many such values reproduced in the urban landscape in communities like Halifax. For example, land-use disputes and their outcomes reflect a cultural commitment to the pre-eminence of private property rights while simultaneously revealing a concern for protecting community amenities. The style and placement of structures on the land often replicate national or international examples. In the 1970s, high-rise office towers came to represent economic success in Halifax much as they did in New York. Accordingly, the skylines of urban North America offered a template against which some sought to judge Market Place Plaza. Trends and values that dominate the economic centre trickle down to affect the periphery.

Several respondents explicitly acknowledged the influence of the national and international context on planning in Halifax. Former Council members discussed the pressure they felt in the 1950s and 1960s from the federal government (in the way of grants for slum clearance) and from the development industry (for project approvals). Citizen activists recall that they followed American civil rights and antiwar protests covered widely in the media, and read the works of Saul Alinski and Jane Jacobs for inspiration. Enthusiasm and commitment to public participation in the late 1960s and early 1970s clearly spread to Halifax via the media and other communication networks. Sometimes a national or international agenda can supersede, at least temporarily, regional traditions and values.

In their fight against Harbour Drive, activists held up the example of the Spadina Expressway to prove the merit of their case. Planners, activists, and politicians all referred to urban forms and experiences in other parts of the world in discussing their image of what would constitute good development for Halifax. Hence we find that decisions about 'appropriate' development often involve references to events, trends, and theories at the national and international level.

Local practice occurs within this international and national context and frequently refers to it. At public meetings, those opposing development projects quote planning theory developed by American authors or promulgated by British royalty. The models discussed reflect our society's attachment to an ideal community of neighbourliness, beauty, security, and good fellowship. In private, planners dismiss such arguments as romantic and naive, but in the public context they cannot respond. They have no equivalent 'popular' theory to cite. The rationale that guides planners' judgment also responds to cultural values, but values about which Canadians tend to be reticent. We do not trumpet the values of capitalism and utilitarianism. Nonetheless, Canadians believe in progress, prosperity, efficiency, and amenity. When planners operate as agents of the municipality, they promote such values. Their arguments for greater density, while phrased in neutral or 'objective' terms, reveal underlying cultural assumptions about economic utility.

Reference to cultural structures and values from international and national contexts depends on the issue. For example, we find more explicit references to national issues and concerns in the Market Place Plaza dispute than in the Mitchell case. Citizen activists fighting Market Place Plaza employed national experts and were assisted in their battle by an agency of the national government: they had no difficulty in arguing a national interest in the issue. In the Mitchell dispute, by contrast, we see little discussion of national values or structures, but considerable reference to international values through the use of planning theory and theorists. By drawing on Jane Jacobs and Prince Charles, citizens sought to broaden the stage for their performances.

In their efforts to pull out national and international stages for the drama, actors create a culture of comparison. Actors invite the audience to compare their experience against the example offered from some other place or time. Actions that may seem inappropriate in one context appear rational on another stage. The ability to draw on a wide range of cultural structures and values to support an argument enhances an actor's persuasiveness. Actors also tread cautiously on foreign stages, however, for fear of losing their footing. In the Halifax context, it may be necessary to seek cultural comparisons, but ultimately an actor must aver regional and local superiority.

The Provincial Context

Under the division of powers in Canada, the provinces have the ability to pass legislation governing the use of land. Control of land in Nova Scotia reflects the province's conservative heritage of Loyalist settlement, late local self-government, limited public landholding, and rampant patronage politics.

The provincial stage for planning rests on the legislative framework of community planning and the values that dominate the public culture. The Planning Act frames roles for the actors: citizens can make their opinions known; planners carry out the technical work; politicians have the power to decide; the province can veto decisions. Citizens find the stage offered by the 1983 Planning Act more constrictive than the stage they had through the 1969 act. Avenues for intervention diminished as modifications in the legislation reflected limited regional sympathy for citizen action.

A fear of mass action, spawned early in a colony of Loyalists to the British Crown, sometimes dominates the provincial agenda. Provincial authorities kept municipalities under central control until the 1880s, and continue to pass legislation that undermines the ability of Nova Scotians to organize collectively.[1] Nova Scotia has no heritage of active participatory democracy in its public culture. The rare examples of collective action in communities around the province receive little public acknowledgment or attention. Politicians and members of the provincial business community usually have little time for cooperatives, protest marches, or public displays of concern.

The prosperity of the province has been closely linked conceptually with the success of Halifax. Designation as a 'growth centre' by the federal government in the 1960s confirmed Halifax's aspirations to serve as a regional capital. Nova Scotians valued development as a sign of prosperity and achievement[2] and wanted their capital to emulate other successful cities. The Halifax establishment feared that the booming cities of central Canada would leave Nova Scotia far behind; Nova Scotians hold central Canada responsible for regional economic failure (see Figure 7.1).

Although Nova Scotians distrusted Upper Canadians, they accepted federal regional planning programs as a way of gaining access to government largesse. The province adopted the necessary legislation to put its communities in a position to take advantage of resources and to keep up with other parts of the country. If Toronto and Montreal had planning, Halifax had to take that seriously. The province

Figure 7.1   Local political cartoon blames Ottawa for Nova Scotia's economic woes. Cartoon by Bruce MacKinnon

could not afford to ignore the tools that other communities used to prosper.

Despite the province's readiness to employ planning as a means to economic growth, Nova Scotians retained a degree of scepticism about planning. Halifax hired planners, but kept them subordinate to the Development Department until the 1970s. Halifax Council wanted development: planning had to prove itself a useful means to that end.

During the 1950s, 1960s, and early 1970s, most Halifax politicians tended to view planners as impractical visionaries. Zoning met local needs in regulating land use. Politicians appreciated the flexibility of life without a plan. However, Councils in the early and mid-1970s moved steadily towards taking planning seriously. Provincial legislation passed in 1969 required that the city prepare a plan. It forced the provincial agenda on a captive municipality. The law also made clear, in the name given to planning documents, that planning could promote development. The 'municipal development plan' would show the way. Powerful Haligonians hoped that planning might help them achieve the dream of a prosperous Halifax.

The Local Context

As in many parts of the country, local politicians in Halifax often have close connections with the development industry. That is not to say that the development industry 'owns' them by any means, but linkages of a social and political nature commonly occur. Influential developers have, on occasion, sought and won political office in Halifax. Politicians and developers generally come from the same social, political, and economic circles.

Even where politicians may not have close ties to developers, most tend to share the values and assumptions of the 'establishment.' They accept the premise that development is good, that the tax base must expand. Often they belong to either the Liberal or the Progressive Conservative parties, although they do not seek office on a party platform basis. Nevertheless, they share the ideology of those parties: the free enterprise ethic.[3]

Local politicians operate within a culture that sees patronage and favouritism as features of the political landscape. People expect that politicians will help their supporters. Citizens believe that politicians should respond to their constituents. The fuzzy line between responsiveness to constituents' needs and supplication to the whim of special interests is the subject of considerable debate and antipathy. What some see as the politician's duty, others may view as influence peddling.

In our brief review of the history of land-use issues in Halifax in the postwar period, we find evidence that circumstances in Halifax reflected events happening and ideas circulating elsewhere. For instance, citizen activists in Halifax were well aware of the opposition to the Spadina Expressway in Toronto as they fought Harbour Drive. Experience also shows, however, that local and regional social and economic realities affect the outcomes of particular land-use disputes. The case-studies illustrate the frustrations that face Haligonians who attempt to participate in the planning process. Citizen activists can count few planning victories in Halifax. It appears that cultural structures and values from the wider stages of the international, national, and provincial contexts can influence the local agenda for a period, but if they do not resonate with local structures and values, then their influence is short-lived or shallow. Legislation that appears to encourage participation in community planning may not, in fact, facilitate certain forms of citizen action. For example, analysis of national and provincial contexts during the late 1970s shows that public rhetoric and planning legislation promoted active public involvement in planning decisions. However, our review of local practice indicates that considerable citizen action did not generally result in outcomes favoured by the activists involved. When Council members are determined to approve a development project, activists may well find it impossible to convince them otherwise. The local political climate proved decidedly pro-growth and antiactivist despite the planning processes and legislation in effect.

Extensive opposition to a development project is enough to kill the project in many communities. That has not proved true in Halifax for three reasons. First, planning legislation in Nova Scotia has been drafted to protect land owners' rights to develop their property while recognizing certain community interests. Hence, councils come under intense scrutiny should they refuse a development. Developments are allowed unless they contravene the intent of the plan.[4]

Second, Council members have reason to believe that they speak for the silent majority in promoting development. They understand that the small number who vote in municipal elections are predominantly those who support growth and progress. In the mid-1980s, Halifax Council approved a project rejected by 11,000 petitioners (about one out of every eleven Haligonians). Yet a few months later, the opponents could not translate signatures on a petition into votes at the ballot-box; antiproject candidates generally lost their efforts to replace sitting members.

Third, Council members know the fiscal strength of the community depends upon the tax base. Development holds the promise of greater revenues so that municipalities can meet their commitments and realize their aims. Balancing the books weighs heavily on decision makers.

Active citizen participation remains a central theme in politics in the 1990s. At every opportunity in Canada, governments are appointing citizens to committees and task forces and inviting them to public meetings. Provincial legislation entrenches citizen involvement by calling for a mandatory 'public participation program' in each municipality. Halifax planners and politicians also affirm their support for citizen participation. Despite the public proclamations, however, the process of planning and procedures for determining outcomes give weak roles to community members. Councils will not and cannot refuse projects simply because some citizens oppose them. Planning gives politicians and bureaucrats the means to promote a pro-development agenda while simultaneously offering them an excuse for their actions: 'We have to support this project despite opposition because of the plan.'

The operation of ward politics in Halifax help account for the way many disputes unfold. Politicians represent geographic regions of the city. They promote neighbourhood interests and concerns on Council. This system allows most politicians to ignore geographically based interest groups from other parts of the city. Politicians typically work with geographically based groups from their own ward and may argue for such groups to Council: after all, they need to secure the support of local voters in the next election. Interest groups with a wide geographic base in the city can expect to find it difficult to gain any Council member's support in opposing a development proposal. Interest groups do not offer a substantial bloc of votes, and helping them could threaten the support a politician might get from pro-development advocates. Thus in the context of a dispute, a neighbourhood-based issue (like the Mitchell dispute) is likely to create a situation in which the local Council member leads the argument in Council. A city-wide issue (such as the Market Place Plaza battle) may result in a split in Council, with members basing their opinions on the merits of the case.

Within Council, alliances rise and fall. Although most Council members support development, a powerful member of Council may convince others to reject a proposed development in the powerful member's neighbourhood. 'You support me on this issue in my area, and I'll support you in your issue.' Less powerful members of Council cannot depend on such support from other aldermen. In any case, however, local residents see their Council member promoting neighbourhood concerns. The problem for Council as a whole is who will advocate the overall interests of the city? The system of alliances promotes neighbourhood agenda, not city-wide concerns.

To a large extent, the City bureaucracy sees itself as protecting the city-wide agenda. City staff review development proposals and formulate a position. To avoid the dissension that characterizes Council discussion of the issues, staff reach a unified position. In selecting the city manager form of municipal administration, Halifax instituted a particular structure within which planners and other municipal employees must operate. Their individual voices and performances adapt to the stage created by the staff structure. The values and the agenda of the corporate unit take precedence over the values of individual actors. Actors speak as agents of the larger corporate body. Internal dissent is discouraged as the actors work together to sustain a unified performance in defence of the values entrenched in municipal policy. Community planning policies and procedures build in values such as growth, efficiency, rationality, stability, and progress.

Many communities develop a system of public structures and values that also affect the staging of performances. Halifax has a number of interest groups concerned with community planning, heritage, and environmental issues. For example, the Community Planning Association of Canada/Nova Scotia Branch (CPAC) operated a storefront office in Halifax until 1991.[5] CPAC supported many neighbourhood groups in their planning activities and supplied skills and resources to citizen activists. While the neighbourhood groups that formed to fight particular battles often advocated particular solutions to planning problems, CPAC members saw the organization's mandate as facilitating participatory democracy.

The Heritage Trust of Nova Scotia lobbies actively on behalf of heritage concerns. Its members keep a watchful eye on planning matters so as to protect the heritage buildings of the province. Heritage Trust advocates a clear and consistent set of values in its activities. Its success in establishing the heritage of Halifax as a key value is evident in many disputes. Even those who advocate demolishing old structures or building new high-rise structures acknowledge a commitment to the heritage of the city. Heritage values are 'motherhood issues.'

A substantial network of environmental groups operate in Halifax. The Ecology Action Centre (EAC) formed in the early 1970s as planning issues came to the fore in Halifax. Its members saw planning as offering the tools to protect urban environments. Over time, EAC moved away from community planning issues to focus on environmental themes, but its staff and members participated actively in the Market Place Plaza dispute: they wanted to safeguard views from the Citadel.

Many of the participants in these citizen networks know each other and cooperate in different planning activities. They share a set of values about means and ends. They believe that citizens should have greater influence, and that the City should promote particular kinds of development. A large percentage of the participants in the citizen networks have moved into Halifax from outside the province. Those who 'come from away' voice a strong commitment to their new home. Many have postsecondary education and are middle-class professionals who lean left in their politics. The well-entrenched political and economic structures of the Halifax establishment exclude them. Citizen activists operate according to values different from those of the local political culture. They construct something of a stage of their own on which to perform, importing international and national values to help them make their points. Perhaps their lack of success in persuading local politicians to take them seriously derives in part from their tendency to play to an external audience.

For the local media, land-use disputes become effective drama and object lessons. People holding picket signs or hugging trees offer compelling images. Newspapers feature the 'battles' prominently, using war metaphors for effect. Editorials and headlines generally reveal that the Halifax print media tends to defend development projects; the media reminds Council regularly of the need for a greater tax base to keep property taxes low. While the visual media give protests great coverage, television viewers tend to take local issues less seriously than they take national issues. Outside of those intimately involved in a planning dispute, few ordinary residents pay much notice.

The Influence of Culture

'Culture' has hardly proven a reductionistic device in our efforts to understand planning practice. Instead, we find ourselves with a plethora of factors used to account for particular human actions. We might well ask which cultural factors are most important influences on planning practice.

Among the factors that come up time and again to account for planning practice are economic structures and values, and political structures and values. We have argued, for instance, that municipalities' reliance on revenues from land taxes leads them to use planning as a tool for development. Municipalities in Nova Scotia have no other significant source of revenue. To meet their obligations for schools, hospitals, public transit, and roads, they must develop their tax base. As federal and provincial governments cut back on transfer payments to lower levels of government, the pressures on municipalities to develop land will, if anything, intensify.

Economic structures and values are significant at the national, international, and provincial levels, as well as locally. Global restructuring by transnational corporations affects the economic stability of communities everywhere. The ascendancy of international capitalism creates a cultural climate in which government intervention (such as planning) receives less support. Local actors operate on a stage where they cannot ignore such international structures and values.

Policies and programs developed by the national government have the ability to set the stage for local planning activities. National regional development programs in the 1960s and 1970s promoted national values and bureaucratic structures. National economic objectives became *de facto* provincial and local objectives.

The incorporation of planning into local political processes means that political structures and values play an especially important role in setting the stage for planning activities. Efforts to make government more rational, with the development of a skilled and independent civil service bureaucracy, provided a place for planning in Canadian culture. Governments adopted planning to increase economic rationality in decisions about the use of land. Unfortunately for planners, however, other rationalities continue to coexist in government processes. Patronage politics did not disappear with the appointment of civil servants, but instead took on new forms (J. Simpson 1988).

Adopting planning as a mechanism for promoting development in the postwar period allowed the federal government to set in motion a series of structures to disseminate new values. Ottawa encouraged municipalities to hire planning staff and prepare redevelopment plans to herald a new era in urban development. By tying access to federal money to planning procedures, the federal government persuaded many Canadians to accept the new rational approach. However, the well-entrenched wariness of Nova Scotians towards ideas (and people) emanating from Upper Canada prevented wholesale conversion.

Our review of the case-study disputes revealed other cultural domains discussed in planning practice. For instance, significant cultural artefacts can become prominent symbols in disputes. In the Market Place Plaza case, the project's opponents argued that development would threaten the Citadel Fortress (a national historic site) and the Old Town Clock. Citizens active in the Mitchell dispute sought to preserve the old estate house as an architectural relic. Planning often involves disputes about major cultural artefacts.

Planning disputes frequently expose conflicting perceptions of social order. Some residents may feel that a project threatens the security of their family and property; as activists, they seek a predictable future in which they have some control over the type of urban environment in which they live. While some people view the neighbourhood as a commodity that they sell along with a building (Bartelt et al. 1987), many residents think of their neighbourhood as a kind of outer sanctuary that protects and buffers their home from the world outside. For some, development threatens the social order. For the advocates of development, growth sustains the social and economic order.

Thus we find that planning disputes reflect a wide range of cultural structures and values that simultaneously set the stage on which planning activities occur and give content to planning disputes. As we consider the roles that actors play and as we review the 'script' of planning disputes, we witness the influence of cultural context on the drama of local democracy.

The Context of Action

Before Halifax fully committed itself to a municipal development plan, local citizen activists and planners advocated community planning as a rational comprehensive process. They believed that, done correctly, planning had the potential to protect community interests, limit developers' political influence, end pressured decisions from councils, set clear criteria for development, allow public consultation and input, and avoid conflicts over land use. Citizens hoped to use planning to protect their rights and to promote their image of the city. Expert planners intended to administer and implement the plan to develop the city in an efficient and rational manner.

After Halifax adopted its Municipal Development Plan (MDP) in 1978, planners and citizen activists found that the plan did not necessarily make land-use planning less contentious. Plan policies proved too vague, ambiguous, and slippery to protect particular images of the city. Plan policies failed to end rancorous debates and delays over projects. The flexibility inherent in plan policies left considerable room for interpretation and subjectivity. Even with the plan in place, politicians had to make tough decisions about development projects.

While the MDP may not have materially affected the outcomes of land-use debates, it altered the discourse of participants in disputes. Plan policies gave citizens, politicians, and developers new terms for packaging their concerns and values. The 'intent' of the plan offered generous substance for political debate. Planning procedures provided new stages for political performances.

Ultimately, the 1978 MDP (and its successor, the 1985 Municipal Planning Strategy) could not meet citizen activists' expectations. When planners came to community meetings asking people to participate in detailed area planning to 'protect' neighbourhoods, participants hoped that planning could help them control change. Later, however, when planners from the same local government argued in public hearings that development projects that activists opposed met the 'intent' of the plan, some participants felt betrayed. Not surprisingly, through the 1980s, citizen activists grew increasingly cynical about the utility of planning and the objectivity of planners.

Planners adjusted better to the new regime 'with a plan' than did citizen activists. Planners accepted the municipality's need for development and growth. They recognized the impossibility of removing 'politics' from planning: rationality often succumbs to pragmatism. Some planners began to believe that citizen activists simply manipulated the planning process to try to prevent certain kinds of developments allowed by the plan. Many came to see public participation as an inherently difficult and reactionary part of the planning process.

Nova Scotian planning legislation requires municipalities to provide citizens with information and opportunities to participate in local planning. Few planners or citizens dispute the importance of public participation in local planning, yet few can deny that public participation in Halifax has had mixed results at best. Citizen activists can point to few 'victories,' even though the local media and developers complain of an 'antidevelopment' climate. In late 1989, Council and planning staff decided to re-evaluate key participatory devices such as the Planning Advisory Committee. Staff recommended that Council disband the PAC, which staff felt had no clear function.[6] By the early 1990s, few seemed satisfied with the state of community planning in Halifax. Activists wanted more influence on outcomes while planners wanted streamlined procedures.

Planning creates activities through which actors play out certain roles in a local drama. In staging events, provincial and federal governments may have given all actors the impression that they have influence in the drama; experience shows that many actors have no real power. Legislation defines the rights of citizens in the planning process in representative democracies. Citizen activists have a strictly limited ability to influence the outcomes of planning disputes in the

Nova Scotia context. Planners wield power only in as much as they support politicians' agendas.

Planning serves a useful political function in modern industrial democracies: it allows politicians to take credit for popular decisions while appearing to employ an open and fair process; it absolves politicians of responsibility for unpopular decisions while providing the mechanisms for enforcing such decisions. By focusing on process rather than outcomes, Nova Scotia planning legislation presumes that participation is an end in itself: participation promotes good citizenship. Politicians need to listen; they need not respond. The ultimate effect of citizen intervention is negligible in Halifax planning disputes. Council approves most development applications regardless of the level of opposition. When Council rules, its members can explain that they simply supported the plan. If people don't like Council decisions, they can blame the plan or the planners. Planning sets the stage for development in Nova Scotia.

Chapter Eight

Command Performance

Many groups of actors play parts in the planning drama. Some, such as planners, play active roles: attending hearings, writing reports, meeting with developers. Others, such as a person reading a meeting advertisement in the local paper, may take a relatively passive role as part of the audience. Regardless of the type of parts actors play, they choose a face to present to others. Participants expect actors to create and sustain performances in a consistent fashion. Through their interactions with other players in the drama, actors craft their characters and utter lines that reveal their deeply held values. They attempt to persuade others to accept their choices.

In this section, we examine three of the main sets of actors in the planning process: planners, politicians, and citizen activists.[1] We describe how actors view themselves and others, and what they see as the function of planning. By examining the ways in which actors talk about and interact with others, we come to understand how their attitudes and assumptions affect the process and outcomes of planning disputes.

Planners' Perspectives

Not all planners respond in the same way to the planning drama. Within the category we call 'planners,' we find actors playing different parts. Planners operate from various positions in society. Some work for municipal councils: here we refer to them 'city planners' for the purpose of differentiation, although in other contexts, we have simply called them 'planners.' Some planners work for private consulting firms or as educators in schools of planning: in this section we call them 'other planners.'[2] Planners' responses often differ according to their employment context, especially in terms of how they view other actors in the drama.

City Planners

City planners see themselves as dispassionate, independent and objective advisers to Council. They are professionals paid to write and interpret planning policies. They believe that elected politicians and residents should establish community vision through adopting plan policies with the planner's help. Planners then execute that vision by implementing the plan.

Within the Development and Planning Department[3] at the City of Halifax, we find a planning division and a development control division, reporting to the city manager through the director of Development and Planning. Planners in the planning (policy) division think of themselves as agents of Council working to put an image of the city into planning policies. They consult with citizen committees in developing plan policies and getting detailed area plans passed by Council. To some extent, they facilitate citizen involvement by providing staff support to planning committees. They also offer technical expertise in writing policies, and advise Council and citizens as to appropriate alternatives.

By contrast, planners in the development control division spend a great deal of their work time with developers. They provide advice on applications for rezoning or development agreements. They hate to delay projects. They understand developers and show considerable empathy for them (Forester 1987; Grant 1990b). When project opponents criticize them for spending so much time with developers they grow angry. Their job requires them to work with developers to see that projects meet plan policies. They cannot do the tasks the City pays them for without meeting developers. Planners in development control do not interact with community residents in the context of policy development meetings. Their contacts with citizens come in public meetings and hearings over disputed projects. Their job requires them to stand up in those meetings to explain the applicant's project and to respond to questions. As a result, tensions between planners and citizens occur frequently, with citizen activists seeing the development planners as 'mouthpieces' for developers.

Baum's (1983) study of planners in Maryland suggested that

planners don't recognize the political nature of their work. Our findings do not substantiate his. Halifax city planners consistently acknowledged their role within an organization with explicit political aims.[4] They work as employees of politicians who operate with a three-year mandate, and who have a narrow geographical focus as the representatives of local neighbourhoods. Planners see planning battles as political fights in which groups with different interests clamour for the attention of Council. Although they see their own function as essentially technical, they know that they operate in a political arena where people battle for high stakes.

In general, planners spoke circumspectly about their views of citizens. They divided citizens into two categories: 'activists' and 'the public.' Planners see 'the public' as disinterested in planning and unknowledgeable about it: Joe and Jane Citizen have few complaints and no reason to get involved in planning disputes unless a project threatens their property values. When people have a problem, they blame 'the City,' not planners. People don't hate planners (see Figure 8.1). Some city planners suggested that a large silent majority supported many development projects, but such people rarely step forward to voice their approval. Activists are another matter, the city planners say. Planners see activists as pro-heritage, antihigh-rise, conservative die-hards. Citizens fear change and may oppose *any* kind of development. They don't offer constructive comments (see Figure 8.2). Activists want to test Council whenever possible, and would prefer to make decisions themselves. They threaten democracy. These 'nettlesome' characters try planners' patience at times. Planners might find life easier if they wrote their reports to please their critics, but they refuse to take the 'coward's way out.'

City planners in Halifax see the plan as promoting growth and development. The plan gives them a set of rules and tools they can use to promote good development. They recognize that the policies in the plan may limit their ability to facilitate good projects. Planners in development control tend to criticize certain plan policies as ineffective or ambiguous. Planners on the policy side believe that the plan reflects what Council and the community wants and serves to help Council make decisions. Development planners prefer flexibility and contract developments; policy planners feel comfortable with as-of-right zoning and few plan amendments.

Few of the planners interviewed talked about 'burn-out' as a serious problem, although the profession acknowledges it as a risk (Finkler 1985). While some staff turnover has occurred, the level of

Figure 8.1

Figure 8.2

attrition in the department is not excessive. Planners who remain with the City adapt to the bureaucratic and political organizations within which they work. They accept the authority structure that concentrates decision-making power within the bureaucracy. They come to adopt the values of those elected through the political process. Survival requires adaptation.

Do city planners have time for 'reflective' consciousness in their practice? Halifax planners are clearly not 'radical' in Beauregard's sense (1980): they do not reflect on their experience with a view to changing society. However, neither are they 'non-reflective': during interviews many of the planners contributed insightful analyses of their own role in community planning. Planners, like most people, reflect on their own experience with a view to putting their own behaviour in a moral context. Their reflections lead them to conclude that they act in a professional and moral fashion.

Other Planners

We find less consistency among the views of other planners because of their divergent experience in consulting, government work, and education. Some have practised as city planners and tend to sympathize with the city planner's problems and perspectives. However, planners who have never worked for municipal governments in Nova Scotia have different expectations and little tolerance for what they see as 'uncreative technical work.'

Other planners often criticize city planners. They see city planners in Halifax as 'politicized,' by which they mean that staff provide the advice politicians want to hear. They believe that city planners should clearly explain trade-offs (with a minimum of technical jargon), offer reasonable alternatives, and recognize their own biases. When other planners look at practice in Halifax, they find city planners committed to high-rise development (to the exclusion of heritage protection). Some other planners complain that city planners have not given people a full range of choices, nor have they implemented the people's agenda. Evidently, other planners consider the appropriate role of the planner to entail a dual function. First, they describe the planner as a facilitator of the will of the people as articulated through Council or through participation programs. Second, they see the planner as a visionary ready to bring new ideas and approaches to direct the community into the future. None of the other planners interviewed reflected on the inherent contradiction in these two functions they give planners. If planners implement the vision of 'the people' (however that is determined), then how can planners simultaneously bring their own vision to bear? Is the strength of the planner's expertise in the communication skills of a facilitator or the creative insights of a visionary?

Some other planners have helped citizen groups oppose particular development projects and tend to share the perspective of citizen activists. Most agree that citizens do not trust city planners. Other planners believe that citizens have a significant role to play in planning matters. Citizens must inform themselves about what is happening in their communities and take advantage of opportunities to get involved. Good citizenship demands active participation.

Those other planners with previous experience as city planners frankly voiced reservations about the motivations of citizen activists. They suggested that some activists want to prevent development and consider only their own interests, not community interests, in opposing projects. Like their colleagues, the city planners, some other planners accept the elitist view that elected politicians ultimately represent the will of the people in democratic societies.

When asked about the function of the plan, other planners suggested that many disputes originate with the vagueness of plan policies. Some respondents thought the plan contained good policies that the City refused to follow. Some suggested that plan policies did not necessarily produce good planning because of inflexibility. Few of the other planners questioned the importance or utility of the plan; they directed most of their criticisms at Council or staff for not using the plan effectively. The problem, they say, is not the game but the players.

One respondent quoted an activist as saying that Halifax engaged in 'planning by development, not developing by plan.' He felt that people's faith in planning had suffered as Halifax misused the process. The plan, treated initially as an almost sacred document, became trivial in practice. Another planner thought that planning too easily degenerated into a bureaucratic exercise in which developers have to jump through hoops. Instead of providing clear rules to facilitate good development, planning may have become an obstacle course that only the fittest can hurdle.

Some of these other planners clearly sustain an image of the planner as a progressive visionary with a role in creating the good community. They do not approve of what they see as the meek behaviour of Halifax city planners whom they believe are overly deferential (either to Council, developers, or to activists). Some of the other planners articulate a different attitude towards planning and its function in a community than do planners in city employment. Many of the harshest critics come from an academic or professional tradition untested by practice in the municipal context in Nova Scotia.

Elected Politicians[5]

Members of City Council had ambivalent feelings about planners. Aldermen who sat on Council in the 1960s and 1970s recall that most Council members did not take planners seriously in the early years. Planners' ideas about reform seemed impractical and the Development Department definitely had the upper hand. Council agreed to planning not out of a sense that it was a desirable end, but because they viewed planning as a means to acquire federal funds for urban redevelopment. Above all, Council members wanted Halifax to enjoy pride of place as a regional centre. They knew that other cities with successful development records had hired planners, so they too decided to employ planning staff. 'Keeping up with Toronto' meant giving planning a chance. To a certain extent, the love/hate relationship Halifax had with 'Upper Canada' rubbed off on planners. Halifax imported planners because the booming cities of central Canada had them. Many of those planners came from central Canada because until the late 1970s, few planners were trained in or were from Nova Scotia. Thus politicians found themselves relying on an ideology and experts imported from a region that Maritimers resent but seek to emulate.

During the early and mid-1970s, planning became increasingly popular in Nova Scotia: the province insisted on it, people agitated for it, and politicians paid attention. The aldermen indicated clearly, however, that their concerns about city planners persisted. Halifax politicians did not want planners to tell them what to do. Planners with grand visions made little headway in Halifax. Aldermen on Council today say that planners have to go along with Council and understand Council values. Planners work for Council (which represents the people): they must know their place. Only practical planners are persuasive.

Those who no longer serve on Council see the planners' willingness to give Council what it wants as the principal weakness of planning in Halifax. They say that people no longer trust planners because staff advice does not seem independent. Perhaps planners

want to produce advice that Council will accept. One former alderman called the planners 'self-serving,' determined to apply their own
agenda to the city. Thus we find that aldermen simultaneously hold
a range of opinions on the role of planners: planners should do what
Council wants; planners who do what Council wants lack independence; planners who promote their own concerns are self-serving.
How can planners win in such circumstances? Whether they kowtow
or promote grand visions, they face frequent criticism.

The aldermen did not agree on whether planning can work in
Halifax. Two respondents seemed to believe that planning means
limiting development. They suggested that planning was impractical
or even doomed because high-rise development is inevitable: the City
needs revenue. Halifax must accept any development it can get or
everyone's taxes will rise. Planning is a luxury for those who can
afford selectivity in seeking development.

Other respondents saw planning as essential for orderly development and good design. One of those aldermen insisted that the city
had to 'plan for reality' (which meant accepting that development
will change some aspects of the city). Planning should not prevent
change, but should channel it into appropriate development. In this
perspective, planning gives communities the tools they need to shape
the kind of places people want to inhabit. Aldermen understand that
the plan provides 'rules for the game.' Those still on Council insist
that those rules have to remain flexible. Planning has to allow and
promote development. Those no longer on Council say the plan
hasn't provided enough protection for neighbourhoods; some of them
advocate stronger policies to protect the city's heritage.

In providing a 'rational' process for Councils to use in considering
development proposals, planning has clearly served a useful purpose
for aldermen. Planning establishes a framework within which cities
make decisions. Although politics and economics remain key factors,
aldermen frame their choices in abstract terms related to the 'intent
of the plan.' Council members can hear from the public, listen to the
developers, seek advice from planners, then make their decisions.
Plan policies remain flexible or vague enough to allow considerable
discretion on the part of Council. Once they reach their decision,
Council members can defend it by pointing to the policies in the plan
or the advice of planners.

Many Council member respondents have, at some point, participated with the ranks of citizen activists on one cause or another. Some
got involved in municipal politics because of concerns about plan-

ning issues. They have had years of interaction with citizens interested in planning matters. Their views of citizen activists vary from considerable admiration to virtual disgust. Those aldermen who respect activists say that citizens love history and willingly fight for the kind of city they want. Over the years, Council members say, citizens have improved their approach. In the early years, citizens taunted, yelled, and even threatened to riot. Now they know how to present logical and respectful arguments, and their voices are more effective. While politicians may not always appreciate criticism, activists have the right to make their concerns known and to lobby aldermen on important issues.

Many politicians, however, see activists as antidevelopment zealots who would destroy the economic base of the city if given their way. Aldermen called some activists 'aggravating bastards' or 'extremists' who 'pick, pick, pick.' They suggest that many of the activists 'come from away.' Some activists, aldermen say, try to delay projects because they don't want anything to change. Time, however, favours developers because eventually protesters tire out and developers can move ahead. In the long run, then, activists make a lot of noise, but do not influence decisions.

For those in a position to decide the outcome of planning disputes, the burden of power weighs heavily. Aldermen understand how important land-use decisions are to everyone involved, and they have many factors to take into account in arriving at decisions. They must evaluate private interests versus other private interests, and private interests versus 'the public interest.' They must judge competing claims about 'the public interest' and render a verdict that can stand the tests of time. Several Council members acknowledged the difficulty of their task.

The nature of the political structure in Halifax makes planning disputes inherently 'political.' Halifax aldermen represent territorially defined 'wards.' Hence, they have a geographic base to protect and defend in order to retain the support of their electorate. When faced with a planning issue in their neighbourhood, they normally articulate the 'neighbourhood view' on that issue. They expect their fellow aldermen to support them when time comes for Council to vote on the matter. When a neighbourhood planning issue has city-wide significance, aldermen may find themselves in a conundrum. Do they articulate the neighbourhood view or look out for the welfare of the city as a whole? Normally, aldermen say, they speak for the neighbourhood view. Several Council respondents complained that some

Council members refuse to take the broader view of what is good for the city. Hence they get caught up in endless petty squabbles over zoning, but give short shrift to community-wide planning issues.

Some of the respondents indicated the pressure aldermen felt to support development. Candidates for municipal office may solicit campaign contributions from the development industry: no rules force disclosure of municipal campaign contributions. Any candidate who does not support development will not likely receive funds from developers. To get elected, candidates also need campaign workers. Although candidates do not run under a Liberal or Conservative banner, their workers often come to them through party connections. Since the mainstream parties tend to value economic development and prosperity, candidates who want their support have to promote development. Some Council member respondents believed that opposition to particular development projects had cost individuals political and financial support, and ultimately elections. They recognized clearly that planning decisions are among the most important decisions aldermen have to make. Jobs, tax revenues, and neighbourhoods are on the line. Opposing development projects in Halifax can carry a high price.

Citizen Activists[6]

Several of the citizen activists who participated in disputes in Halifax have maintained an interest in planning issues for more than twenty years. Such citizens see planning as a cause worth championing, almost as an end in itself. Others participated in a single land-use dispute in their neighbourhood because they perceived a threat; they see planning as the means to fight just battles.

Of the thousands of people who live in our communities, few choose to take an active role in the planning process. Most pass their lives oblivious of planning issues. Out of the masses come a few brave souls for whom planning seems a matter of importance, worth giving up weekends and evenings to countless meetings. All of the citizen activists interviewed believe that participating in planning disputes constitutes part of the civic duty of citizens in a democratic society. They see involvement as invigorating and expect abundant opportunities for the public to participate in the planning process. Some engaged in citizen action rather reluctantly to fight a project with an immediate impact on their neighbourhood. Others, however, clearly enjoy 'a good fight' and willingly enter the fray at any opportunity.

Citizen activists share a consistent image of Halifax that they expect the plan to protect. They cherish its natural and architectural heritage. They see Halifax as an intimate, family-oriented, small-scale community, distinct from the 'big city' of faceless high-rises. They view the community as a moral object that embodies key social values. They generally oppose high-rise development and the loss of older buildings or structures. They believe that most Haligonians share their perspective, and at times they have tried to demonstrate that with petitions. They are prepared to protect their sacred concepts with what borders on missionary zeal.

Quite often citizens discuss their ideal image of Halifax in terms of contrasts with Toronto or Montreal or Vancouver. They don't want to emulate Mississauga or Calgary. They may, however, also use other cities as examples to frame the possibilities for good new development on heritage themes: they point to the Old City in Montreal, or the market district in Boston. Many of them have travelled widely and refer to European and American cities as evidence of opportunities Halifax has forsaken.

While citizen activists agree on their ultimate aims, they do not agree on methods or approaches. Some prefer concrete action: try to buy the land in dispute to control what will go on it. Others, without the resources to wield such influence, launch publicity and lobbying campaigns to convince Council to turn a project down. Over the years, citizens learned that they had to develop persuasive arguments and present them effectively. They do their homework. They prepare briefs and exhibits. They know the plan inside out.

Many respondents who have worked on dozens of disputes through the years feel that citizens have grown disillusioned with the planning process over time. People pick their fights carefully now because they know how hard it is to win. When the City first adopted the plan, activists had great hopes about the kinds of developments policies would allow. They hoped for an end to ugly high-rise towers and apartment buildings. Seeing the plan in operation through the years, though, they have lost faith in the ability of planning to help them realize their aims for the city. Planning has not given citizens the power to determine the outcomes of disputes. As a consequence, many people have dropped out of the fight after losing battles. Those who stayed in have done so because they feel they must save as much heritage as they can.

Planning disputes provide excitement and drama that a small number of the citizens[7] find stimulating. For them, collective action becomes both a social activity and an intellectual challenge. One respondent called it 'a real turn-on.' Such activists derive a sense of accomplishment and well-being from their performances. Not only do they see the issues as vitally important and worth championing, they relish the challenge of the part they play.

Like most of the participants in planning disputes, citizen activists generally hold university degrees and enjoy comfortable lives; high-status people seem most likely to participate in community and political activities (Huckfeldt 1986; Kornberg et al. 1982). Participation in planning activities does not often appeal to the poor or the working class in Halifax. The level of skill required to mount persuasive performances is enough to dissuade most citizens from taking leading roles in the drama.

Citizens who participated in developing the Halifax plan have a sense of ownership of the document. Most view the plan as a positive statement designed to promote their image of the city. They feel betrayed that the City has not 'stuck to the plan' and enforced its provisions as they understand them. They expect municipal government to serve the people, and see planning as one of the tools cities can use to protect themselves from rapacious developers. Many citizen activists feel discouraged that planning has failed to protect things that some feel make Halifax special. They believed that planning would give them a strong shield to protect their community; instead, they got a leaky sieve. Activists cannot understand why Council refused to reject developments that they believe contravene plan policies. They expected results that planning has not delivered.

Many of the activists in Halifax have read popular planning literature and followed the pronouncements of gurus such as Jane Jacobs and Prince Charles. They readily blame planners and planning for the wrongs of modern urban environments: high-rise buildings destroy social fabric; planners create suburban sprawl. Planning and its practitioners become lightning-rods for complaints about the ills of industrial capitalism. In becoming institutionalized as part of the tool kit of community management, planning furnished a good target for the critics of the status quo. Those on the right dislike planning as they detest most government intervention. Let the market decide, they say. Planning artificially restricts markets. Set the minimal rules we need for public safety and amenity, and leave it there. Those on the left say planning has not accomplished nearly enough. It should put the wishes of the people ahead of the avarice of developers.

Planning should promote better ways of doing things and result in a good community. Everyone has a pet theory of planning.

One citizen indicated her concern that instead of building better environments, planning has become a tool of discrimination in our communities. Citizens can use planning policies to keep certain people out of neighbourhoods. Citizens who work together on one battle may turn against each other when faced with cooperative housing projects in their own neighbourhood. Self-interest certainly plays a significant role in disputes about projects in residential areas. Citizens may attempt to use planning policies and procedures to promote their own interests. As Pross (1981) notes, a fine line separates self-interest and public interest. Citizens may believe that they stand for the good of the community even as they promote solutions that work against the needs and interests of others. In planning disputes, citizens argue dramatically divergent interests. The concerns of disadvantaged groups within the community may not surface in the discussion.

Citizen activists maintain superficially good relations with planning staff and Council, but they sometimes distrust representatives of the City. Some feel staff misrepresent plan policies and intent. A few even suggest that staff are corrupt and in the pocket of developers. Activists feel uncomfortable with their own cynicism and their growing readiness to compromise on important principles to make relatively minor gains. A few have not mastered the fine art of debating: some individuals call planning staff names in public while their fellow activists wince with embarrassment. Coalitions that develop spontaneously around an issue have no way of distancing themselves from participants whose methods may alienate decision makers and others. In the drama of public hearings, anyone has the right to take the stage and perform. Unlike the planners whose performances are tightly stage-managed by their supervisors, citizens improvise with limited direction.

Virtually none of the citizen activists interviewed had a positive attitude towards Halifax planning staff.[8] They saw City staff as unconcerned bureaucrats playing to Council and to the development lobby. Planners, they say, treat citizens as naive, romantic nuisances. Staff withhold information, misrepresent policies, and have their own agenda to promote high-rise development. Derisive epithets used by some respondents indicated the depth of mistrust. Respondents suggested various reasons for their negative feelings towards planners: planners pay lip-service to public participation; planners bend regulations to get the maximum benefit for developers; planners speak indecipherable jargon in public meetings to confuse and bore people. Planners don't understand what Haligonians value. Planners come from away. Planners stay too long and become entrenched in their positions so the City does not get new ideas or approaches.

A few activists alleged corruption or impropriety on the part of city planners. They suggested that City staff had inappropriate social connections with developers. Because planning staff present development projects at public meetings, many citizens feel uncomfortable and suspicious about the real motives of planners. For these activists, the planner appears as the villainous accomplice to the nasty developer. All of the citizens interviewed clearly expect that planners should 'work for the people.' They see themselves, as part of the electorate in a democratic society, as the ultimate employers of the civic bureaucracy.[9] When bureaucrats do not act as citizens expect they should, then citizens feel morally outraged. 'Our taxes pay their salary!'

Citizens have a different view than planners have of participation in planning. Planners see participation as a means to an end (a plan or decision). Citizen activists consider participation a vital process in achieving an ideal community in a democratic society: it is a means as well as an end. They feel frustrated that their input does not have greater effect. Some burn out or quit in frustration. Others go on with the attitude that they can't afford to quit.

Activists in Halifax make many of the same kinds of arguments that activists make in other urban centres. They read the same planning gurus. Yet they do not feel they have had the same impact on urban development as have their counterparts in other cities. In many communities, sustained protest stops projects; not in Halifax. Efforts to elect 'progressive' candidates to Council have generally proved unsuccessful. Halifax has not supported progressive politics, nor progressive planning practice. Decision makers in Halifax do not find activists persuasive.

Actors in Interaction

The actors in the planning drama play complex roles. They frame their performances as they explore the stage on which dramas unfold, as they interact with other actors, and as they prepare the scripts they deliver. Our analysis of the perceptions of the actors

TABLE 8.1
Actors' views of self and others

	Perceived role of city planner	Perceived role of politician	Perceived role of citizen
City planner's view	Objective Independent Expert	Legitimate Arbiter Judge	Selfish Conservative Subjective
Politician's view	Politicized Expert Employee	Legitimate Independent Objective	Concerned Vociferous Selfish
Citizen's view	Pro-growth Conservative Subjective	Pro-growth Conservative Weak-kneed	Concerned Legitimate Independent

showed some consistent themes in their evaluations of each other. The key features used to differentiate categories of actors included reasoning style (objective/subjective), interests articulated (public/self), and claim to legitimacy (legitimate/illegitimate). In each case, actors themselves laid claim to the positive trait, while describing other actors in terms that implied negative traits (see Table 8.1). Their own performances take on a moral tone in relation to the performances of others. They neither understand nor appreciate each others' motivations and perceptions. Their faith in their own righteousness can blind them to the potential arbitrariness of their positions.

All of the actors see their own role in positive terms, while using nouns and adjectives with negative connotations to refer to some of the others. The word 'conservative' is interesting in this context. It has different meanings, depending on who uses it. When citizens call planners 'conservative,' they mean that planners do not innovate but promote high-rise development. When planners call citizens 'conservative,' they refer to citizens' dislike of high-rise development and their commitment to tradition. The same word has almost opposite meanings, yet offers a convenient negative label that satisfies both parties.

Planners see themselves as objective experts, treat politicians as legitimate arbiters, and look at citizens as self-interested partisans. Politicians see themselves as independent arbiters trying to weigh the arguments of vociferous residents and self-serving planners. Citizens see both planners and politicians as conservative and pro-development, while they view themselves as having the legitimate interests

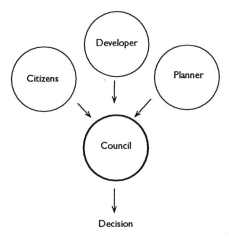

Figure 8.3   Politicians' view of decision context. Politicians balance multiple interests and then render judgment.

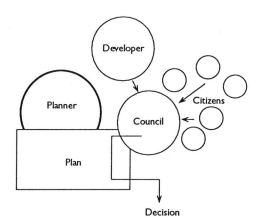

Figure 8.4   Planners' view of decision context. Planners filter the inputs to Council through the policies of the plan. Council's decision responds to plan policies.

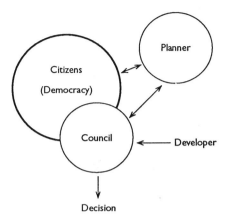

Figure 8.5   Citizen activists' view of decision context. Citizens reveal their concerns to the council they elected to represent them. Planners are responsible to both citizens and council. Developers lobby from outside.

of the community at heart. The actors seldom appreciate each others' perspectives or understand the value base from which they operate. While they all have roles in the same drama, they rarely work together to achieve harmony of purpose.

We have seen from the descriptions of actors' concerns that various actors in the planning drama differ also in their interpretations of the context in which decisions are made. They view their own role and the role of other actors in radically different ways. Figures 8.3, 8.4, and 8.5 illustrate their perspectives.

Politicians believe that they alone have the ultimate responsibility for making decisions (see Figure 8.3). Developers bring forward their applications for consideration. Citizens present their views. Planners explain plan policies and other technical constraints. Then politicians put all of the factors together, balance them, and come up with a decision good for the community. In this view, the key element in the outcome is the evaluation made by Council. As central players, aldermen may draw upon a wide range of inputs in determining 'the public interest.' The political structure, which gives elected representatives power, is the organizing element in the process.

Planners' cognitive maps of the decision context differ dramatically from politicians' (see Figure 8.4). While planners see politicians as responsible for making decisions, they believe that politicians must operate within the policy environment of the plan. Politicians listen to the many concerns articulated by citizens interested in the outcome. Then they hear the planner's advice about whether the developer's proposed project meets the intent of the plan. Politicians then weigh the choices and make their tough decisions. From the planner's perspective, the policies and procedures set out by municipal and provincial legislation form the parameters within which the interaction occurs. All of the participants may bring their concerns to the discussion, but the outcome must reflect the application of rational rules.

Citizen activists have another view of the decision context (see Figure 8.5). They believe that in a democratic society, politicians must implement the will of the people. If the people mobilize to press for certain actions, then politicians should respond accordingly. Planners should serve the democratic interests of the community by providing expert advice and support. Developers, with their own interests, attempt to influence politicians, but should operate outside of the decision context.[10] This view employs the concept of 'democracy' as its organizing principle. Politicians should make their decisions based on what 'the people' say. The rationale for the outcome should reflect the nature and number of interactions in the process: if a large number of citizens speak out against a proposal, Council should refuse it.

We find that the view of the decision context articulated by citizen activists resembles the philosophy of much of the recent planning literature dealing with the role of the planner: the planner should promote democracy (Beauregard 1980; Forester 1982a, 1989; Hoch 1984b; Marris 1982a). The problem with employing this perspective as the basis for a theory of practice is its partiality: it gives only a partial understanding of the nature of practice, and it embodies the value judgments of only one set of the players.[11]

American authors have published much of the theoretical literature and case-studies of the role of planners. In American ideology, grounded in a national history of revolutionary action, the people are sovereign. Citizens have the right and the power to make decisions. Depending on jurisdiction, Americans can vote in referenda on planning issues, hold town hall meetings to decide important matters, and impeach elected officials who displease the community. Citizens can act in a democratic fashion to realize their concerns. American planning literature reflects this rich experience and ideology. It sees a role for the planner in facilitating independent citizen action. When we try to apply that approach in Canada, however, we run into ideological and institutional barriers. Despite the penetration of American media and values in Canadian society, Canadian legislation and political organization does not revere citizen sovereignty to the same extent. Canadian planning works through the institutions of elitist representative government. Canadians use referenda sparingly and with great reticence. The 1992 constitutional referendum confirmed the experts' disdain for popular sovereignty: the people refused the compromise offered them, and in the bargain rebuffed the decision-making process. Those who hope the referendum constituted progress towards greater participation by voters on matters of national importance may well worry that they've had a once-in-a-lifetime experience.

Canadians have no mechanisms to impeach elected officials or bureaucrats. We have a reputation for accepting authority. Self-government came late to Canada; the town hall meeting tradition bypassed most regions. The patterns of interactions in Canadian planning reflect Canadian experience and values. That context leaves little room for the planner to 'promote democracy.'

In order to make sense of the behaviour of politicians, citizens, and planners in community planning in Halifax, we have explored their perspectives on the decision-making process as well as their views of the roles of various actors. If we judge the actors in our drama by some idealistic moral standard, we inevitably find them wanting. If we interpret their behaviour in the context in which they act and interact, we discover another logic at work in the situation. We may not agree with the actions of some of the actors in this drama, but we gain a better understanding of how they frame their performances.

Performances present an actor's idealized view of self (Goffman 1959). As actors take the stage, they affirm important moral values in officially credible ways. The strategies that actors use to validate their performances reflect their assessment of an implicit hierarchy of cultural values. Disagreement over hierarchies of values and their application in particular instances sustains disputes. We will discuss values in some detail in the next chapter, but at this point, we might note that all of the actors interviewed would probably agree that planning should promote or enhance efficiency, amenity, equity, and democracy. Unfortunately, such agreement proves misleading, as the actors rank and apply the concepts differently. As actors face the difficult task of framing and sustaining moral performances, they wrestle with how to present their values in a persuasive manner.

Our analysis of the key actors in planning dramas reveals that all of the categories of actors make tough choices in framing their performances. Planners face a common tension of casting themselves (or being cast as) one of two characters: the visionary equipped with professional values drawn from experience and academia, or the municipal employee tethered to an expedient political agenda. In either case, planners may promote efficiency, amenity, and democracy, but define those concepts differently. For example, in the moral system of the professional planner, high-density residential development in the urban core promotes efficiency; for the municipal employee whose Council favours low-density development, zoning for single detached housing makes life easier.

Citizens also make choices in framing and sustaining their performances. Do they cloak themselves in the shades of cool reason or don a daring mask of passionate concern? The citizen who performs with careful logic in some ways emulates the planner's style and substance. Citizens who speak emotionally of their commitment to a cause draw on a wide range of social values and institutions to validate their participation. Within the range of extremes, citizens select styles of performance to suit the stage and to sway outcomes. In the divergent styles that result, we find evidence of value consensus breaking down. Although citizens may share concern for equity when they expect Council to heed numbers in arriving at a decision, concern for equity may disappear when one member of the group attempts to organize a cooperative housing project in the neighbourhood.

Politicians experience the daunting task of sustaining a consistent face in divergent contexts. For instance, the same individual may, in the course of a single dispute, play the part of representative, employer, judge, advocate, and supplicant (for votes). As a result, politicians typically attempt to validate their actions in a variety of ways; they sustain their performances by drawing on a wide range of values. Thus we can expect politicians to attempt to address both local and community-wide concerns, to talk about self- and public interest, and to refer to both professional and political values. Perhaps the central concept politicians use in sustaining their performances is the metaphor of the scales of justice: balancing divergent interests. Above all else, the politician hopes to perform as a fair judge.

Actors have a vast array of strategies for validating their action and experience. Planners rely predominantly on professional and bureaucratic validation: their training gives them expert knowledge, technical skills, and the objectivity necessary for rational action; the structures and policies of their employment organization provide rules for public behaviour and 'common sense' interpretations of everyday activity.

Citizen activists validate their performances by reference to personal, professional, political, and cultural factors. Length of residence and roots in the community confer credibility on participants in a planning dispute, as do various forms of personal or professional expertise. Political validation derives from popular interpretations of the nature of democracy, the moral virtue of civic action, and the legitimate rights of taxpayers. In certain circumstances, citizens may have recourse to cultural validations, such as a reference to the planning theories of Prince Charles.

Politicians enjoy the legitimacy accorded to elected political representatives in our system of government. Democratic process validates their actions. During disputes, however, politicians also attempt to justify their actions through reference to economic and professional values. They often discuss the importance of economic prosperity and positive tax revenues. They may explain the choices they make in contentious disputes by pointing to the expert advice they receive from professional staff.

In the next chapter we will explore actors' validations in greater detail as we look at the meanings transacted through planning disputes. Articulating the script of the planning drama reveals the heart of the drama: the values actors hold so dear.

Chapter Nine

Scripts and Values

As actors participate in the planning drama, they reveal their values and beliefs through the lines they deliver. Planning disputes have no set script. Instead, actors improvise around particular themes and share elements of a common language: they script their performances as they act. In engaging in planning activities, people transact significant cultural meanings and values that we can retrieve through analysing situations.

Values, Beliefs, and Meanings

Throughout this book, we have seen examples of the ways in which values, beliefs, and meanings suffuse planning practice and theory. Interviews with participants in the planning process show that some (but not all) of the participants in planning disputes know that cultural values and beliefs influence performances. Several respondents acknowledged that planning involves debates about what makes communities work; they readily pointed to the values motivating other actors, but did not explicitly recognize the influence of their own values. Few of the participants interviewed understood the nature of the meanings they transacted with others through their planning activities.

Some of the planners discussed the significance of values in some detail. They saw the plan as embodying certain community values determined by Council as the City's agenda: for example, they held that the plan promoted increasing densities in peninsular Halifax.

Planners thought of public hearings as venues in which different participants bring their values to bear before Council. The planners, however, did not recognize their own values. They saw themselves as 'objective' and 'independent.' They did not acknowledge that their interpretations of plan policies or their evaluation of proposed developments involved value judgments. When they used terms like 'complementary' design or 'moderate' height, they believed they were making simple technical judgments.

Citizen activists in Halifax assumed that planners had their own agenda in favour of high-rise development. They saw developers as motivated solely by profit. We might characterize many, though by no means all, citizens who oppose major development projects as social democrats or small L liberals. They spoke about fairness and government that works for the people. Those citizens who examined their own motivations usually articulated their love of heritage, sometimes providing vivid details of childhood memories to account for their passion.

Land-use disputes clearly involve normative debates. They may involve conflicts over use values, as in the Mitchell property case: 'Is this piece of land best left as an open, tree-covered area so that the community can enjoy a park-like setting, or is it best developed in heritage town houses so that it fits the character of the streetscape opposite?' Disputes may involve fights about use value versus exchange value, as in the Market Place Plaza case: 'Is it appropriate to allow a developer to build a lucrative high-rise tower if that building might affect the public's view from the Citadel?' No single answer can result from such normative choices. Preferred options depend on the actors' values.

Planning attempts to regulate the use of land to preserve community amenities. It continually confronts the dilemma of public versus private rights in land. Because Canadian jurisdictions tend to zone land for present use (not for some future vision), we create through planning a context in which owners can apply to change the use of a piece of land (to increase its exchange value). We generate opportunities and public forums in which debates can occur (about use values). Before institutionalized planning, communities had no clearly defined venues for articulating conflicting values about land. Rather than ending disputes about the use of particular pieces of land, planning has institutionalized debate about land use. Politicians must render verdicts on appropriate outcomes in the face of tough choices and occasionally abundant publicity.

Complex Value Sets

Much of the discourse of planning disputes in Halifax reflects widely held values and beliefs in our society. Although we use slightly different terms, our findings generally corroborate Alterman and Page's (1973) assertion that values having to do with individualism, democracy, and scientism figure prominently in planning.

In their study of Canadian values, Blishen and Atkinson (1980) found that while most Canadians share the same set of basic values,[1] they differ in the degree to which they appreciate certain things. For instance, Maritimers value the family slightly more strongly than do Canadians from other regions. Like other Canadians, Maritimers place family security, economic stability, and love highest in their ranking of personal values.

Contention and dispute in Halifax revolve around a number of interrelated and complex value sets: free enterprise values, values of science and rationality, community and other social values, power and political values, and aesthetic values.

Free Enterprise Values

Many actors in the planning process (especially politicians, developers, and planners) share some of the underlying premises and values of mainstream capitalistic, free enterprise ideology. They believe in modernism and progress, as evidenced by high-rise buildings, rapid growth, and industrial development. They hope for prosperity, profit, jobs, and growth. They value individual initiative, freedom, and representative government. They talk about the importance of 'pragmatism,' 'realism,' and 'practical' action. They view those who think differently than they do as 'naive,' 'impractical,' or 'irrational.'

The values associated with free enterprise ideology continue to dominate Canadian society, even in recessionary times. Free market ideology structures public policy and permeates the mass media. Given the demise of socialism in eastern Europe in recent years and the ascendancy of a global economy, capitalist values have surged to new prominence in the 1990s.

Even actors who want to limit the rights of private entrepreneurs may nonetheless exhibit values that we associate with the free enterprise set. For instance, most citizens value private property and the rights it confers. Residents fighting height changes to the Mitchell estate attempted to buy the property (or parts of it) in order to influence its development: they accepted the premise that only ownership gives adequate control. Ownership of private property remains ideologically linked with personal independence and good citizenship.[2]

Many of the participants in planning disputes assume that change inevitably results from progress and prosperity. They believe that the tools of science, which for some include planning, allow us to control the direction of that change.

Values of Science and Rationality

Our modern society has great faith in science and technology. Planning lays claim to rationality and objectivity as it draws on the techniques (and the aura) of science. All of the participants in the planning process seem to accept that science holds the answers to key questions. Few dispute the necessity of logical analysis.

As an 'expert,' the planner seeks to establish credibility through the use of information: statistics, charts, and consultants' reports. Technical jargon, acronyms, and formulas bring sophisticated codes to presentations.[3] Planners view objectivity and detachment as essential. Fact demolishes opinion. Actors who value science operate in rhetorical styles that rely on the appearance of syllogistic reasoning. In their efforts to influence decisions, citizen activists clearly accept scientific values as paramount. They bring in their own 'experts.'[4] They use the same standards of logical argumentation and presentation as do the planners. Activists differ only in their beliefs about who should benefit from decisions reached.

While reason is the dominant paradigm in planning argumentation, in some contexts passion flourishes. Indeed, at points in disputes, passion is expected (or even required) of certain participants. By expressing emotion, citizens and politicians demonstrate commitment and concern. Emotion registers the importance attributed to outcomes. Those who employ emotion in their rhetoric strive for an appropriate balance between reason and passion. Citizens feel more comfortable with intense passion than do politicians who seem compelled to blend reason and passion for effect. As F.G. Bailey (1983) suggests, the use of passion as a rhetorical style has clear limits. Some players avoid passion entirely. Planners who dare to express emotion in a public context risk the contempt of professional colleagues. Planners may experience intense emotions in the context of planning disputes, but their role requires that they suppress or ignore their feelings. The planning process, with its reliance on laws and regulations, is designed to operate primarily in the rational mode; the planner is the key enforcer of the rational rhetorical style.

Community and Social Values

Our society has many values that revolve around the importance of social institutions like community, neighbourhood, and family. Although all of the actors acknowledge the same values, they employ them differently in the context of planning disputes. Debates about community and neighbourhood reveal the moral significance we give such social units in our cultural tradition. Communities and neighbourhoods are more than just places in which we live: they reveal our deeply held ideas about relationships between people, and about the connections between people and place.

The concept of 'community' embodies concerns about class, tradition, and common interest. It implies that people of like backgrounds, common heritage, and similar circumstances share a sense of place. Maritimers have a well-developed sense of place often associated with the rugged coastal landscapes and small traditional towns of the region. The values connected to community often include pride of origin and mistrust of those who 'come from away.' Those with several generations of ancestors in Nova Scotia claim roots in the community, and enjoy considerable authority in speaking about the community interest.

Values connected with heritage seem closely linked to social values about community. Many people with a strong attachment to place want physical links with the past preserved. They fear the loss of buildings that connect them to distant times and revered ancestors. For them, urban structures and patterns represent communal resources that define community and neighbourhood character. Destroying the physical manifestations of the past means denying community heritage to subsequent generations.

People take their civic duties seriously in a community: they vote, they perform community service, they protect important common symbols. They enjoy a measure of local control over their lives. A community entails reciprocal moral obligations among those who live within it. Community members pay taxes and receive services. People consent to be governed and expect to be consulted. The neighbourhood as a geographic notion also carries with it many values and beliefs. It implies small defined areas where people know each other and interact on a regular basis. Neighbourhoods, like communities, should offer safe, stable, secure places for raising families. People help each other in neighbourhoods. Strangers do not intrude into neighbourhoods.

Our notions of community and neighbourhood often encapsulate nostalgia for the small towns of a bygone era. In the early 1990s, such nostalgia came to permeate the latest planning approach: neotraditional town planning. Across the continent planners call for picket fences and small town centres to promote social harmony and community control. Although previous efforts to achieve the good community through better design have failed, the planning profession seems ready to give environmental determinism yet another chance. Planning approaches that embed powerful cultural values about place often prove highly persuasive.

Household structure changed markedly in the postwar period, but we still value the family, especially the nuclear family of parents with children. Our popular culture tends to treat other forms of households as secondary. The family, people say, gives children security and stability; we use planning to guarantee the security and stability that the family deserves as the central social institution in our society. Increasingly, however, 'non-family' households form a significant proportion of the social units in our communities. Our policies and regulations have not always responded adequately to such demographic changes (Hayden 1984). We continue to talk about 'single-family detached' residential districts. Our image of the nuclear family as a moral unit leads us to treat it as normative in everyday life as well as in planning activities.[5]

Zoning regulations reflect some of the values associated with community, neighbourhood, and family. We separate home and work by keeping residential areas away from industrial zones. We avoid mixing up 'families' with 'non-family households' by enforcing exclusively single-family housing areas. We do everything possible to use planning to protect families, neighbourhoods, and communities.

Attempts to preserve community, neighbourhood, and family sometimes reflect underlying class biases and racial inequalities. Residents often seek to preserve class and race homogeneity in their residential environments. They cannot acknowledge their exclusivity, however, because the myths of the public culture deny racial and class discrimination. Discussions about preserving character and maintaining security can, however, mask efforts to keep 'others' out.

Xenophobia thus appears in a benign form cloaked in rhetoric about protecting sacred spaces, moral units, and community tradition.

Unfortunately, allegiance to community values can rationalize excluding people from a community or neighbourhood. The Mitchell property case showed both residents and planners suggesting that planning regulations could encourage desirable types of people to live in the neighbourhood. Planners advocated high-rise development so that the owners could build luxury condominium units. Residents asked for low-rise development so that the owners might build expensive family-style townhouses. None of the participants wanted rental apartments on the site: small units would bring in 'transients' who might make the neighbourhood less desirable and less safe for families.

Power and Political Values

Planning disputes often reflect political values and debates about the nature and exercise of power. In our society few people want to acknowledge their power. Politicians claim that the people hold power through electing representatives to office for a limited period. Politicians argue that they have responsibility rather than power. Planners see Council as holding power to make decisions about whether a particular project meets plan policies; they do not see their advisory capacity as bestowing power. Citizens understand that politicians have the ultimate power to decide, but they also believe that planners have considerable power in their control of information and advice. Many citizens see themselves as having insufficient power; they think that politicians and planners should share power with citizens. All of the parties recognize the power of the media to create and control information and to focus community attention in certain directions.

Participants in disputes enjoy painting themselves as underdogs, threatened from all sides by forces with much greater power. Various actors raise questions about legitimacy: who has the ultimate right to decide? Who should wield power? Inevitably the issue of democracy arises. Our society prides itself on its democratic nature. Planning disputes clearly reveal, however, that while people value democracy, they do not agree on what it means.

Council members understand democracy to mean the election of representatives to make decisions on behalf of the community. They value a system that legitimates their power and authority. Their view reflects the elitist model of representative democracy that characterizes Canadian politics (Kornberg et al. 1982). Planners share politicians' view that given the pluralistic nature of Canadian society, a structure of authority is essential. They see citizen activists as representing only one of many claims that might arise in planning matters. They fear giving undue attention to a 'squeaky wheel' at the expense of 'the silent majority.' While planners believe citizens must have the right to participate, they do not think that politicians should bow to what a few people want.

By contrast, citizen activists often refer to their faith in participatory democracy. They believe that citizens have a right and duty to participate in the political process in representative democracies. Moreover, they argue that elected politicians have a responsibility to listen to what citizens say and respond directly.

Developers and Council members sometimes link the value of democracy with free enterprise values. They argue that constitutional democracy depends on the 'fragmentation of political power and widespread distribution of property rights' (Windsor 1988: 108). Such linkages between capitalism and democracy occur frequently in our culture, especially in the popular media. Those in positions of authority view the protection of individual rights and a free market as key features of democratic government.

Occasionally respondents referred to the effects of political patronage in community planning. Patronage may not figure as prominently in municipal politics as it does in provincial affairs, but it can affect planning disputes. City Council appoints members to the Planning Advisory Committee and to other citizen advisory committees. Provincial patronage, in the form of appointments to the Municipal Board (and the Planning Appeal Board before it), may affect the outcome of appeals. Whether patronage occurs or not, or whether it affects the outcome of planning disputes or not, players in the planning process believe that in certain circumstances, authorities make decisions not based on the evidence but because of favours owed. Nova Scotians expect to find patronage wherever they find politicians, in community planning as well as in highway building. Hence 'the patronage' becomes a convenient explanatory device to account for unpopular decisions. It fuels growing cynicism about political and bureaucratic processes.

Aesthetic Values

Many planners, politicians, and citizens suggested that planning primarily serves to ensure order and predictability in our communities. As a species, humans tend to value order. Planning has become a useful tool for perpetuating order in urban environments. People also value beauty and nature. Debates about aesthetic issues figured prominently in the case-study disputes examined. What is good design? Participants in the planning process have obvious disagreements about the answer to that question. Citizen activists believe that Victorian architecture shines in comparison with modern architecture. They value heritage and tradition highly. They vehemently dislike high-rise buildings, especially those with concrete or glass facades. Their evaluation of a design often derives from the anticipated effects of the structure on neighbourhoods or on public amenities.

Planners often suggest that their aesthetic values do not matter in the context of their work, but their advice necessitates many value judgments. Their comments indicate that they do not dislike high rise buildings. They argue that 'complementary' design may mean different things, depending on perspective; they won't be tied to a Victorian image. They place great importance on landscaping the grounds around structures. They value the trees and open space left by the 'small imprint' of a tall building.

Values and Visions

How do people come to hold the values that matter to them? Most of the value sets that influence planning practice reflect dominant themes in our public culture. As Horne (1986) argues, we absorb values and beliefs as we learn to become members of our communities. Institutions such as school, church, government, and media transmit values along with their other messages. Within the 'folk culture' of individual contacts and social ties, communities pass on traditional meanings and develop a local 'common sense' that members use to validate their experience. As we play our roles in the planning drama, we act on our values, sometimes transforming them in the process.

In his work on Canadian political culture, Bell (1981) suggests several features of societies that might affect the values people hold. The cultural context of a community may limit the range of values. In the Nova Scotia context, British and Scots ancestry looms large. Some respondents specifically referred to their Scottish forefathers to explain their own attitudes towards planning issues. The hardy Highlanders evicted by their lairds in the eighteenth and nineteenth centuries carried with them loyalty to their clans and a fatalistic acceptance of events (Prebble 1963), characteristics that contributed to Nova Scotian patronage politics.

Formative events in the history of a community may also affect community values. Certainly the rebellious but short-lived participatory democracy of Halifax in the early 1970s found a good deal of its inspiration in the widely publicized 'Encounter Week' of 1970. The economic infrastructure that dominates a community also contributes to the values people hold. Nova Scotians believe in the free market system that operates in Canada. With Halifax's large military and government presence, Haligonian society has developed values that support authority and bureaucracy. The conservatism of the region is legendary.

Other factors may also contribute to value formation. Professional education, for example, may encourage individuals to adopt values that diverge from the mainstream. Some individuals choose to adopt minority value sets, such as social democratic ideology, despite the disparagement they may face from other community members. We cannot always predict or explain why people value the things they do. Sometimes articulate, well-placed actors can affect significant community values or their expression. When those actors piggyback on cultural trends or events, they may help to change values. Thus in the late 1960s and early 1970s, citizen participation in local government came to the fore in Halifax. The value change, which emphasized the significance of citizen action, ran headlong into relatively unsupportive bureaucratic, political, and social structures that over time limited its impact.

Certainly the values that motivate actors are intrinsically linked to their interest base. For example, residents seeking to protect their residential environment from change may draw heavily on values connected to family, security, neighbourhood, and heritage. Citizens fighting to prevent a high-rise structure from obstructing public views will argue aesthetic, community, heritage, and technical values. Various actors in the drama may employ the same range of values, but apply them in different measure and to divergent ends.

Actors tend to validate their actions according to their interest bases. Planners may legitimate their activities by appealing to various value sets, such as their professional expertise (scientific or rational), or their employment status (political or bureaucratic).[6] In certain contexts, planners validate their contributions based on their specialized knowledge of the plan and the values it embodies.

Citizen activists validate their lines in the drama by reference to their place in the political economy of the community (as taxpayers and voters), by allegiance to high moral principles, and by virtue of their residency or roots in the community. At times, they may also validate their preferred choices by pointing to planning theories and theorists whose philosophy and values they share.[7]

Politicians validate their actions by appealing to democratic processes and to scientific expertise. They defend their activities by explaining that communities elect them to make difficult decisions. Once politicians make their choices, they can use plan policies, public input, and staff advice to legitimate their decisions. In framing their validation of a decision, politicians direct community members to read the script in a particular way. Thus, if the local papers quote the aldermen as saying they made their choice based on strong advice from planning staff, the perceptions of community members about the relative importance of various inputs into the decision may be significantly affected. Politicians can lay the blame for unpopular choices in a number of places; if they choose to deposit blame on the planners, they divert any animosity to paid employees who have no ability to respond.

Values and concomitant beliefs other than those we have summarized undoubtedly appear during planning disputes. We have presented some of the key value sets noted in documents and interviews. Some of these values enjoy widespread agreement. Others indicate conflicting notions of how the world should operate and what matters in life. Participants in the planning process have disparate visions that they articulate during debates about development projects. Not only do their images of the city differ, in fact their understandings of issues vary. As they argue about what constitutes 'good development,' their language reflects the different meanings they attach to particular concepts.

Language and Meaning

To understand planning practice from the point of view of the actors in it, we need to examine the language that actors use. Indeed, in this research, discourse fragments constitute our primary data source. If we want to understand what planning disputes involve and what people transact through planning, then we must look at language and its meanings. Students of language know that language is far from neutral (Brown and Yule 1983). It embeds values and judgments within it. The terms of discourse reveal the structures of meaning of political debate (Connolly 1974).

As we explored the language used during the two planning disputes presented in Part 2, we found that participants in the cases often used similar terms in radically different ways. Key concepts in the planning and political process become contested. Gallie (1956) explains that 'essentially contested concepts' are appraisive, open to interpretation, internally complex, and debatable. Respondents may use them both aggressively and defensively. People fight about their values and their influence on outcomes through arguments over language.

What does a concept 'really' mean? Concepts mean what those using them intend. Since various players have different agendas and different values, they often attempt to communicate wildly different messages using essentially similar terms. We have no way to determine 'which of them is right,' if any of them are: 'It is quite impossible to find a *general principle* for deciding which of two contestant uses of an essentially contested concept really "uses it best." If no such principle can be found or fixed, then how can the arguments of the contestants in such a dispute be subject to logical appraisal' (Gallie 1956: 189)?

Among the concepts contested during planning disputes, we find political terms like 'democracy' and 'the public interest.'[8] Participants argue about who speaks for 'the public' or 'the community.' Actors do not agree on what constitutes 'good development,' or 'sound planning.' They spend hours debating what 'the plan' means, and what 'the character' of a neighbourhood might be. In the following sections, we briefly discuss some of the essentially contested concepts we discovered recurring in the Halifax context.

Democracy

The participants in planning disputes allude to democracy when they want to make a particular course of action appear legitimate. Politicians and planners remind others that citizens elect Council to make decisions: democracy comes every three years at the ballot-box. Paying undue attention to protestors would subvert and undermine democracy, which in its appropriate application implies due process and regard for the rights of all the players. As used by planners, politicians, and developers, 'democracy' supports the status quo. It legitimates existing structures and processes for arriving at decisions.

Citizen activists use democracy in a radically different way. They want to restructure society: 'give power to the people.' They expect politicians to listen and respond to the voiced wishes of those attending hearings and meetings. Their view of participatory democracy clashes with the elitist perspective that sees full participation as unworkable and even dangerous. Activists see politicians and planners as frustrating opportunities for open government and meaningful participation.

The rhetoric about 'democracy' masks significant problems that some respondents noted. Representative democracy in our society has resulted in the dominance of white, middle-aged, middle-class, Christian males in elected office. Municipal elections seldom bring out more than 35 per cent of the electorate. A minority of community members selects an unrepresentative sample of the population to 'represent' them.

Those who advocate grass-roots participatory democracy assume that people will participate if given appropriate opportunities. Planners and politicians who spoke critically of participatory democracy noted that most citizens have little interest in casting ballots and even less desire for active involvement in civic affairs; they fear that participatory democracy will allow powerful groups undue influence in a community.[9] Do we want a political system where the masses, easily swayed by manipulation and 'friendly fascism' (Gross 1980), determine the agenda?

Can we trust that the people are good and wise? Given the xenophobia that often prevails among citizens defending their neighbourhoods, can we expect participatory democracy to result in greater equity? The advocates of 'democratic planning' often link democracy to equity, but evidence from practice should make us sceptical about the extent to which those who participate in planning activities want to promote the interests of the disadvantaged. We will return to these themes in Chapter 10.

The Public Interest

We consistently justify planning in our society by its claim to safeguard 'the public interest.' In certain circumstances, we are prepared to limit the rights of private property owners because of a greater community good. Inevitably, however, debates rage over what decision would best serve the public interest. How much restraint on individual rights and interests can we tolerate in a democratic society?

During interviews, planners suggested that the outcome Council favours becomes, *de facto*, the public interest. Transcripts of disputes and staff reports clearly indicate, though, that planners do evaluate circumstances and make judgments about whether proposed changes to plans or land use regulations serve the public interest. Planners link the public interest to planning principles. 'The city should increase density': efficiency is in the public interest.[10] The planner's task in giving advice to Council is to interpret the public interest based on knowledge of the community, plan policies, and planning principles.

Citizens articulate a normative vision of the public interest that may reflect their own self-interest (especially if the dispute occurs in a residential area). Indeed, as Reagan and Fedor-Thurman (1987) show, citizen participation is strongest where self-interest is at stake, yet participants may feel they have to define some threatened common interest as well. So, for example, in the Mitchell property dispute, citizens opposing changes to the area argued that the old house constituted a treasure for the community as a whole. Arguments about community interest generate greater public support and may have greater hope of influencing outcomes, than would private interests.

Developers pursue projects as business activities, yet they invariably promote the 'public' benefits of their projects: jobs, tax revenues, housing. In making their decisions about what constitutes 'the public interest,' politicians may find the economic concerns persuasive. Because the municipality derives its economic revenues from taxes on land, Council has a significant interest in strengthening the tax base.

None of the actors want to stand accused of pursuing anything other than the public interest. In the rhetoric of disputes, promoting one's own interest is commonly acknowledged as a weak strategy. Opponents may be attacked as showing only concern for their own self-interest. One of the strongest epithets used to discredit others during a dispute is to suggest that they represent 'special interests.' In certain contexts, the term 'special interest group' refers to a category of political lobbying organization widely distrusted (Etzioni 1985; Pross 1981). When actors use the term in the context of local planning disputes, they attempt to give a negative connotation to those they label.

All of the participants accept that planning should serve the public interest, but no empirical test to determine the public good exists.[11]

Accordingly, actors attribute to their own favoured solutions the esteem associated with 'the public interest.' Thus the concept provides abundant ground for contention and dispute.

The Public

A relatively small number of actors participate in planning disputes, yet all parties agree that a much greater number of people have an interest in decision outcomes. Actors frequently refer to 'the public,' 'the community,' 'ordinary people,' or 'Joe Citizen' as rhetorical devices to bolster an argument.

What does the public say or think about a particular case? None of the actors knows for sure, although they all hear from community members from time to time. When they believe that they enjoy widespread support for their position, they may call upon 'that old standby, the "silent majority"' (Loney 1977: 458) to make their case for them. They cannot conceive of the possibility that the public would not share their view (see Figure 9.1). All of the actors assert their legitimacy in speaking for the public. They all think that they understand the people, but perhaps they only express their own opinions.

The public elects Council. Politicians see themselves as selected to make decisions on behalf of the public they represent. In our political system, they legitimately speak for the public. They enjoy what we might call 'representative legitimacy.'

Planners study public views through surveys and other scientific means. They believe that they understand what the people want, and can therefore reflect public opinion in reporting to Council. They ensure that Council does not simply hear from the 'special interests' who lobby strenuously, and who may block the voices of the silent majority. Planners claim a kind of 'technical legitimacy' in speaking for the public.

Citizens and developers are members of the public. As members of the public, citizens see themselves as voicing public concerns to politicians and planners. They belong to the sovereign people. We might call their claim 'membership legitimacy': they speak for the category from which they come.

All of the actors believe that they know the public mind and can speak for the community. Increasingly, participants in disputes use petitions and surveys to impress upon others their understanding of the wishes and desires of the public. Until the mid-1980s, citizen activists monopolized such devices. In recent years, however, developers

Figure 9.1   Everyone shares my views. Drawing by Kerri Allen

have also adopted the techniques with some measure of success. It is no mean feat to determine what 'the public' wants, but all of the participants in the planning drama certainly claim to know.

Good Development

In any dispute, actors hold divergent views on what should happen on a particular piece of land. They often phrase their debate in terms of what constitutes good or appropriate development. The concept 'good development' may refer to much more than simply the building that might go on a site. In fact, it may embody a host of values about family, neighbourhood, and community. When citizens say they do not want high-rise buildings, they reveal their fear of strangers who may differ from them in class, race, family status, or origins. They indicate their reluctance to accept change in the places they know and love. They talk about good development, but they fight for a sense of place and the security of tradition and home.

Planners have a different idea of the meaning of good development. They can accept a wider scope of options within the category. As long as a project will not cause obvious problems (like sewer overflows or traffic hazards), then it may be good. They have decided that market factors should not influence their judgment: as far as they are concerned, a good development can stand vacant for years.[12] Good development is less an intrinsic feature of a project than the result of the fair application of rules.

Politicians see development as enhancing the tax base, providing jobs and housing: by definition, most development is good. In certain contexts, however, when properties run down or projects fail, politicians may admit that poor developments can occur.

Sound Planning

None of the respondents interviewed and none of the documents reviewed seriously challenged the legitimacy or appropriateness of planning, yet 'sound planning' or 'good planning' may mean different things to different people. When actors refer to 'basic planning principles,' they may hold radically divergent precepts.

Interestingly, planners seemed the most reluctant to say what they thought constituted 'good planning.' Several of them asked rhetorically whether planning principles existed. Yet their advice to Council and the policies inherent in the plan indicated that they do accept certain principles as paramount: for instance, planners wanted to promote commercial growth in the Central Business District and to increase density on the peninsula. Council members affirmed the importance of flexibility as a planning principle. If Council followed procedures, listened to staff and the public, and had a decision approved by the minister without appeal, then that confirmed sound planning. Good planning should facilitate development and not require that Council have to hear too many contentious cases.

Citizen activists adhere to alternative planning principles than those held by planners and Council. They see sound planning in the Jane Jacobs and Prince Charles mode: it promotes small-scale, low-rise, heritage-based development. Activists talk about 'human' scale.[13] They want busy streets, urban vitality, safe neighbourhoods. They may merge elements of different planning models to come up with a set of planning principles that, on occasion, prove self-contradictory (Grant 1991).

Although politicians seem reasonably happy with the kind of planning process operating in Halifax, planners and citizens voiced concerns about procedures. Procedures used by the City of Halifax promote adversarial relationships between planners and citizens when disputes arise. While planners seemed reticent to offer alternatives to present modes of operating, citizen activists generally advocated an enhanced role for citizens.

The Plan

Actors in planning disputes all read the same plan or plans, yet their understandings of the meaning and implications of plan policies vary wildly. They disagree about which policies should apply and what particular words imply. They have different interpretations of 'the intent' of the plan. They argue about how to define vague objectives. Actors' ideas about the kind of document the plan is or should be affect their use of the plan in debate.

Planners do not treat all policies in the plan as equal. Some policies carry greater weight in an implicit hierarchy. In judging particular proposals, then, planners may determine that some policies do not apply. They may interpret words like 'complementary' to apply to the proposed project. Certain policies they may dismiss as irrelevant or inapplicable. Plan policies (and accompanying regulations) offer a kit of tools of varying function and finesse.

Citizen activists have their own idea of what the plan means. They search the plan for policies to use to attack a proposal and have a particular understanding of what words in policies denote. They believe the plan should protect the city from certain kinds of projects: they originally pushed for a community plan in order to resist undesirable change. Citizens want shields and spears from the plan to aid them in their battles. By contrast, developers may see the plan and its policies as hurdles to get over, or roadblocks to avoid. They read policies carefully and selectively, and they employ experts to argue that their projects meet the intent of the plan.

The plan gives actors a common language to use in debates. Instead of openly arguing about values, means, and ends, actors bicker about the meaning of words and the application of policies and regulations. The metaphors of 'tools' and 'weapons' indicates some of the differences in the ways actors use the plan to script their performances.

The Character of the Community

Participants in a dispute often argue about the character of the community or neighbourhood. People's images of a community differ according to whether they live in it or not. People have particular ways of visualizing a community that may lead them to judge its character differently than others do. Those who share the antiurban bias that has long dominated our culture may harbour nostalgia for the moral rural community of the small town (Hadden and Barton 1973). People who enjoy big city life value bustling streets.

Residents of a community normally evaluate their area positively. The places around our homes tend to provide important geographic and social contexts for our lives (Agnew 1984). Through various situations, such as a chat between neighbours over the backyard fence, people transact the meaning and significance of their neighbourhood. Collectively, they determine what gives their area its special nature or character. They may, for example, value its heritage architecture or its shady streets.

People who do not live in the area may value or devalue other attributes: for instance, they may dislike the busy streets, or appreciate ready access to public transit. The choice of terms used to describe an area projects moral judgments (Guttenberg 1968). For instance, those who called Africville a 'slum' in the 1960s experienced relief when the bulldozers moved in; the residents of Africville found their social networks and sense of place shattered because they lost their homes.[14] When actors with divergent images of a community try to make decisions about appropriate development projects in the area, they cannot agree. One may argue the area is a 'heritage district'; the other says it forms 'the urban core.' Neither can understand what the other is thinking; both presume the other is misguided, corrupted, or preoccupied with self-interest.

Professional planners spend many hours pouring over maps and symbolic representations of communities. When they develop a land-use map or a zoning map, they look at the community in 'plan view' from above. They see areas as spatial patterns of different uses. Changing one or two of the elements in the pattern does not seem a problem to them. While most residents can read maps and locate places in their communities, they do not normally think of their neighbourhoods in plan view. They see streetscapes and vistas from ground level. Their mental image of the changes development projects can render in their neighbourhood bears little resemblance to the image in the mind of the planner. An intrusive element in an idealized landscape can threaten citizens' understanding of their community. Thus, while all the actors may refer to the 'character of the neighbourhood,' they talk past each other. They don't see or feel the same place.

Communication and Miscommunication

Exploring the context of planning disputes forces us to conclude that considerable miscommunication occurs about and during the planning process. The actors involved in planning activities often do not understand or respect each other. They suspect hidden agendas and identify 'special interests' lurking everywhere. They baffle and confuse each other. They do not see their own values and do not recognize the values of others as legitimate. They think of their own beliefs as 'facts,' while others espouse mere 'opinion.' Divergent views of the world lead actors to see planning issues in wholly different terms. Little wonder they find it so difficult to come to mutually agreeable resolutions. They cannot find common ground.

Communicative problems that occur during planning disputes reflect in large part the inevitable outcome of debates over essentially contested cultural concepts. Participants in planning activities battle over divergent images of the city and different expectations of democratic process. Ultimately, community planning cannot resolve debates about fundamental principles, regardless of the promises and assumptions people may have made about what planning would mean. Many of the problems of planning derive not from planning itself but from the culture that has adopted planning as a useful institution. Planning activities merely provide the stage upon which actors play out a script of competing values, beliefs, and meanings.

The script of the planning drama derives from many sources. Local factors clearly play a significant part in framing the issues and themes that dominate the discourse. In Halifax, for instance, a history of limited economic development left the community with a substantial stock of vacant land and old buildings, the future of which people could debate. We also recognize that themes developing in the national or international context can affect the ways in which actors think and talk about planning issues: Haligonians pointed to the Spadina Expressway as a colossal white elephant.

The rhetoric of contention and dispute is a moral rhetoric (F.G. Bailey 1983: 135). It conveys belonging, legitimacy, and identity. We find little evidence of the rhetoric of compromise in planning disputes. Actors remain convinced of their own openness, honesty, and veracity, but show no trust in other categories of actors. People do not seek to work together to achieve common goals but compete in their efforts to persuade others of the truth of their cause.

Despite adopting planning policies and planning procedures in communities like Halifax, we have not ended contention. Planning disputes continue to reflect fundamental disagreements about community means and ends. The planning process gives communities a set of means by which they can arrive at decisions, but not all actors accept the legitimacy of the political and bureaucratic procedures. The presence of an approved community plan may signify that a community has reached some level of consensus about a set of ends, but debates about how to interpret plan policies reveal substantive differences of opinions concealed within vague or ambiguous language. People disagree on where they're going and how to get there.

The 'wicked problems' that plague our communities show no signs of disappearing. Adopting a plan and planning procedures does not solve disputes over the use of land but rather institutionalizes debate in a new process with new language. As each dispute arises, community members frame it in the context of their knowledge of the planning activities and outcomes that preceded it. Actors' decisions about how to script performances in new scenes reflect some of the lessons taken from previous acts. Thus the process of improvisation continues.

Part 4

Planning in a
Democratic Society

Chapter Ten

Democracy in Myth and Practice

The perils of democracy in practice are many. So are the perils of democracy in definition. Even in the West where we think we use the word rationally, few people give it the same meaning. And many people give it no meaning at all. They use it as a talisman, or charm, which if worn conspicuously will make them better citizens. Vain hope, for the charm is useless until its intricate workings are understood.

(Agar 1965: Preface)

Democracy is a *cause célèbre* in Western society. Everyone supports democracy. In practice, however, we find no consensus on the meaning of the term. Democracy surfaces in our societies as a value-laden contested concept. Most Canadians believe that citizens have the right to participate in making important decisions about the future of their communities, yet community residents often feel powerless to prevent unwanted changes. Although Canadians have unprecedented opportunities to appear before city councils, travelling government commissions, and other official bodies, they have no assurance that their comments will influence those with the power to decide. Governments at all levels frequently impose policies and projects on people who may not want them. Democracy in Canada does not mean citizen power by any stretch of the imagination: should it?

In its most general sense, democracy means the sovereignty of the people. A democratic government is one 'of the people, by the people, for the people.' Such agreement about the fundamental nature of democracy masks considerable debate about how to determine the will of the people. The particular application of democracy in a polity entails choices and compromises.

The Process of Democracy

Dahl (1989) argues that the process is the key feature of democracy. In democratic societies, citizens select their leaders through electoral processes, and participate in various political activities. All democratic societies engage in some kind of voting behaviour, but their processes differ in a number of ways. Polities characterized by what Dahl (1989) calls 'polyarchy' employ mass suffrage[1] and political parties in a form of representative democracy. Leaders elected to office for prescribed terms make decisions on behalf of the electorate.

The electorate continues to influence decision makers between elections in some polities. Some jurisdictions give voters the right to recall or impeach politicians who fail to meet community standards. Referenda or plebiscites may allow voters to make binding decisions on planning or other matters.

Kornberg et al. (1982) argue that while Canada approximates a system of representative democracy, it remains imperfect. Our government is less open to participation than is ideal. Voters generally cannot impeach politicians or insist on referenda. Parliamentary government limits the rights of voters: after casting ballots, voters must wait until a politician's term expires before receiving another opportunity to sanction the politician. While voters in some areas can exercise influence through lobbying activities, the political process limits opportunities for democratic intervention. Elected politicians, not the masses, determine the 'will of the people' between elections. Even the 1992 constitutional referendum did not transfer decision-making responsibility: before the vote, politicians argued that they need not be bound to the results; after, however, politicians bowed to the inevitable and accepted the verdict of the people.

Does democracy mean 'majority rule'? Many polities allow candidates to claim office without winning a majority of the ballots cast. A 'first past the post' system within a multiparty democracy can result in the election of candidates who receive fewer than 50 per cent of the votes. Hence the majority of electors find themselves with no representative to voice their concerns in government. Because of the regional nature of Canadian politics, such circumstances are commonplace. American voters less frequently elect politicians with fewer than 50 per cent of the votes cast because of the absence of effective third parties[2]. Some multiparty polities, such as Israel, require voters to cast ballots for political parties rather than for local representatives: then each party is allocated seats according to its percent of the popular vote. Other multi-party polities, such as France, hold run-off elections: voters choose from among the top two vote-getters from a preliminary round.

Are all voters equal? Not all votes have equal import in a Canadian election. Small northern ridings may have one-tenth the number of voters as large urban ridings. Urban voters traditionally have been underrepresented in Canadian legislatures. Furthermore, the continued practice of appointing unelected persons to the Senate denies both voter equality and regional equality: patronage politics favours the few over the many.

Democracy in the former East-bloc nations operated differently than Western models. In fact, Western governments did not view communist nations as democratic polities. Political parties other than the Communist Party could not contest elections, and voters often had a single choice on the ballot. However, in some cases voters could refuse a candidate by voting no. A candidate with a majority of no votes could not win an election. Voters in Western polities do not have the right to refuse candidates: an uncontested candidate is acclaimed to office.

Given the 'sameness' of candidates seeking election, we might ask whether voters face real choices when they enter the ballot-box in contested Western elections: voters can choose from an array of candidates, almost all of whom are white, affluent, conservative, telegenic, middle-aged, family men. The myth of democracy speaks of diversity, but the practice reveals homogeneity.

The myth of democracy holds that people cherish the right to vote and the right to participate in civic affairs. Some polities enforce the myth by requiring citizens to vote: Australia has laws to impose fines on those who fail to cast a ballot in national elections. In the U.S., where the myth of democracy pervades the mass media and popular culture, the reality of practice reveals disillusionment. Fewer than half of eligible voters cast ballots in congressional elections in the U.S.[3] The practice of registering voters systematically excludes significant numbers of potential voters, many of them members of minority populations. Citizens evidently feel a significant level of disaffection if they choose not to exercise their basic right in a democratic society. As a headline in TIME announced in early 1992, people are simply 'FED UP!' (Walsh 1992).

People often speak of local politics as the heart of democracy. At the local level you can know your political representatives: they live in your neighbourhood; they shop in the local supermarket. Local politics have the potential to represent the grass roots. Again we find divergence between the myth and the reality of democracy when we look at local politics. Voter turnout is generally lower in local elections than in provincial or federal elections. Fewer than 40 per cent of eligible voters typically cast ballots in Halifax elections, while 75 per cent to 80 per cent vote in provincial and federal elections. Voters show little interest and knowledge about local politics. Many people don't know what ward they live in or who their local alderman is. The majority of community residents seem disinterested in local democracy.

Is participation by the people just a normative concept (Stankiewicz 1980): a good idea, but impractical? Or should it remain the heart of the concept of representative democracy (Kornberg et al. 1982)? Canadian governments offer citizens relatively few opportunities to participate directly in governance. Governments 'consult' the people through commissions, polls, and task forces, but the people do not decide. The balance of powers in our polity shows that early political leaders distrusted the people. Through the years, mass civic action in the form of protests, blockades, illegal strikes, or sit-ins have met severe resistance and repression. Governments fear anarchy as the logical (or illogical) extreme of democracy. Citizens who find existing channels inadequate are inevitably characterized as radical or even dangerous. Every polity, Canada included, limits the kinds of participation it accepts from its citizens.

Many commentators on democracy suggest that the people cannot take more power than they currently enjoy without threatening democracy (e.g., Stankiewicz 1980). Those who advocate enhanced rights for citizens often assume that participatory democracy will result in a better society. Unfortunately, practice leads us to question such presumptions. The people may not be selfless and 'good' in their behaviour. Apathy, petty jealousy, tyranny, selfishness, and xenophobia occur with some frequency in human populations. While we cannot assume such traits constitute 'human nature,' they do reveal common cultural values and behaviours. Unfortunately, participation in political activities or planning processes does not convert people into wise and moral citizens. Fundamental inequities and ideological differences remain.

The Substance of Democracy

Against those who argue that democracy is fundamentally a process are those who suggest that the primary aim of democracy is substantive: to protect rights. 'So we may hazard one statement about democracy: it is a means toward an end, and the end is freedom. It is freedom which men have always wanted and upon which they must always insist, for without freedom human beings cannot become fully human' (Agar 1965: 18). Democracy may involve protecting human rights such as the right of free speech, the right to a fair trial, and the right to live where one chooses. Some commentators insist that democracy must also protect property rights from 'majoritarian tyranny' (Windsor 1988: 108): they link the concept tightly to capitalism. Perceptions that planning may limit property rights often underline allegations that planning is antidemocratic.

Debates about the substance of democracy reveal different priorities that people place on 'rights.' Societies have fundamental disagreements about what people should expect as their share of the social contract. We also find many examples of conflicting rights: the rights of the community versus the individual; the right of one individual versus those of another. Moral debates over issues such as abortion reflect the dilemma spawned by conflicting rights: a woman's right to control her body; a right of the unborn to live. Who has what rights?

Implicit in many discussions of the nature of democracy are arguments about social rights. Should citizens have the right to health, education, employment, or shelter? Many Western polities do not guarantee citizens such rights. Millions of Americans have no health coverage. Illiteracy rates are soaring in developed industrial nations. Structural unemployment in the range of 10 per cent of the workforce is commonplace. Workers face shrinking incomes, declining job security, and a disappearing social safety net. Tens of thousands of citizens in affluent societies have no homes. Despite their optimistic rhetoric, Western democratic societies have not promoted equity. Capitalist democracies speak of 'equality of opportunity' rather than equality of results. Ideological commitments to equity are more strongly linked to socialism than to democracy.

We find no consensus on what democracy means, either in theory or practice. Is it a process for selecting governments? Which method of selecting governments is the most democratic? If democracy means government by the people, then what role do the people play? Does democracy mean protecting rights and, if so, what rights and whose rights? Does democracy imply greater equity? The essentially contested nature of the concept of 'democracy' among the participants in planning disputes reflects broad disagreements within our culture about the answers to these and other questions.

Promoting Democracy in the 1990s

Despite the lack of consensus on the meaning of democracy, democracy is a powerful ideological construct in Western societies. Even 'totalitarian governments oppress their peoples "in the name of democracy"' (World Monitor 1991: 9). With the fall of communism as an economic system, Western definitions of democracy gained in influence. The media invariably illustrates stories of the heroic struggles of former communist nations with accounts of the success of democracy against all odds. The 'transition to democracy' in newspeak marks the ascendance of market economics and electoral politics.

Democracy in the 1990s hides a host of problems its proponents cannot easily deny. Although heralded as a political system where the people rule, democracy coexists with oligarchy and inequality. The ruling elites in most Western societies constitute an exclusive affluent class closely aligned with corporate interests. Citizens in many democracies defer to authority, to celebrity, and the military. When the federal government suspended civil liberties and arrested hundreds of people without trial in Quebec during the October Crisis of 1970, Canadians welcomed the heavy hand. During the 1991 Gulf War, Americans supported military censorship of broadcast transmissions. In a time when actors become presidents and political leaders look like actors, citizens have forgotten how to be sceptical.

Global economic restructuring and depressed industrial economies have combined to render communities vulnerable to decisions taken in boardrooms half way around the world. International corporations have the power to destroy the economies of our communities; they play communities against each other as they seek financial and environmental concessions. Is it possible to nurture democracy when people have so little control over their economic fate? Did the peoples of eastern Europe mobilize for democracy only to impoverish themselves? Mass unemployment and hopelessness undermine faith in democracy as a political system. The poor in Western societies have grown so disaffected they opt out of the political system: they don't vote; they don't participate. In the face of hunger, warfare, or powerlessness, people can't worry about democratic process or rights.

We might argue that communities have to some extent used planning to undermine the potential of minorities and the poor to participate in democratic community politics. Urban renewal schemes in the 1960s destroyed poor neighbourhoods and often scattered residents throughout urban areas. Without a localized base, the poor find it difficult to organize mass action. Policies from the 1970s that promoted 'social mix' and recent initiatives advocating integration continue the philosophy of separating the poor from each other. Social planning policies have failed to provide the resources people need to live healthful lives. Little wonder that the poor fail to participate in civic affairs. Participation in planning is a luxury they can't afford.

Participation in a Democratic Society

Many of those who advocate greater public participation in the planning process assert that democracy is good for people. 'Political participation is a tonic,' says Mishler (1981: 140). It promotes self-esteem and a sense of efficacy for participants. While participation entails considerable self-sacrifice, its proponents say it promotes good citizenship. Unfortunately, we find little evidence that the majority of community residents buy such arguments.

Citizens who want to participate in civic affairs have lots of opportunities today. They can volunteer for municipal boards, committees, and commissions. They can attend workshops, task force meetings, and open houses. Lots of government-appointed groups want public input in their processes. Many such groups are discovering, however, that although the polls indicate that people want to be consulted, relatively few ordinary citizens show up for most public meetings. The big crowds appear only for contentious disputes.

Despite the opportunities provided to citizens, most citizens do not participate. The silent majority parks in front of the television for the latest episode of 'Star Trek.' In the television age, the residents of Western societies would rather watch a protest march on the tube than participate in one. The threshold for generating political action from citizens is high in a narcissistic society that values leisure time but can't afford many leisure activities (Lasch 1979). Those who do participate in civic affairs find that democracy does not generate consensus: it fuels conflict (Barber 1988). Well-financed interests can participate effectively and see that decision makers address their concerns (Etzioni 1985; Nagel 1987). Citizens without resources often grow cynical and frustrated in the face of their inability to influence outcomes.

Participation is a luxury for citizens in modern industrial societies. It requires skills (e.g., in public speaking), resources (e.g., for child care), money (e.g., for legal advice), and time. Can we legitimately speak of democratic participation when so few citizens can take advantage of the opportunities provided?

Democratic Spaces

Democracy occurs within geopolitical units. The earliest democratic states were the cities of ancient Greece. In this century, nation states became the typical democratic units. Many of the modern nation state democracies are currently in the process of fracturing: geopolitical units within them employ the ideology of democratic nationalism to subvert existing power arrangements. Canada's constitutional crisis with Quebec reveals strong connections between territory and democracy. Democracy (like nationalism) proves a powerful but fractious concept.

Human societies often form intense attachments to place. People value the places they inhabit; they derive meaning and identity from the land (Marris 1982a, 1982b). Through democratic planning processes they attempt to control the use and disposition of land. However, they face a basic dilemma: '... how can the small community function autonomously and determine its own destiny when it is subject to the powerful external economic control of finance capitalism and the cultural influence of the mass media' (Johnson 1987: 296)? People cannot control the spaces they value. They can't prevent the destruction of valued structures. They can't guarantee the preservation of public amenities. Democratic government does not give people the power to decide the fate of their communities: neither does planning.[4]

Economic restructuring unravels the threads that bind people to place. Industrial nations have accepted the premise that both capital and labour must be mobile: no more regional economic development. People now have to move to find jobs because jobs will not come to them. A society that believes corporate bottom lines, not local employment rates, define economic success tends to devalue peripheral areas. Marginalized places breed people who feel increasingly marginalized. In such a context, planners find themselves caught between the economic imperatives of their employers and the spatial values of community residents.

Manipulation of the Masses

Many social commentators have suggested that citizen participation is increasing in Western societies. Alvin Toffler (1978) forecast an era of 'anticipatory democracy.' John Naisbitt (1984) included the development of a participatory culture among his American 'megatrends.' Behind these myths of strengthening democracy, however, we find evidence of the manipulation of public perception. Ronald Reagan's 1980 election staff handbook put it best: 'There is a tendency in our increasingly complex and highly technological society to forget that American democracy is less a form of government than a romantic preference for a particular value structure' (quoted in J. Nelson 1987: 109). At the same time as business and government become more powerful, the ideology of individualism and democracy strengthen (Murphy 1971). Riessman (1987) indicates, however, that much of the citizen energy and enthusiasm generated during the past two decades has gone into consumerism and self-actualization, not into collective community-based action. We have participatory theory in ideology, elitist democracy in practice.

During the 1980s, planners joined other professionals in talking about the importance of empowerment and community initiative. Unfortunately, legitimate efforts to help people develop their strength and gain control over their lives can be manipulated by those looking for excuses to cut programs or staff. Blaney and McFarland (1988) explain, for instance, that the province of New Brunswick used the idea of community-based services as a way of ending payments and programs for those in need. The rhetoric of independence can cloak a philosophy of abandonment.

Bertram Gross (1980) asks us to assess carefully the message of those who promise us greater democracy.

There is an old adage that the cure for the weaknesses of democracy is more democracy. The reason it sounds hollow is that 'democracy,' like 'fascism,' is used in many entirely different – even contradictory – ways. When one uses the term to refer only to the formal machinery of representative government, the maxim is a meaningless cliché. Much tinkering with, and perhaps improvement in, democratic machinery might even be expected on the road to serfdom. But if democracy is seen in terms of the decentralization and counterbalancing of power, then the subject for analysis is the reconstructing of society itself (Gross 1980: 7).

Those with power do not offer a reconstructed society that would give ordinary citizens more influence. *Au contraire.* The global restructuring underway today concentrates wealth and power in the hands of a small elite. Corporate influence has grown to such an extent that the corporate agenda has become the international agenda of Western societies (Bagdikian 1987); the messages of the mega-corporations fill the airwaves night and day.

With the power of the mass media held by a small number of corporations, people have little hope of receiving the information they need to make considered choices. Hairstyle politics, knee-jerk conservatism, and rampant xenophobia replace substantive debate. Ku Klux Klan leaders run for prominent political offices and sometimes win. Former Eastern bloc states herald their new-found democracy and freedom by banning the Communist Party: people can only accept so much freedom. Rational argumentation and tolerance for dissenting opinions are endangered in what passes for democracy today. Rather than contributing to democratic debate and discussion, the mass media pander to base pleasures and fears with diversionary tactics and stereotyped solutions.

What Is Democracy?

The $64,000 question. Who knows what democracy is or what it should be? Certainly we cannot expect planners to 'promote' what others continue to debate! To charge the planner with restoring or nurturing democracy is to expect the planner to have a vision absent in other members of society. While the planning profession is full of talented and intelligent people, is it fair to expect them to have the wisdom of Solomon? No one gives planners the right to impose their value judgments on others, even if they claim to act on behalf of 'democracy.'

Does this mean, then, that planners must simply operate within the 'democracy' in place in our communities? Should planners ignore the inequities and the manipulation that our systems have produced? Surely not. Yet inequities and manipulation are products of our culture. We find little evidence to indicate that the people would change circumstances or outcomes if only they participated more actively in civic affairs. Participation won't solve all of the problems of community planning, although it may alleviate a few.

How far can planners take their professional concern about equity? Many of the academics who advocate 'planners as democrats' link democracy and equity, but we cannot assume that ordinary citizens do. Can planners assume their understanding of equity reflects anything other than personal or professional opinion? What do we mean by 'equity' anyway? Equity is yet another concept people would contest if it reached a significant threshold of importance. In modern industrial societies, equity concerns rarely progress beyond the rhetoric stage.

What does planning in a democratic society require? In the final chapter we consider what planning can and cannot achieve.

Chapter Eleven

Planning Myths and Reality

Throughout this book we have argued that the problems and the prospects of planning make sense only when examined within the matrix of cultural context. Planning occurs within a web of social, political, and economic relations between people. Planning activities, like other cultural activities, allow people to produce and reproduce meanings and places that reflect deeply held cultural values. The interpretive approach we have employed leads us to see planning as providing venues and processes through which actors argue about the values they connect to places, resources, and people. Our central metaphor, the drama, shows that planning constitutes socially constructed behaviour and interactions. People build the stages on which they perform; they hone the characters they play; they formulate the lines they deliver. People make planning into what they need to make communities work effectively. Planners who think they can shape planning in their own professional image fail to recognize this reality.

Planning serves our communities well as a process for mediating conflicts over allocating valued resources. It does not eliminate contention, but rather channels it into socially acceptable forms. Governments institutionalized planning not because they were dazzled by the rationality and profundity of planning theory, but because planning proved useful as a legitimated means of reaching difficult decisions about distributing limited resources. Official plans have come to imply consensus on the ends a community will pursue. Planning processes provide the means by which community members debate how to achieve communal ends.

Lessons for Planning Theory and Practice

Can the results of this research shed light on planning theory and practice? Much modern planning theory with its optimistic rhetoric about 'radical' practice (see, e.g., Forester 1989; Friedmann 1987) seems hopelessly naive given the reality of planning practice in Halifax.

Planning finds its roots in the Progressive Era of the 1890s, when it seemed reasonable to think that reason could transform society. As governments extended the franchise widely through the male population, faith in democracy blossomed. Technological breakthroughs proved that communities could achieve greater efficiency and amenity. Advocates of workers and the poor spoke eloquently of the need for social justice and equity. The professional values spawned in those early days of planning continue to pervade mainstream planning theory.

When we compare planning theory to planning practice, though, we note that some values translated effectively into practice while others found an unsympathetic reception. Accordingly, planners face an ideological crisis: they can stick to the gamut of professional values (efficiency, amenity, equity) and consider themselves 'progressive,' or they can adapt their opinions to accord with mainstream values in their community. Progressive planners see adapted planners as having sold their souls to the devil; mainstream planners see the progressives as naive dreamers.

Can planners operate as reflective and progressive practitioners, as Schon (1983) or Forester (1989) argue? Although Kraushaar (1988) sounds a sceptical note in suggesting that 'progressive planning' may be an oxymoron, some communities may welcome such interventions. Clavel (1986) gives hope to those who long for progressive communities; unfortunately, the cities he discusses represent exceptions rather than the rule. Most communities do not tolerate planners who promote radical initiatives.

When we examine the term 'progressive,' we find many of the same semantic problems we identified with concepts like 'democracy': actors don't agree about what it means. The definition an actor prefers reflects the actor's value and interest base. Within the planning profession, 'progressive' has meant different things through the years. In the 1950s and 1960s, slum clearance seemed progressive. Thirty years later, some planners suggest that recreating old-fashioned small towns or 'restoring democracy' indicate progressive practice. With 20/20 hindsight, thirty years from now, will we criticize the progressive notions of the 1990s? Does the term 'progressive' simply mask a preference for one set of cultural values over another?

Can planners promote democracy? Given that we have found no consensus on what people mean by 'democracy,' we may not be able to answer that question. The appropriate role for citizens in democratic planning remains somewhat fuzzy. By and large, citizens lack the information, interest, and opportunities they need to participate effectively in community decision making. Planners lack the resources to overcome values and processes that limit the roles citizens play in community power structures. Without consensus on common ends, planners and citizens can hardly work together to achieve change.

Planning has not played a radical role in most communities. As a socio-historical phenomenon, it has served the status quo. In Halifax, as in other Canadian communities, land-use planning has protected the interests of municipal governments and the development industry, and has prevented certain uses and people from moving into affluent neighbourhoods. Critics might argue that planning has protected development from the people by facilitating the development of land (regardless of the wishes of the neighbourhood or the needs of the masses).

If we judge planning practice in Halifax according to theoretical criteria developed within an explicitly ideological framework that says planners should empower 'the public,' then we would render an exceedingly harsh judgment on planners. Planning practice in Halifax is not 'organizing and democratizing.' Nonetheless, we have seen that it has a clear internal logic that we need to understand. Planning may not promote equity and citizen power, but it does foster other significant cultural values and meanings. Theoretical proclamations about the role of the planner, which make existing practice seem villainous, disempower planners and citizens who believe in 'democratic planning.' Planners working for municipal governments recognize the real constraints on their role; even if they want to 'restore democracy' (whatever that means), they have few opportunities to alter the decision-making structure or processes in their community. Planners work within bureaucratic and political structures that limit their ability to innovate (Baum 1987); they must push the values of their employers.

This is not to say, however, that planners have no power to improve their practice. Clearly, they need to develop their communication skills so that they can hear what people say to them and avoid boggling people with jargon. They can press their employers for new procedures and regulations to facilitate public participation in decision making. They should examine and explain the distributive effects of planning decisions on groups within the community. They must work with community values and community members. Where their values differ from community values, planners must make both sets of values explicit to the community. They cannot impose ideology suggested by planning theory and expect it to ameliorate planning practice in a community with its own agenda. They must strive to be open, fair, honest, and sincere (Forester 1989).

Our analysis offers a fresh perspective on planning theory. Popular planning theory does not provide explicit guidance for planning practice; rather, it constitutes part of the cultural context in which community planning occurs. Planning theory, especially that embodying a normative framework, may become a rhetorical device used by participants in disputes to lend credibility or authority to particular arguments. Given the wealth of divergent views within the profession, actors can pick and choose their planning theory to suit their case. Experts called to testify at appeals can justify almost any course of action as 'good planning' based on 'sound theory.' Professional theory does not directly affect the choices communities make about either means or ends in planning disputes, but may provide a resource to the actors engaged in planning activities.

Planning and Capitalism

Planning and capitalism make uneasy companions. As Scott and Roweis (1977: 1107) indicate, capitalist urbanization simultaneously requires and resists planning. Planning operates as part of the state apparatus to stabilize conditions for capital (Harvey 1978), yet the advocates of a free market resent the limitations planning imposes. While some suggest that planning in a democratic society means improving conditions for powerless peoples, others aver that it requires protecting freedom of action and free enterprise. Critics claim that because planning inhibits free choice and imposes professional values on a community, it should be strictly limited (Churchill 1954; Kelly 1986). Few commentators, however, advocate abandoning planning entirely. Planning and zoning have become too important to the system of setting land values in our society for anyone to forsake them.

People in our communities may not understand planning. They sometimes resent planners who tell them they need permission to make certain changes to their structures. However, when citizens purchase a home, they pay careful attention to the zoning of the lot. They expect planning to protect their neighbourhoods from unwanted intrusions. They accept that planning defends them from the extremes of laissez-faire capitalism.

Discussions about the role of planning in democratic societies reflect the tension between collective and individual rights over land (Foglesong 1986). States have institutionalized planning to help reproduce existing social and economic orders. Governments use planning as a tool to stabilize or control growth. In boom times, collective concerns take precedence as communities fight the negative consequences of rapid growth. In bust periods, communities seek to promote growth through favouring individual development rights. The debate about the appropriate nature of planning never ends, but is continually rechanneled to meet changing circumstances.

Planning and Participation

Why do some citizens choose to get involved in planning activities while others take no interest? The factors that motivate people to attend meetings, prepare briefs, or organize protests are complex and varied. Some people undoubtedly operate out of self-interest, while others may have the sense that they want to safeguard community interests (Lewin 1991). We know that most people take no active role in planning activities. The best efforts to promote citizen participation usually result in low rates of involvement. The town hall meetings that bring out entire communities in rural New England do not occur in most parts of North America. Planners continue to face uncertainty about what 'the silent majority' thinks, expects, and wants.

Although the Halifax case-study yielded many insights, we still cannot say definitively how participation affects outcomes in planning disputes. In some communities, politicians respond to public displays of concern. Lengthy petitions, packed public meetings, and court challenges have had little effect in Halifax. Certain factors clearly play a significant role: economic conditions, political structures, community values, and the nature of the issue at hand all affect how politicians respond. If the ends promoted by the institutionalized planning process receive the tacit support of community members, then other interventions by organized minorities seem unlikely to succeed. However, we would predict that if the ends of planning are not widely supported, then citizen interventions may well prevail.

Planning is most effective when it supports community values. In Halifax, that means promoting growth and development. Perhaps in other communities supporting public values would require 'promoting democracy,' or it could mean abandoning planning processes entirely. If community values do not nurture citizen participation and democratic involvement, then planners or citizens who want public input face an enormous task. They will have to help create conditions in which broad community concerns are represented in the planning process.

It is increasingly difficult for those who espouse elitist models of representative government to find firm moral ground from which to defend their position. Surely we have room in our decision-making processes for greater participation from the members of our communities. Those who promote participatory models of representative government have trouble explaining why people don't get involved. Many commentators from both camps will undoubtedly argue that we need more public information: the elitists suggest that if people understand the issues, they will support political decisions; the participation advocates say that if people understand the issues, they will demand a role in the process. Perhaps both groups are wrong. 'Education' and 'information' may be the standard remedy prescribed for all the ills of our society, but they won't always cure the patient. The media inundates people with information every day. Information is not the problem.

We might argue instead that what will make planning more democratic, even in the communities that resist participation, are more venues for meaningful public involvement. But how will we get the venues without a local commitment? Planners can continue to go through the empty motions of holding public meetings where the participants talk past each other, or they can begin to suggest alternative forums that offer greater opportunities for dialogue and negotiation. Planners can encourage councils to promote locally based action and neighbourhood planning. Rather than viewing activists as enemies, planners can draw all of those interested in issues into discussions about options and alternatives. Opening up planning will require that planners develop their communication and listening skills, but may reward the community with a less elitist decision-making process.

The planner's role in this vision of a more participatory process changes from that of technical adviser to that of 'technical adviser plus.' As municipal employees, planners cannot abandon their traditional concerns, but they can add dimensions to their practice. They can facilitate public discussion of alternatives and impacts so that community members recognize the consequences of the choices they face. Planners can help council members and community residents move beyond mere 'public opinion' to what Yankelovich (1991) calls 'public judgment.' They can expose moral choices so that people understand the values and interests they advocate. Coming to public judgment doesn't end contention or dispute, but it can improve the quality of the discussion. Planners have a role to play in ensuring that opportunities for democratic debate are available and utilized.

Planning in Halifax

Studying planning disputes reveals the details of community arguments about means and ends. We found people in Halifax hotly contesting the meaning of democracy: how should communities arrive at important decisions? What kind of spaces and relationships should result from democratic processes? The problems planners and citizens encounter derive in part from uncertainty over the function of democratic planning in the local cultural context.

Several kinds of constraints operate in Halifax to limit democratic participation and effectiveness. The local electoral system creates a structure of territorially based politics: neighbourhoods fight each other for amenities and ignore each other's problems. A legacy of patronage politics has created a populace that expects politicians to dispense favours differentially.

Provincial legislation has framed planning as a process for regulating the use of land. Planning in Nova Scotia is not designed to regulate social and economic concerns. Citizens or planners who want to raise equity issues find such matters outside the normal purview of the planning process. Citizens who seek active roles in the planning process find their opportunities constrained by legislation that views planning as primarily a mechanism for facilitating developer and government interactions. Economic dependency and regional underdevelopment have created circumstances that make power brokers in Halifax anxious for any kind of growth or development. Local governments depend upon the revenues from land taxes to meet their expenditure requirements. Promoting growth takes priority in the face of fiscal need. Given that the most active public participation comes from those who oppose development projects, power brokers have little interest in promoting democratic involvement.

Social networks within Halifax also constrain democratic participation in planning activities. Citizens active in planning disputes are often perceived as outsiders; those who originate in Halifax take pains to proclaim their roots. Politicians and other power brokers see protest against established interests as unrepresentative, ill-informed, and illegitimate. The people most affected by development find themselves unable to protect their image of the local residential environment: their participation in civic affairs may take them outside the protective mesh of social networks. Those who form part of the 'establishment' might find themselves ostracized for fighting development in their neighbourhood. Those outside the 'establishment' have less to lose and often form alternative social networks to support each other in their efforts to preserve their sense of place. While some citizens relish the role of 'public watchdog,' others have no wish to suffer social stigma.

In small communities, planners can find themselves isolated by social and political networks that exclude them. Halifax planners find their legitimacy undermined by their external origins; if they push too far with professional values and ideas, politicians quickly put them back in their place. Their position outside of established networks makes them vulnerable targets. Planners hoe a difficult row in the field of community planning. They have few supporters in Halifax. Citizens distrust and suspect them. Politicians divert blame to them. Yet Halifax planners are ordinary people performing thankless jobs. Their behaviour makes complete sense in the context within which they operate. As Healey (1992) found in her study of a planner at work, it is easy to sympathize with practising planners: they act in a principled, honest, open, and reasoned manner. They have no horns on their heads. If they do not meet certain expectations we have of them, we should not assume their failures result from malice aforethought. Like other community members, they play minor parts in a local drama that someone else directs.

Citizens active in planning matters in Halifax often find participation frustrating and alienating. Has participation in planning benefited those who participated? Many respondents saw participation in community planning as a 'good deed,' as community service. Having observed outcomes that challenged their image of the city and that violated their sense of what the plan stood for, many have grown cynical about the benefits of participation. Participation without success undermines people's faith in planning. Cynicism and disaffection grow among those who fail to protect their neighbourhoods from unwanted change. Activists who promote community-wide issues, such as those who advocate heritage preservation, take losses better than do citizens fighting for residential environments. The myth of democracy suffers a severe bleaching in the harsh light of community practice: rather than strengthening the fabric of citizen action and initiative, participation in planning disputes may weaken the fibres that sustain democratic ideology. Can planning create participation processes that will reinforce democratic commitment?

In presenting this case-study of community planning in Halifax, we have not provided definitive responses to the question of what democratic planning should mean. No doubt we have raised more questions than we have answered. The possibilities for further research are considerable. We might, for instance, hope to learn more about communication in planning disputes by conducting detailed discourse analyses. We need to compare and contrast the values and meanings operating in Halifax with circumstances in other communities to build our understanding of the problems and prospects of planning. Do actors in other communities frame their roles in similar ways? Do the same or different themes feature in the scripts of other planning dramas?

We have a lot to learn about how planners work in our communities. During interviews we just began to touch on 'the folklore of the profession': the ideas that planners have about what people are like, about what kinds of communities work best, and about the function of planning in city management. Where do planners seek their knowledge in practising their craft? How do they validate knowledge? How do they develop theories of effective action? How do they justify their advice and decisions? These and many other questions remain as we try to understand the roles of planners and other actors in the drama of community planning.

In arguing that cultural context conditions the success of particular planning interventions, we must not forget that social change results from individual and collective actions. Cultural values and beliefs may influence the outcomes of planning disputes, but they do not determine them. We should not reify 'culture' but recognize it as a body of knowledge and artefacts transacted between its members. The values and meanings shared by actors in the planning process in Halifax today may not be those familiar to actors in other local arenas. To build our understanding of the range and pervasiveness of such cultural meanings, we need more case-studies of practice.

Towards a Theory of Practice

Empirical case-studies provide some of the data we need to develop a theory of planning practice. We have attempted to interpret one community's experience to develop insights into practice; now we must discover whether such findings help us explain and account for practice in other communities.

In building a theory of practice, we will need to articulate an understanding of what happens in community planning. Explanations should be clear both to practitioners and to academics. Theory must make sense of practice. A theory of practice should account for the role of the planner, the citizen, and the politician in community planning. It should clarify the nature of decision making and illuminate the values and meanings transacted through planning activities. It should reveal the context in which planning occurs.

Building a theory of practice is a necessary step in any discipline. However, planners will not rest with a theory of practice because planning is inevitably ideological. Different planners, depending on their own and their community's values and beliefs, will want to frame a normative theory of action to accompany their theory of practice, for it is only by combining a compelling understanding of the nature of practice with an effective strategy for action that we can use planning to create the kinds of communities we desire.

Unfortunately for planners, consensus on the values that should frame planning has proven impossible to achieve. While ethics has become a hot topic in planning discussions, planners cannot formulate a clear professional ethic. What values should the planner promote? Is there a clearly superior moral framework? Who has the authority to determine which values will prevail? Debate over value positions seems unlikely to resolve itself. How can planners determine a moral position when they work within communities that have no sense of what the 'good society' might be? Ultimately, planning provides the means to an end. If we have no shared vision of a desirable end state, then how can we expect planning to show us how to get there?

As we unravel the mysteries of the drama of democracy, we find bizarre plot twists, stages with hidden compartments, and actors with complex characters. We do not find a single villain to blame for the problems of planning. Planners share responsibility for creating expectations that planning cannot hope to fulfil; citizens allow themselves to be manipulated and excluded; politicians use planning for various ends. In our drama, as in Agatha Christie's famous mystery on the Orient Express, all the characters are guilty: they all participate in the crime. Perhaps that is the moral of the story.

Our communities will not likely abandon planning in the near future. People prefer predictability over chaos. We accept the superiority of reason over passion. We acknowledge the need to protect community rights from individual rights. We find planning useful. We will, however, continue to fight about planning and the future of our communities. Contention and dispute about the use and disposition of community resources are eternal themes in the drama of democracy.

Appendix
Glossary of Terms
and Short Forms

CBD   Central Business District. The central part or downtown area of the city where office buildings are expected to locate.

CMHC   Canada Mortgage and Housing Corporation (formerly Central Mortgage and Housing), an agency of the federal government that provides mortgage insurance for low- and moderate-cost housing. Its regulations for site planning determined early planning standards in Canada.

Concerned Citizens for the Mitchell Property
A lobby group of people formed in an effort to save the Mitchell house from destruction and prevent high-rise development on the site.

CPAC   Community Planning Association of Canada. Originally formed as a national organization in 1946 with CMHC assistance. In 1979, the federal government cut funding for the national organization, and only provincial affiliates survived in some regions. The Nova Scotia division maintained a strong presence (through volunteer and provincial funding). It lobbies for citizen involvement in community planning.

CRA   Central redevelopment area. Following the Stevenson Report, in the late 1950s the City of Halifax declared a large portion of the downtown as an area for slum clearance and redevelopment. With federal funds, the area was razed in preparation for major redevelopment.

EAC   Ecology Action Centre, a volunteer-funded action network begun around 1969. Over the years, it has lobbied effectively on various planning and environmental issues.

Friends of the Public Gardens
A lobby group formed to prevent the redesignation of the land at the corner of Summer Street and Spring Garden Road. It continues to operate, now focusing its efforts on supporting the Public Gardens and fighting development projects around the park periphery.

Heritage Trust of Nova Scotia
A lobby group that fights for heritage protection. It brings forward properties to the province and the city for heritage designation, and opposes projects that threaten Nova Scotian heritage.

LUB   Land-use by-law (formerly the zoning by-law). The 1983 Planning Act required that each municipality adopt a land-use by-law to implement its plan.

MDP   Municipal development plan. The 1969 Planning Act required municipalities to prepare plans to promote and facilitate development.

MOVE   MOVEment for Citizen Voice and Action. A network of agencies formed in the early 1970s with funding and support from the federal and provincial governments. It lobbied intensely on several planning issues, but folded when its funding disappeared later in the decade.

MPS   Municipal Planning Strategy. The 1983 Planning Act enabled municipalities to prepare plans to facilitate development.

PAC   Planning Advisory Committee. Nova Scotia planning legislation allows municipal councils to appoint PACs to advise them on planning matters. PACs must include at least two members of Council and citizens from the community.

R-3   High-density residential. This was the highest density residential zone under the 1978 and 1985 plans. It allows 250 people per acre.

Notes

Chapter 1: The Planning Drama

1 Baum (1987) offers such an analysis of planners and planning administrators in Maryland.

2 Even science has its problems with interpretation. As Polanyi (1946) and Kuhn (1970) have argued, scientists' facts and approaches are subject to considerable interpretation.

3 Those data may come from a wide variety of sources when we talk about a phenomenon as general as 'culture.' All kinds of disparate factors contribute to the matrix within which humans act. We attempt to understand as much as we can and acknowledge that we will never explain everything.

4 This section draws substantively on my paper, 'Understanding the Social Context of Planning,' in *Environments* (Grant 1990a).

5 In anthropological terms, we take something of a functionalist approach here, accepting that institutions like 'community planning' have particular social functions that we can determine through investigation. Generally, our approach recognizes that while we can understand institutions as having functions, individuals who belong to the society sustain and reproduce institutions through their interactions (Blumer 1969).

6 Americans tout democracy loudly, yet their voting record in presidential and congressional elections is abysmal. We find a similar problem with local governments in Canada. Municipalities often find fewer than half of eligible voters casting ballots for local Council members.

7 Forester's recent work in 'critical ethnography' (1992) begins to reveal the potential for critical theory to lead to useful applications for studying planning practice.

8 Because American planners do not work for line departments of a municipal administration, they have different problems in their practice than Canadian planners face. Such differences may account in part for the irrelevance of some American planning theory to inform Canadian planners.

9 This is not an argument for naive functionalism. We would not hold that every aspect of planning must have some past or present function. Rather, we suggest that social and political structures, traditional ways of doing things, and other cultural variables constrain the choices that people make. This does not preclude innovation or occasionally atypical responses. Individual actors operate within given structures and traditions, interpret them, and change them in a dynamic, transactive process.

Chapter 2: Stages, Actors, and Scripts

1 By 1992, the New Democrats formed governments in three provinces: Ontario, British Columbia, and Saskatchewan.

2 In 1993, the government of Nova Scotia announced that it would take over responsibility for social assistance under a municipal restructuring program.

3 Blishen and Atkinson's (1980) study looks at a small number of values, however, and does not discuss the beliefs and meanings that accompany the values in different areas of the country.

4 The Canadian electoral system is based on the premise of regional representation. Simultaneously, however, the parliamentary system runs on a party basis. While the political strength of some parties is regionally concentrated, governments have historically enjoyed representation from across the nation. Recently, though, regionalism has grown in Canada, and traditional parties may find it difficult to build a national coalition in years to come.

5 Many communities enforce deference to politicians through the use of honorific titles, such as 'Your Honour' or 'Your Worship' (to refer to the mayor).

6 Sticking to the party platform is more important in Canadian than in American politics. The structure of Canadian parties makes it difficult for renegades to maintain membership and its privileges. This reality makes it more difficult for Canadian politicians to take personal positions on important local issues.

7 In this context, 'democratize' seems to mean subverting the status quo. The authors seek a society of greater equity and social justice where individuals engage freely in civic action for the pleasure of it.

8 We borrow this term from F.G. Bailey (1983).

9 Archives collected by planning departments or agencies, or files kept by community groups usually contain documentary evidence about planning activities.

10 Mass culture frequently deals with the theme of the 'dispassionate' character. The psychopath is perhaps the most feared of all killers because of a lack of emotional depth. In science fiction, the rational android or alien often longs for human 'feelings.'

Chapter 3: Desperately Seeking Development

1 Ralph Matthews (1977) documents the disastrous impacts of the growth centre philosophy on rural settlements in Newfoundland. In the Maritimes as well, concentrating investment in urban centres had the effect of undermining the attractiveness of small communities for their residents.

2 Translated into everyday English, this means 'let people move to where the jobs are.' In the depressed modern global economy, fewer and fewer jobs are in Canada, especially in peripheral regions.

3 Many of the Acadians later returned to the province, but some moved south to the U.S. where they became known as 'Cajuns.'

4 In the 1990s, such voter disaffection has become widespread in Canada. Surprisingly, the cynicism has not apparently reduced voter turnout in federal or provincial elections.

5 For a few weeks, public sector workers protested loudly and in considerable numbers around the legislature, but they failed to gain the kind of public support they needed to force the government to reconsider its action.

6 It is, of course, impossible to predict how Nova Scotians will vote in the next election. Traditionally, they have returned Liberal or Conservative governments that have promoted a business agenda. Given the kind of political changes seen in Ontario, for years a bastion of conservatism but now graced with a majority socialist government, it is conceivable that Nova Scotia could also elect a left-of-centre government. We should keep in mind, though, that Nova Scotians have elected few socialists in the past, and would have to make a major shift in their voting patterns to do so.

7 This section summarizes findings documented in an article published in *Plan Canada* (Grant 1988a).

8 I have not found any analysis to explain why the province decided to adopt planning legislation at this time. Given that some other provinces did the same, perhaps government officials had been discussing the idea. This period was, of course, a time of great interest in the potential of town planning to solve the problems of the city. In Britain, Ebenezer Howard and his cronies were building garden cities (Creese 1966), and the city beautification movement inspired similar schemes across North America. 'Town planning' was a popular idea, fusing values of progress, efficiency, and science in what many saw as a practical way. Nova Scotian legislators must have shared the optimism.

Chapter 4: Planning Issues in Peninsular Halifax

1 Documents reviewed include clipping files, pamphlets, books, journals, handwritten notes, and well-worn manuscripts. Because of the unusual nature of some of the materials, references coded in the text appear in a separate 'clipping file' section at the end of the bibliography.

   Throughout the book quotations from documents are indented. To conceal the identity of participants in the disputes, names included in published quotes have been deleted or altered. Minor typographical errors have been corrected; the use of '[sic]' would have taken away from the flow and impact of the discourse.

2 Respondents' comments appear throughout the text. We reproduce the texts with minimal editing. Most interviews took place in 1990.

   Normally an identifier code indicates whether the respondent is: a Council member (alderman or mayor, past or present) [A]; a city planner [P]; an 'other' planner (consultant or educator) [O]; a developer [D]; or a citizen active in planning issues [C]. To protect the identity of respondents, no further identifying codes are offered. Where the content of the text may identify a speaker, or where the number of members in a category is very small, we omit identifying codes.

3 Coded references are explained in the clipping file section at the end of the bibliography.

4 One respondent, who first moved to Halifax immediately after the clearance, said the site looked like bombed-out London.

5 In early 1990, the hotel launched an advertising campaign with huge billboards around the city that boasted 'See our stunning example of urban renewal.'

6 [Q:] Indicates a question from the interviewer.

7 Voluntary Planning includes people from the private sector, non-

governmental organizations, and academics who advise the provincial government on economic planning matters (Lamport 1988).

8 It appears that the Planning Department had only one or two planners until the mid-1970s when it began to grow. By the late 1980s, the City employed ten to twelve planners.

9 Residents groups attempting to appeal under the 1983 act often had trouble gaining standing before the Municipal Board. In 1987, the province amended the act to define 'aggrieved persons' in such a way as to allow interested parties to appeal.

10 During the 1985 municipal election campaign in Halifax, the Friends of the Public Gardens supported a slate of candidates who stood against Summer Gardens. They circulated political buttons with the logo, 'If City Council won't plan, plan to change the Council.' By and large, their candidates lost to others supported by the mainstream political party machines.

11 Canada Mortgage and Housing Corporation, the housing agency of the federal government.

12 Nova Scotia has two planning schools, but the City rarely hires local graduates.

13 The building is now known as the North American Life Building, named after its principal tenant.

Chapter 5: Market Place Plaza

1 The developer had served as an alderman on Halifax City Council earlier in the decade.

2 Coded references (from clipping file data) are located at the end of the bibliography.

3 This is a variant on the 'come from away' theme. Haligonian heritage and people are most highly valued.

4 Under the 1969 act, property owners could apply for contract zoning in designated areas. Contract zoning, also known as spot rezoning, allowed Council to change allowable heights, density, and uses on the site.

5 Groups opposing the project included the Community Planning Association of Canada (Nova Scotia Division), Heritage Trust (Nova Scotia), Ecology Action Centre, and Parks Canada (Citadel).

6 Under the 1983 Planning Act, 'contract zoning' gave way to 'development agreements.' Both imply contracts arranged between a land owner and Council to waive the normal zoning or land-use regulations.

7 It seems more probable that the *courts* awarded costs after the appellants unsuccessfully attempted to overturn the Planning Appeal Board's ruling.

Chapter 6: Mitchell Property

1 Where a plan allows development agreements, normal planning regulations do not apply. The property owner negotiates a contract with the municipality to determine site-specific regulations for development.
2 This would allow 250 people per acre.
3 Halifax prepared detailed area plans for several neighbourhoods, including the south end of the peninsula.
4 The planner's words and tone betray him. His careful choice of language and reluctance to discuss the citizens who opposed the project seem to reflect deep wounds that he does not care to reveal.
5 Quotations in which speakers are identified as 'Citizen #' or 'Planner' refer to the minutes of Planning Advisory Committee public meetings. City staff provide typed transcripts of the tapes recorded at PAC public meetings.
6 Given the fate of some of the planners who lost their jobs in the early 1970s because Council didn't support their approach, we might not be surprised that planners worry about Council approval.
7 The most commonly cited works included McHarg (1969), Friedmann (1973), Jacobs (1961), and Lynch (1960).
8 We might speculate that planners develop a body of 'folk wisdom' or 'common sense' within the context of their daily work. How that conventional wisdom may be affected by their contacts with other professionals and their interactions with the public would be a fruitful area for further research.
9 The by-law calculated height from the lower limit of the roof-line. An amendment in 1990 revised this provision.
10 The reader may recall that in a staff report on the Time Square proposal, discussed in the Chapter 7, staff *did* consider the developer's economic circumstances in deciding what kinds of uses the project should include.

Chapter 7: Staging Planning Activities

1 To attract an international corporation to build factories in Nova Scotia during the 1960s and 1970s, the provincial government passed special labour legislation to limit the ability of unions to organize workers. In

1991, the province suspended the rights of 40,000 provincial employees by freezing collective agreements for a two-year period.

2 Perhaps the province is doomed forever to attempt to overcome its early reputation as 'Nova Scarcity' (Haliburton 1829).

3 While some aldermen with New Democratic Party (social democrat) connections have served on Halifax Council, they have always constituted a small minority.

4 Even if Council refuses a project, the provincial Municipal Board may entertain an appeal and approve the development. In a decision in early 1992, the Board ruled that public opposition to a project was not sufficient grounds for Council to refuse an application to amend zoning regulations (Nova Scotia 1992).

5 CPAC received federal funding through Central Mortgage and Housing Corporation from 1946 until the late 1970s. The province of Nova Scotia then provided a grant for CPAC's planning advisory service until 1991 when all government funding ceased.

6 Staff revealed its position in a staff report dated 12 January 1990. Council did not accept staff advice, but it did revise the terms of reference of the PAC and reduced the number of Council members appointed to it.

Chapter 8: Command Performance

1 Because of the small number of developers and their agents in our interview sample, we cannot safely make general statements about their views.

2 The sample for detailed interviews included eleven planners: six urban planners and five 'other' planners (consultants or educators).

3 The two departments merged during the late 1980s after the retirement of the man who directed the Development Department for approximately three decades. Even the name of the department creates contention. Across Nova Scotia, many planning departments are called 'Planning and Development.' Halifax reverses the order. Planning staff explain the name as a matter of internal politics: the name of the larger section came first when the departments merged. Citizens see the name as evidence that planning has become subservient to development. While Development is the larger division, Planning has more planners (approximately six to eight positions).

4 In part, these differences reflect the employment context of Canadian versus American planners. As municipal civil servants, Canadian planners cannot escape the political environment.

5 Only four members of Halifax Council contacted agreed to an interview. The sample, which includes both past and present members (mayors and aldermen), is small and not necessarily representative. Nonetheless, respondents had reasonably consistent views.

Respondents could probably be categorized as somewhat liberal (in a small L sense). They may be more sympathetic to citizen activists than those who declined to participate in the survey.

6 Twelve citizen activists participated in detailed interviews.

7 Some of the most committed activists are willing to devote a great deal of time to planning issues. One of the respondents noted, 'Thank God XX doesn't have any children or the city would be a lot worse off today.'

8 Particular planners were especially vilified by a number of respondents.

9 Citizens tend not to understand the 'city manager' form of civic administration that is designed to separate political and bureaucratic responsibilities. The electorate selects the Council, which sets policies and tax rates. Council appoints a city manager who runs the civic administration. Staff report to the city manager, who reports to Council. Hence the planning staff are at several removes from citizen control.

10 When citizens allege corruption, then they presume that developers have interfered with the decision context by inappropriately pushing inside it.

11 Some might argue that although citizens are only one of the sets of players, their views should prevail because they constitute a majority. There are problems with this argument, however. First, we do not know whether the views of respondents interviewed are shared beyond the sample. Second, we only interviewed citizen activists. Those who do not participate may not share the views of activists.

Chapter 9: Scripts and Values

1 Blishen and Atkinson (1980) measured eleven values. Many of the values we describe do not appear in their list.

2 In the wake of the Los Angeles riots of May 1992, an aide to President Bush affirmed this premise. He suggested that greater home ownership among the poor would lessen the likelihood of such civil unrest.

3 Such codes can alienate an inexperienced audience. Planners use them not to prevent communication but to aver their commitment to a rhetorical style. They believe that a rational argument that uses correct

terms gives the most accurate account of the choices a community faces.

4 Citizens obviously may employ different strategies in public meetings. Some may give 'homey poetry readings' or display heart-warming landscape paintings for effect. Citizen organizers believe, though, that they must 'fight fire with fire' and provide experts to challenge the developer's experts.

5 For example, many planning departments do not provide resources for single parents to participate in planning activities. Adults in two-parent families can attend evening meetings, but single parents would need assistance with child care in order to participate.

6 Patsy Healey (1992) found the same legitimating strategies used by a planner in Manchester: (1) procedural norms set by council, (2) ethical or professional principles.

7 In studies of Kingston and Cincinnati, Harris (1988) and Davis (1991) argue that collective citizen action derives from property-based class interests. However, our data clearly indicate two forms of collective action: one locally based and one community based. While locally based collective action develops at least in part out of a concern for property, community-based action does not. Community-based collective action responds to principles shared within socially reinforced community networks.

8 Variants on this term include the common good, the public will, and the common weal.

9 For example, the polls indicate that most Canadians feel that abortion should be a matter between a woman and her doctor. Nevertheless, well-organized pro-life groups managed to convince the federal government and many provincial governments to attempt to restrict access to abortion in the late 1980s.

10 The 1985 plan includes policies that confirm this definition of the public interest. In recent years, however, Council has made several decisions that undermine support for increasing density. Hence, planners face a conundrum: they say that it is Council's job to determine the public interest, yet they disagree with some of Council's judgments.

11 The planning literature nonetheless abounds with efforts to clarify the public interest (e.g., Klosterman 1980).

12 This may seem somewhat contradictory, given the importance staff attach to potential tax revenues in their reports on the merits of a proposed development project. In effect, staff only examines the potential tax base, but cannot forecast the more relevant 'business occupancy tax' revenues.

13 It might seem that high-rise development is uniquely 'human,' but the use of the word in this context is meant to set the scale apart from that possible with modern technology.

14 In their analysis of neighbourhood planning in Ottawa during the 1970s, Andrew and Milroy (1986) noted that while citizens viewed the neighbourhood as a central geographic unit, planners saw it as a residual category. Accordingly, plans for neighbourhoods developed into detailed land-use plans instead of dealing with the social and environmental matters that most troubled residents.

Chapter 10: Democracy in Myth and Practice

1 Democracy does not mean that everyone in the community has the right to vote. Youths, immigrants, and convicts have lesser rights in our society and may be excluded from 'mass suffrage.'

2 The 1992 presidential elections made Bill Clinton president with approximately 43 per cent of votes cast; Ross Perot made a strong showing as an independent candidate.

3 Green and Ledbetter (1988) report that in 1888 approximately 80 per cent of eligible voters voted in the U.S. national elections. In 1986, only 37 per cent of eligible voters cast a ballot. The 1992 presidential election showed a high turnout for American elections: 54 per cent of eligible voters cast ballots (16 November, *TIME*, 1992).

4 Porteous (1989) demonstrated in Howdendyke (U.K.) and Matthews (1977) showed in Newfoundland that planning contributed to the process of community destruction initiated by democratically elected governments.

Bibliography

Agar, Herbert. 1965. *The Perils of Democracy*. Chester Springs, PA: Dufour Editions.

Agnew, J.A. 1984. 'Devaluing place: "people prosperity versus place prosperity."' *Environment and Planning D: Society and Space* 1: 35–45.

Ahlbrandt, Roger S., Jr. 1984. *Neighborhoods, People, and Community*. New York: Plenum Press.

Andrew, Caroline, and Beth Moore Milroy. 1986. 'Making Policies and Plans for Neighbourhoods: Ottawa's Experience.' *Plan Canada* 26(2): 34–9.

Alterman, Rachel, and John E. Page. 1973. 'The Ubiquity of Values and the Planning Process.' *Plan Canada* 13(1): 13–26.

Altshuler, Alan A. 1965. *The City Planning Process: A Political Analysis*. Ithaca, NY: Cornell University Press.

Armstrong, Alan H. 1959. 'Thomas Adams and the Commission of Conservation.' *Plan Canada* 1(1): 14–32.

Arnstein, Sherry R. 1969. 'A Ladder of Citizen Participation.' *Journal of the American Institute of Planners* 35(4): 216–24.

Axworthy, Lloyd. 1979. 'The Politics of Urban Populism.' In W. Perks and I.M. Robinson (eds), *Urban and Regional Planning in a Federal State*. Stroudsburg, PA: Dowden, Hutchinson & Ross, 282–92.

Babcock, Richard. 1966. *The Zoning Game: Municipal Practices and Policies*. Milwaukee: University of Wisconsin Press.

Bagdikian, Ben. 1987. *The Media Monopoly* (2nd ed. Boston: Beacon Press.

Bailey, F.G. 1983. *The Tactical Uses of Passion: An Essay on Power, Reason, and Reality*. Ithaca, NY: Cornell University Press.

Bailey, Joe. 1975. *Social Theory of Planning*. London: Routledge and Kegan Paul.

Barber, James David. 1988. *Politics by Humans: Research on American Leadership*. Durham: Duke University Press.

Bartelt, David, et al. 1987. 'Islands in the Stream: Neighborhoods and the Political Economy of the City.' In I. Altmann and A. Wandersman (eds), *Neighborhood and Community Environments*. New York: Plenum Press, 163–89.

Baum, Howell S. 1980. 'Sensitizing Planners to Organization.' In P. Clavel, J. Forester, W. Goldsmith (eds), *Urban and Regional Planning in an Age of Austerity*. New York: Pergamon Press, 279–307.

– 1983. *Planners and Public Expectations*. Cambridge, MA: Schenkman Publishing Company.

– 1987. *The Invisible Bureaucracy: The Unconscious in Organizational Problem Solving*. New York: Oxford University Press.

Beauregard, Robert A. 1980. 'Thinking About Practicing Planning.' In P. Clavel, J. Forester, W. Goldsmith (eds), *Urban and Regional Planning in an Age of Austerity*. New York: Pergamon, 308–25.

– 1988. 'In the Absence of Practice: The Locality Research Debate.' *Antipode* 20(1): 52–9.

Beck, J. Murray. 1973. *The Evolution of Municipal Government in Nova Scotia, 1749–1973* A study prepared for the Nova Scotia Royal Commission on Education, Public Services and Provincial-Municipal Relations. Halifax: Government of Nova Scotia.

– 1988. 'Nova Scotia.' *The Canadian Encyclopedia*. Edmonton: Hurtig Publishers, 1526–34.

Bell, David V.J. 1981. 'Political Culture in Canada.' In M.S. Whittington and G. Williams (eds), *Canadian Politics in the 1980s* Toronto: Methuen, 108–25.

Berry, Jeffrey M., et al. 1984. 'Public Involvement in Administration: The Structural Determinants of Effective Citizen Participation.' *Journal of Voluntary Action Research* 13(2): 7–23.

Blais, Andre, and Elisabeth Gidengil. 1993. 'Making Representative Democracy Work: A Study of Canadians' Views.' *Institute for Social Research Newsletter* 8(1): 1, 4.

Blaney, Elizabeth, and Nancy MacFarland. 1988. 'The Self-Help Illusion: "Community Voluntary Action" and the Decline of Social Services in New Brunswick.' *New Maritimes* (March): 8–9.

Blishen, Bernard R., and Tom Atkinson. 1980. *Regional and Status Differences in Canadian Values*. Toronto: Institute for Social Research, York University.

Blumer, Herbert. 1969. *Symbolic Interactionism: Perspective and Method*. Berkeley: University of California Press.

Bolan, Richard S. 1969. 'Community Decision Behavior: The Culture of Planning.' *Journal of the American Institute of Planners* 35(3): 301–10.

Bolan, Richard S. 1980. 'The Practitioner as Theorist: The Phenomenology of the Professional Episode.' *Journal of the American Planning Association* 46(3): 261–74.

Boyer, M. Christine. 1983. *Dreaming the Rational City: The Myth of American City Planning.* Cambridge, MA: MIT Press.

Boyte, Harry C., Heather Booth, and Steve Max. 1986. *Citizen Action and the New American Populism.* Philadelphia: Temple University Press.

Breheny, M.J. 1984. 'A Practical View of Planning Theory.' *Environment and Planning B: Planning and Design* 10: 101–15.

Brown, Gillian, and George Yule. 1983. *Discourse Analysis.* Cambridge: Cambridge University Press.

Brym, Robert J. 1979. 'Political Conservatism in Atlantic Canada.' In Robert Brym and James Sacouman (eds), *Underdevelopment and Social Movements in Atlantic Canada.* Toronto: New Hogtown Press, 59–79.

Burton, Dudley J., and M. Brian Murphy. 1980. 'Democratic Planning in Austerity: Practices and Theory.' In P. Clavel, J. Forester, M. Goldsmith (eds), *Urban and Regional Planning in an Age of Austerity.* New York: Pergamon, 177–205.

Cartwright, T.J. 1973. 'Problems, Solutions and Strategies: A Contribution to the Theory and Practice of Planning.' *Journal of the American Institute of Planners* 39(2): 179–87.

Christiansen-Ruffman, Linda. 1981. 'Models, Ideologies and Counter-ideologies of Citizen Participation.' Paper presented at Canadian Sociology and Anthropology Association meetings.

Churchill, Henry S. 1954. 'Planning in a Free Society.' *Journal of the American Institute of Planners* 20(4): 189–91.

Clairmont, Donald H., and Dennis W. Magill. 1971. *Africville Relocation Report.* Halifax: Institute of Public Affairs, Dalhousie University.

– 1987. *Africville: The Life and Death of a Canadian Black Community* (rev. ed.). Toronto: Canadian Scholar's Press.

Clavel, Pierre. 1986. *The Progressive City: Planning and Participation 1969–1984.* New Brunswick, NJ: Rutgers University Press.

Collier, Robert. 1974. *Contemporary Cathedrals.* Montreal: Harvest House.

Community Planning Association of Canada (CPAC). n.d. *What Can One Man Do?* Ottawa: CPAC.

Connolly, William E. 1974. *The Terms of Political Discourse.* Lexington, MA: D.C. Heath and Company.

Crapo, R.H. 1990. *Cultural Anthropology: Understanding Ourselves and Others.* Guilford, Conn.: Dushkin Publishing.

Creese, Walter L. 1966. *The Search for Environment. The Garden City: Before and After.* New Haven: Yale University Press.

Cullingworth, J.B. 1972. *Problems of an Urban Society, Volume II: The Social Content of Planning.* London: George Allen and Unwin.

Cullingworth, J. Barry. 1987. *Urban and Regional Planning in Canada.* New Brunswick, NJ: Transaction Books.

Cullum, Miles Stanton. 1978. 'Human Values in the Design and Use of Suburbia: An Exploratory Study of City Planners, Land Developers and Home-Buyers.' Unpublished MA thesis, School of Urban and Regional Planning, University of Waterloo.

Dahl, Robert A. 1989. *Democracy and Its Critics.* New Haven: Yale University Press.

Dalton, Linda. 1989. 'Emerging Knowledge About Planning Practice.' *Journal of Planning Education and Research* 9(1): 29–44.

Davidoff, Leonore, Jean L'Esperance, and Howard Newby. 1976. 'Landscape with Figures: Home and Community in English Society.' In J. Mitchell and A. Oakley (eds), *The Rights and Wrongs of Women.* Harmondsworth and New York: Penguin, 139–75.

Davidoff, Paul. 1965. 'Advocacy and Pluralism in Planning.' *Journal of the American Institute of Planners* 31(4): 331–37.

Davidoff, Paul, and Thomas A. Reiner. 1962. 'A Choice Theory of Planning.' *Journal of the American Institute of Planners.* 28(2): 103–15.

Davis, John Emmeus. 1991. *Contested Ground: Collective Action and the Urban Neighborhood.* Ithaca, NY: Cornell University Press.

Dear, Michael, and Glenda Laws. 1986. 'The Social Theory of Planning.' *Plan Canada* 26(9): 246–51.

de Neufville, Judith Innes. 1983. 'Planning Theory and Practice: Bridging the Gap.' *Journal of Planning Education and Research* 3(1): 35–45.

Dyckman, John W. 1983. 'Reflections on Planning Practice in an Age of Reason.' *Journal of Planning Education and Research* 3(1): 5–12.

Etzioni, Amitai. 1985. 'Special Interest Groups Versus Constituency Representation.' *Research in Social Movements, Conflicts and Change* 8: 171–95.

Fagence, Michael. 1977. *Citizen Participation in Planning.* Oxford: Pergamon Press.

Finkler, Earl. 1985. 'Avoid Scorch City.' *Planning* 51(5): 20–2.

Foglesong, Richard E. 1986. *Planning the Capitalist City: The Colonial Era to the 1920s.* Princeton, NJ: Princeton University Press.

Foote, G. 1979. 'Council Facing Reams of Reports, Briefs in Study of Canterbury Controversy,' *Mail Star,* 8 December 1979.

Forester, John. 1980. 'Critical Theory and Planning Practice.' *Journal of the American Planning Association* 46(3): 275–86.

- 1982a. 'Understanding Planning Practice: An Empirical, Practical and Normative Account.' *Journal of Planning Education and Research* 1(2): 59–71.
- 1982b. 'Know Your Organizations: Planning and the Reproduction of Social and Political Relations.' *Plan Canada* 22(1): 3–13.
- 1986. 'Politics, Power, Ethics and Practice: Abiding Problems for the Future of Planning.' *Plan Canada* 26(9): 224–7.
- 1987. 'Planning in the Face of Conflict: Negotiation and Mediation Strategies in Local Land Use Regulation.' *Journal of the American Planning Association* 53(3): 303–14.
- 1989. *Planning in the Face of Power*. Berkeley: University of California Press.
- 1992. 'Critical Ethnography: On Fieldwork in a Habermasian Way.' In M. Alvesson and H. Wilmott (eds), *Critical Management Studies*. Beverly Hills: Sage, 46–65.
Friedenberg, Edgar. 1980. *Deference to Authority: The Case of Canada*. White Plains, NY: M.E. Sharpe Inc.
Friedmann, John. 1973. *Retracking America: A Theory of Transactive Planning*. Garden City, NY: Anchor Press/Doubleday.
- 1987. *Planning in the Public Domain: From Knowledge to Action*. Princeton, NJ: Princeton University Press.
Fulton, William. 1987. 'The Profit Motive: Across the Country, Cities Are Becoming Real Estate Developers, and Planners Are Leading the Way.' *Planning* 53(10): 6–10.
Gall, Margaret A. 1974. 'MOVEment for Citizens Voice and Action: A Case Study on Citizen Participation.' MA Unpublished thesis, Sociology, Dalhousie University, Halifax.
Gallie, W. B. 1956. 'Essentially contested concepts.' *Proceedings of the Aristotelian Society* 56: 167–98.
Galloway, Thomas D., and Riad G. Mahayni. 1977. 'Planning Theory in Retrospect: The Process of Paradigm Change.' *Journal of the American Institute of Planners* 43(1): 62–71.
Gans, Herbert J. 1968. *People and Plans: Essays on Urban Problems and Solutions*. New York: Basic Books.
Geertz, Clifford. 1973. *The Interpretation of Cultures*. New York: Basic Books.
- 1983. *Local Knowledge: Further Essays in Interpretive Anthropology*. New York: Basic Books Inc.
Gerecke, Kent. 1973. 'An Evaluation of Canadian Urban Planning.' *Contact* 5(6): 1–12.
- 1984. 'New Directions for City Planning.' *City Magazine* VII(4): 35–7.

Goffman, Erving. 1959. *The Presentation of Self in Everyday Life*. Garden City, NY: Doubleday Anchor.

Goldberg, Michael A., and John Mercer. 1986. *The Myth of the North American City: Continentalism Challenged*. Vancouver: University of British Columbia Press.

Goldberg, Michael A., and Douglas Webster. 1977. *The Atlantic Provinces: Canada's New Amenity Region*. Vancouver: Urban Land Economics Publications, University of British Columbia.

Goldstein, H.A. 1984. 'Planning as Argumentation.' *Environment and Planning B: Planning and Design* 11: 297–312.

Goodenough, Ward H. 1981. *Culture, Language, and Society*. Menlo Park: The Benjamin/Cummings Publishing Company.

Grant, Jill. 1988a. 'They Say "You Can't Legislate Public Participation": The Nova Scotia Experience.' *Plan Canada* 27(10): 260–7.

– 1988b. 'Helter Shelter: The Housing Crisis and the Decline of Community Planning.' *New Maritimes* 6(8): 12–13.

– 1989a. 'Hard Luck: The Failure of Regional Planning in Nova Scotia.' *Canadian Journal of Regional Science* XII(2): 273–84.

– 1989b. 'From "Human Values" to "Human Resources": Planners' Perceptions of Public Role and Public Interest.' *Plan Canada* 29(6): 11–18.

– 1990a. 'Understanding the Social Context of Planning.' *Environments* 20(3): 10–19.

– 1990b. 'Planning Ethics: Dealing with Developers.' *Plan Canada* 30(2): 30–2.

– 1991. 'Contradictions in the Neighbourhood: Planning Residential Environments.' *Plan Canada* 31(1): 16–20.

Green, Mark, and James Ledbetter. 1988. '20 Solutions.' *Mother Jones* 13(6) (July–August): 24–37.

Gross, Bertram. 1980. *Friendly Fascism: The New Face of Power in America*. Montreal: Black Rose Books.

Guttenberg, Albert Z. 1968. 'The Social Uses of City Planning: A Preliminary Inquiry.' *Plan Canada* 9(1): 6–14.

Hadden, Jeffrey K., and Josef J. Barton. 1973. 'An Image That Will Not Die: Thoughts on the History of Anti-urban Ideology.' In L.H. Masotti and J.K. Hadden (eds), *The Urbanization of the Suburbs* Beverly Hills: Sage, 79–116.

Haliburton, Thomas C. 1829 [1973]. *An Historical and Statistical Account of Nova-Scotia* (in two volumes). Halifax: Joseph Howe Publisher. Canadiana Reprint Series. Belleville, ON: Mika Publishing.

Halifax, City of. 1969. 'The Master Plan!' Halifax: Planning Department.

– 1978. *Municipal Development Plan*. Halifax: Planning Department.

– 1985. *Municipal Planning Strategy*. Halifax: Planning Department.

Harris, Richard. 1988. *Democracy in Kingston: A Social Movement in Urban Politics, 1965–1970*. Montreal: McGill-Queen's University Press.

Hartnett, Ken O. 1970. *Encounter on Urban Environment: Historian's Report. Documentary of a Community's Week Long Confrontation With Itself*. Halifax: Voluntary Economic Planning.

Harvey, David. 1978. 'On Planning the Ideology of Planning.' In R.W. Burchell and G. Sternlieb (eds), *Planning Theory in the 1980s* New Brunswick, NJ: Center for Urban Policy Research.

– 1987. 'Flexible Accumulation through Urbanization: Reflections on "Post-Modernism" in the American City.' *Antipode* 19(3): 260–86.

Hawboldt, Stephen. 1976. 'Regional Development: Provincial Initiatives and Local Reactions.' *The Mirror* (Annapolis Valley, Nova Scotia), 29 December.

Hayden, Dolores. 1984. *Redesigning the American Dream: The Future of Housing, Work, and Family Life*. New York: Norton.

Healey, Patsy. 1992. 'A Planner's Day: Knowledge and Action in Communicative Practice.' *American Planning Association Journal* 58(1): 9–20.

Hedman, Richard, and Fred Bair, Jr. 1967. *And on the Eighth Day: Series of Essays and Tableaux on Planner and Planning*. Chicago: American Society of Planning Officials.

Herman, Edward S., and James Petras. 1985. ' "Resurgent democracy": Rhetoric and Reality.' *New Left Review* 154: 83–98.

Heseltine, John. 1982. *Citizen Participation in Land Use Control Procedures: Discussion Paper*. Halifax: City of Halifax Planning Department.

Higgins, Donald. 1981. 'Progressive City Politics and the Citizen Movement: A Status Report.' *City Magazine* V(1): 84–95.

– 1985. 'Urban Citizen Movements.' *The Canadian Encyclopedia* (1st ed.) 3: 1883.

– 1986. *Local and Urban Politics in Canada*. Toronto: Gage Educational Publishing.

Hiss, Tony. 1990. *The Experience of Place*. New York: Alfred A. Knopf.

Hoch, Charles J. 1984a. 'Pragmatism, Planning, and Power.' *Journal of Planning Education and Research* 4(2): 86–95.

– 1984b. 'Doing Good and Being Right: The Pragmatic Connection in Planning Theory.' *Journal of the American Planning Association* 50(3): 335–45.

Hodge, Gerald. 1985. 'The Roots of Canadian Planning.' *Journal of the American Planning Association* 51(1): 8–22.

– 1986. *Planning Canadian Communities: An Introduction to the Principles, Practice and Participants*. Toronto: Methuen Publications.

Horne, Donald. 1986. *The Public Culture: The Triumph of Industrialism*. London: Pluto Press.

Howard, Ebenezer. 1902. *Garden Cities of To-morrow* (New rev. ed.). Eastbourne, U.K.: Attic Books.

– 1923. 'Land Ownership in Garden Cities and the Value of Zoning.' *Town Planning Institute of Canada Journal* 2(2): 1–2.

Howe, Elizabeth. 1992. 'Professional Roles and the Public Interest in Planning.' *Journal of Planning Literature* 6(3): 230–48.

Howe, Elizabeth, and Jerome Kaufman. 1981. 'The Values of Contemporary American Planners.' *Journal of the American Planning Association* 47(3): 266–78.

Howland, R.D. 1957. *Some Regional Aspects of Canada's Economic Development*. Ottawa: Royal Commission on Canada's Economic Prospects (Government of Canada).

Huckfeldt, Robert. 1986. *Politics in Context: Assimilation and Conflict in Urban Neighborhoods*. New York: Agathon Press, Inc.

Jacobs, Jane. 1961. *The Death and Life of Great American Cities*. New York: Vintage Books, Random House.

Jarvie, I.C. 1972. *Concepts and Society*. London: Routledge and Kegan Paul.

Johnson, D.A. 1987. 'Review of Arthur E. Morgan. 1942. "The Small Community: Foundation of Democratic Life."' *Journal of the American Planning Association* 53(2): 295–6.

Kaufman, Jerome L. 1986. 'Making Planners More Effective Strategists.' In Barry Checkoway (ed.), *Strategic Perspectives on Planning Practice*. Lexington, MS: Lexington Books, D.C. Heath and Co., 87–104.

Kelly, Eric Damian. 1986. 'Planning vs. democracy.' *Land Use Law and Zoning Digest* 38(7): 3–5.

Kiernan, M.J. 1983. 'Ideology, Politics, and Planning: Reflections on the Theory and Practice of Urban Planning.' *Environment and Planning B: Planning and Design* 10(1): 71–87.

– 1990. 'Urban Planning in Canada: A Synopsis and Some Future Directions.' *Plan Canada* 30(1): 11–22.

Klosterman, Richard E. 1980. 'A Public Interest Criterion.' *Journal of the American Planning Association* 46(3): 323–33.

– 1983. 'Fact and Value in Planning.' *Journal of the American Planning Association* 49(2): 216–25.

Kornberg, Allan, William Mishler, and Harold D. Clarke. 1982. *Representative Democracy in the Canadian Provinces*. Scarborough, ON: Prentice-Hall Canada.

Kraushaar, Robert. 1988. 'Outside the Whale: Progressive Planning and the

Dilemmas of Radical Reform.' *Journal of the American Planning Association* 54(1): 91–100.

Krueckeberg, Donald A. 1983. 'The Culture of Planning.' In D. Krueckeberg (ed.), *Introduction to Planning History*. New Brunswick, NJ: Center for Urban Policy Research, 1–12.

Kuhn, Thomas S. 1970. *The Structure of Scientific Revolutions* (2nd ed., enlarged). International Encyclopedia of Unified Science, 2(2). Chicago: University of Chicago Press.

Lamport, Anthony. 1988. *Common Ground: 25 Years of Voluntary Planning in Nova Scotia*. Halifax: Department of Small Business Development.

Lang, R.S. 1972. *Nova Scotia Municipal and Regional Planning in the Seventies*. Halifax: Department of Municipal Affairs.

Lasch, Christopher. 1979. *The Culture of Narcissism: American Life in an Age of Diminishing Expectations*. New York: Warner Books.

Lash, Harry. 1977. *Planning in a Human Way: Personal Reflections on the Regional Planning Experience in Greater Vancouver*. Urban Prospects Series. Ottawa: Ministry of State for Urban Affairs.

League For Social Reconstruction. 1935. *Social Planning for Canada*. Toronto: Thomas Nelson and Sons Ltd.

Leiss, William, Stephen Kline, and Sut Jhally. 1990. *Social Communication in Advertising: Persons, Products and Images of Well-Being* (2nd ed.) Scarborough, ON: Nelson.

Lewin, Leif. 1991. *Self-Interest and Public Interest in Western Politics*. New York: Oxford University Press.

Logan, John, and Harvey L. Molotch. 1987. *Urban Fortunes: The Political Economy of Place*. Berkeley: University of California Press.

Loney, Martin. 1977. 'A Political Economy of Citizen Participation.' In L. Panitch (ed.), *The Canadian State: Political Economy and Political Power*. Toronto: University of Toronto Press, 446–72.

Long, Norton E. 1968. 'The Local Community as an Ecology of Games.' In W.D. Hawley and F.M. Wirt (eds), *The Search for Community Power*. Englewood Cliffs, NJ: Prentice Hall, 228–38.

Longhini, Gregory. 1985. 'Ballot Box Zoning.' *Planning* 51(5): 11–13.

Lukes, Stephen. 1974. *Power: A Radical View*. London: Macmillan.

Lynch, Kevin. 1960. *The Image of the City*. Cambridge, MA: The MIT Press.

Marris, Peter. 1982a. *Community Planning and Conceptions of Change*. London: Routledge and Kegan Paul.

– 1982b. 'Social Change and Reintegration.' *Journal of Planning Education and Research* 2(1): 54–61.

Martin, Larry R.G., Pierre Filion, and Eric S. Higgs. 1988. 'A Survey of the Preferred Literature of Canadian Planners.' *Plan Canada* 28(1): 6–11.

Matthews, Ralph. 1977. 'Growth and No-Growth in Atlantic Canada.' *City Magazine* 2(8): 45–7.

McGee, Harold. 1987. 'A Sense of Place.' In G. Peabody, C. MacGregor, R. Thorne (eds), *The Maritimes: Tradition, Challenge and Change*. Halifax: Maritext Ltd, 192–3.

McHarg, Ian L. 1969. *Design with Nature*. Garden City, NY: Doubleday/Natural History Press.

Miller, Donald L. 1986. *The Lewis Mumford Reader*. New York: Pantheon Books.

Mills, C. Wright. 1963. 'The Structure of Power in American Society.' *Power Politics and People: The Collected Essays of C. Wright Mills*. New York: Oxford University Press, 23–38.

Mishler, William. 1981. 'Political Participation and Democracy.' In M.S. Whittington and G. Williams (eds), *Canadian Politics in the 1980s*. Toronto: Methuen, 126–41.

Moffit, Leonard C. 1975. 'Value Implications for Public Planning: Some Thoughts and Questions.' *Journal of the American Institute of Planning* 41(6): 397–405.

Moore, Peter W. 1979. 'Zoning and Planning: The Toronto Experience, 1904–1970.' In A. Artibise and G. Stelter (eds), *The Usable Urban Past*. Toronto: Macmillan of Canada, 316–41.

Morrione, Thomas J. 1988. 'Herbert G. Blumer (1900–1987): A Legacy of Concepts, Criticisms, and Contributions.' *Symbolic Interactionism* 11(1): 1–12.

Murphy, Robert F. 1971. *The Dialectics of Social Life: Alarms and Excursions in Anthropological Theory*. New York: Basic Books Inc.

Nagel, Jack H. 1987. *Participation*. Foundations of Modern Political Science Series. Englewood Cliffs, NJ: Prentice-Hall Inc.

Naisbitt, John. 1984. *Megatrends: Ten New Directions Transforming our Lives*. New York: Warner Books.

Needleman, Martin L., and Carolyn Emerson Needleman. 1974. *Guerrillas in the Bureaucracy: The Community Planning Experiment in the United States*. New York: John Wiley and Sons.

Nelson, Joyce. 1987. *The Perfect Machine: TV in the Nuclear Age*. Toronto: Between the Lines.

Nelson, William N. 1980. *On Justifying Democracy*. Boston: Routledge and Kegan Paul.

Nova Scotia. 1912. *An Act Respecting Town Planning*. Statutes of Nova Scotia, 1912, Chapter 6.

– 1915. *An Act Respecting Town Planning*. Revised Statutes of Nova Scotia, 1915, Chapter 3.

– 1939. *Town Planning Act*. Statutes of Nova Scotia, 1939, Chapter 8. (Revised 1954, Chapter 292).

– 1969. *The Planning Act*. Statutes of Nova Scotia, 1969, Chapter 16.

– 1983. *The Planning Act*. Statutes of Nova Scotia, 1983, Chapter 9.

Nova Scotia, Municipal Affairs. 1992. 'Municipal Board, Recent Decisions.' *Planning Developments* 4(1): 9–11.

Pacey, Elizabeth. 1979. *The Battle of Citadel Hill*. Hantsport, NS: Lancelot Press.

Pateman, Carole. 1970. *Participation and Democratic Theory*. New York: Cambridge University Press.

Perin, Constance. 1977. *Everything in Its Place: Social Order and Land Use in America*. Princeton, NJ: Princeton University Press.

Perry, Stewart E. 1987. *Communities on the Way: Rebuilding Local Economies in the United States and Canada*. Albany: State University of New York Press.

Polanyi, Michael. 1946. *Science, Faith and Society*. Chicago: University of Chicago Press.

Porteous, J. Douglas. 1989. *Planned to Death: The Annihilation of a Place Called Howdendyke*. Manchester: Manchester University Press.

Prebble, John. 1963. *The Highland Clearances*. Harmondsworth, U.K.: Penguin Books.

Pross, Paul. 1981. 'Pressure Groups: Talking Chameleons.' In M. Whittington and G. Williams (eds), *Canadian Politics in the 1980s*. Toronto: Methuen, 221–59.

Rapoport, Amos. 1984. 'Culture and the Rrban Order,' In J.A. Agnew, J. Mercer, D. Sopher (eds), *The City in Cultural Context*. Boston: Allen and Unwin, 50–75.

Ravetz, Alison. 1986. *The Government of Space: Town Planning in Modern Society*. London: Faber and Faber.

Reagan, Michael, and Victoria Lynn Fedor-Thurman. 1987. 'Public Participation: Reflections on the California Energy Policy Experience.' In J. Desario and S. Langton (eds), *Citizen Participation in Public Decision Making*. New York: Greenwood Press, 89–113.

Rejai, M. 1967. *Democracy: The Contemporary Theories*. New York: Atherton Press.

Richardson, N.H. 1967. 'Editorial: A Goal for the Second Century.' *Plan Canada* 8(1): 3.

– 1968. 'Editorial: Municipal Muddle.' *Plan Canada* 9(2): 50–1.

– 1985. 'Canadian Institute of Municipal Planners.' *CIP Forum* 1985(4): 2.

– 1987. 'Address.' Student Planning Conference, School of Urban and Regional Planning, University of Waterloo.

Riessman, Frank. 1987. 'A New Political Culture.' *Social Policy* 18(1): 2–3.

Rittel, Horst W.J., and Melvin M. Webber. 1973. 'Dilemmas in a General Theory of Planning.' *Policy Sciences* 4: 155–69.

Roweis, S.T. 1983. 'Urban Planning as Professional Mediation of Territorial Politics.' *Environment and Planning D: Society and Space* 1: 139–62.

Savoie, Donald J. 1986. *Regional Economic Development: Canada's Search for Solutions.* Toronto: University of Toronto Press.

Schon, Donald A. 1982. 'Some of What a Planner Knows: A Case Study of Knowing-in-Practice.' *Journal of the American Planning Association* 48(3): 351–64.

– 1983. *The Reflective Practitioner: How Professionals Think in Action.* New York: Basic Books, Inc.

Scott, A.J., and S.T. Roweis. 1977. 'Urban Planning in Theory and Practice: A Reappraisal.' *Environment and Planning A* 9: 1097–1119.

Shrivani, Hamid. 1985. 'Insiders' Views on Planning Practice.' *Journal of the American Planning Association* 51(4): 486–95.

Simpson, Jeffrey. 1988. *Spoils of Power: The Politics of Patronage.* Toronto: Collins.

Simpson, Michael. 1985. *Thomas Adams and the Modern Planning Movement: Britain, Canada and the United States, 1900–1940.* London: Alexandrine Press Book.

Spragge, Godfrey L. 1975. 'Canadian Planners' Goals: Deep Roots and Fuzzy Thinking.' *Canadian Public Administration* 18(2): 216–34.

Stankiewicz, W.J. 1980. *Approaches to Democracy: Philosophy of Government at the Close of the Twentieth Century.* London: Edward Arnold.

Stelter, Gilbert A. 1986. 'Power and Place in Urban History.' In G. Stelter and A. Artibise (eds), *Power and Place.* Vancouver: University of British Columbia Press, 1–15.

Stephenson, Gordon. 1957. *A Redevelopment Study of Halifax, Nova Scotia.* Halifax: City of Halifax.

Surette, Ralph. 1988. 'Debunking Special Status.' *Atlantic Insight* (October) 30.

Swain, Harry. 1979. 'The Halifax–Dartmouth Waterfront Project.' In W.T. Perks and I.M. Robinson (eds), *Urban and Regional Planning in a Federal State: The Canadian Experience.* Stroudsburg, PA: Dowden, Hutchinson and Ross Inc., 271–81.

Throgmorton, James A. 1992. 'Planning as Persuasive Storytelling About the Future: Negotiating an Electric Power Rate Settlement in Illinois.' *Journal of Planning Education and Research* 12(1): 17–31.

TIME. 1992. 'The Week: US Elections.' *TIME,* 16 November: 22–4.

Toffler, Alvin. 1978. 'Introduction' and 'What Is Anticipatory Democracy?'.

In Clement Bezold (ed.), *Anticipatory Democracy: People in the Politics of the Future*. New York: Random House, xi–xxii, 361–5.

Udy, John. 1980. 'Why Plan? Planning and the Eternal Values.' *Plan Canada* 20(3): 176–83.

Williams, Rick. 1987. 'And Then There's the Banks ...' *New Maritimes* 5(10): 11.

– 1988. 'Malign Neglect.' *New Maritimes* (March): 11–12.

Walsh, James. 1992. 'Fed Up!' *TIME* (20 April): 28–30, 35.

Windsor, Duane. 1988. 'Why Planners Need Economics.' *Journal of the American Planning Association* 54(1): 107–8.

World Monitor. 1991. *World Monitor* (December): Untitled news item on the 2500th anniversary of democracy in Greece.

Yankelovich, Daniel. 1991. *Coming to Public Judgement: Making Democracy Work in a Complex World*. Syracuse, NY: Syracuse University Press.

Zierler, Amy. 1979. 'Another Time, Another Place.' *Halifax* (October): 10–11.

References from Clipping Files

The documents listed in this section came from clipping files kept by the City of Halifax (Development and Planning Department) and by the Community Planning Association of Canada (Nova Scotia Division). Code numbers refer to notes in the chapters on Halifax.

A1   A. Zierler, 'Halifax: Plan Just the Beginning,' *City Magazine* (1978) 3(8): 3–6.

B26   Halifax Planning Department, 'Discussion paper,' March 1973.

B27   Halifax Planning Department, staff report, September 1977.

B33   CPAC, 'What Can One Man Do?' Pamphlet. (ca. 1950s, early 1960s)

B33B   C. Hoy, article from *Toronto Star*, 24 February 1973 (title missing).

B35B   Clipped article, 'Vaughan Suggests Scaled Down Plan' *Mail-Star*, 20 March 1963.

B35D   Staff report, 'Harbour Drive,' 31 May 1963.

B35E   Staff report, 'Cogswell Street Interchange,' 14 March 1968.

B41   CPAC, 'Nova Scotia.' *Community Planning Review* (1964) XIV (1): 31.

D10   CPAC, January 1973, brief to Council.

Market Place Plaza Dispute

D17   City of Halifax, staff report, 'Contract Development and lot Consolidation – Brunswick and George Streets.' 20 June 1979.

D18   Community Planning Association, brief, 'The Citadel – Our Sense of Place.' 22 August 1979.

D19   B. Allen, Acting city solicitor report, 'Time Square,' 28 August 1979.

D21   A. Zierler, 'Another Time, Another Place,' *Halifax* (October 1979): 10–11

D22   S. Kimber, 'On Tour With [the Developer],' *Halifax* (October 1979): 29–31.

D23B   Senior planner, staff memo, 22 November 1979.

D23D   Senior planner, staff memo, 'Case #3799 – Contract Development/ Lot Consolidation: George/Brunswick Streets.' 30 October 1979.

D24B   Citizen letter to Council, 12 November 1979.

D24D   Director of planning, staff memo, 'Contract Development/Lot Consolidation: Corner of Brunswick and George Streets,' 29 November 1979.

D25   Citizen letter to Council, 3 December 1979.

D26   Citizen letter to Council, 3 December 1979.

D27A   Halifax Homeowners' Association, brief, 4 December 1979.

D27B   Citizen letter to Council, 4 December 1979.

D28B   Citizen brief, 5 December 1979.

D29   Citizen Brief, 5 December 1979.

D32   G. Foote, 'Council Facing Reams of Reports, Briefs in Study of Canterbury Controversy,' *Mail-Star*, 8 December 1979.

D33   Citizen letter to Council, 10 December 1979.

D37   J. White, 'Dollars and Sense,' *Mail-Star* (incomplete date, ca. February 1980).

D39   Community Planning Association, 'Notice of Appeal' to the Provincial Planning Appeal Board, 27 March 1980.

Mitchell Property Dispute

C2   Citizen letter to editor, *Daily News*, 8 January 1987.

C4A   Planning, staff report, 'Request for Amendment to MPS, Section
            V (South End Area Plan) for Property at 1044/1010 Tower Road
            and 1049 Wellington Street,' 27 February 1987.

C6   J. Tibbetts, 'Neighbors Ready to Fight Mitchell Property High-
            Rise,' *Daily News*, 7 March 1987.

C7A   L. Wild, 'Mitchell Development Plan Quashed,' *Daily News*, 23
            April 1987.

C7B   Citizen letter to editor, *Mail Star*, 18 March 1987.

C11   Citizen letter to editor, *Mail Star*, 26 May 1987.

C13A   R. Roberts, 'Old Mitchell House to Be Torn Down' *Daily News*, 3
            December 1987.

C13B   'Demolition Plan Opposed,' *Mail-Star*, 4 December 1987.

C14   'Supporters of Mitchell House Hope to Gather 3,000-Signature
            Petition.' *Mail-Star*, 16 December 1987.

C19A   R. Roberts, 'Mitchell House Gets 30–Day Reprieve,' *Daily News*, 4
            December 1987.

C19B   E. MacLellan and J. Jacobson, 'Demolition of Mitchell Mansion Is
            Protested,' *Mail-Star*, 3 December 1987.

C24   R. Roberts, 'Mitchell House to Be Demolished This Morning,
            Lobby Group Says,' *Daily News*, 30 April 1988.

C26   R. Roberts, 'Mitchell House Razed – "Horrible Sight",' *Daily
            News*, 2 May 1988.

C28   Citizen editorial, 'Nothing Left But Rubble, Memories,' *Mail Star*,
            11 May 1988.

C29AA   'Mitchell Lot Move Curbs Public Rights.' *Daily News*, 17 May
            1989.

C30   M. Blanchard, 'Sparks Fly Over Mitchell Site Ashes,' *Daily News*,
            16 May 1989.

C32   B. Bateman, 'Neighbors to Fight Plan for Mitchell Property,'
            Daily News 27 June 1989.

C33   M. Stephenson, 'Gloves Come Off in Mitchell Property Scrap,' *Mail-Star*, 27 June 1989.

C36   City of Halifax, Planning Advisory Committee, PAC public meeting, minutes, 25 July 1989.

C38   PAC public meeting, minutes, 5 September 1989.

C42   Planning Advisory Committee (report to Council), 'Amendment to the Height Precinct Map (ZM–17) – Mitchell Property, Tower Road.' 4 October 1989.

C45   M. Stephenson, 'Mitchell Height Restriction Lifted: South-End Opponents "Shocked, Discouraged," May Appeal; Family "Relieved," ' *Mail-Star*, 13 October 1989.

D2   Staff report – supplementary, 'Amendment to Height Precinct Map (ZM–17) – Mitchell Property, Tower Road: Amendment to Section 44F of the Land Use Bylaw (Peninsula),' 15 June 1989.

Index